PERSPECTIVES IN SOCIAL WORK

PERSPECTIVES IN SOCIAL WORK

Noel and Rita Timms

Illustrated by Chris Blow

Routledge & Kegan Paul
London, Henley and Boston

First published in 1977
by Routledge & Kegan Paul Ltd
39 Store Street,
London WC1E 7DD,
Broadway House,
Newtown Road,
Henley-on-Thames,
Oxon RG9 1EN and
9 Park Street,
Boston, Mass. 02108, USA
Set in 11/12 pt Imprint
and printed in Great Britain by
Butler & Tanner Ltd, Frome and London
© Noel and Rita Timms 1977

ISBN 0 7100 8505 2 (c)
ISBN 0 7100 8519 2 (p)

CONTENTS

ACKNOWLEDGMENTS

We are very grateful to the following who have read an earlier draft of the manuscript: the late Dorothea Storey; Robert Carew; Graham Parker and William Roberts. They have commented very helpfully on our ideas but, it goes without saying, bear no responsibility for what follows. We are in the debt of two consumers whose accounts of service we have used in this book, and of Hazel Cleghorn who has worked hard and patiently at our drafts.

INTRODUCTION

Our objective in writing this text is to enable students on courses of training in social work to acquire an adequate idea of what they (courses and students) are about. We hope to stimulate students to identify and appraise the 'work' of social work. We do not assume this to be an easy task – training for social work is not just a question of communicating a set of skills, even though the acquisition of some skills, administrative and technical (such as recording), is a necessary part of the process; skills are necessary but they are not sufficient for social work training and practice. In our view the 'field' of social work has yet to be cultivated, a great deal of digging and refining is required in many areas of study and practice: social policies require reformulation; imagination and determination are required if the basic groundwork for training in social *service* is to be secured.

We do not pretend, therefore, that anyone can confidently assert that current social work practice or training is a 'success' story. Indeed we believe that there are genuine grounds for criticism and disquiet at many levels. We can understand why students and practitioners feel driven, some finally, some occasionally, to withdraw from what seems such an unsatisfactory field of action and enquiry, in favour of an alternative occupation or the establishment of an alternative society.

Equally we can understand the resentment of social workers who remain in the field attempting work they believe is both arduous and undervalued by the society in which they operate. There are many allusions now to the 'battered' social worker who struggles with maximum caseloads and minimum resources in a social context of optimum disparagement. The self-righteousness of much recent press reporting on child battering has exploited the sensational at the expense of encompassing the real issues

3

inherent in such tragedies. Yet we believe there are vital issues to be discussed if human life is to be protected and human suffering alleviated, for that is the central justification for the existence of 'social work' itself: i.e. it makes some impact on that problem. Essential to this discussion is the 'understanding' of student and social worker of what he is about in the social context in which he operates – both situation and context require familiarisation. An example of this is the 'understanding' which social workers require in the face of current criticisms of their effectiveness.

There are many reasons why social workers are the target of abuse or criticism. Many members of the public believe that the 'Welfare State' was created to be a panacea for all social ills. They believe that large social service departments are financed by heavy taxation and at the cost of diminishing earnings for themselves. They have high expectations of the 'productivity' of social workers so that all manner of deprivations are seen to be their province. Functions of neighbourliness are now believed to be the responsibility of the 'welfare', visiting the old and infirm the responsibility of the social services. They are, therefore, suitably outraged when old people die alone or young people are neglected. They cannot envisage the magnitude of the 'need' to be met by the voluntary and statutory social services or the poverty of resources to meet it. Social workers from this perspective seem to them to be failing to 'work'. The media contribute to the myth of 'social work' as a means of salvation through general inadvertence that has surprisingly failed.

The situation of public apathy and ignorance is not of the public's own making. Social workers have a responsibility to communicate the nature of their task because they are employed under 'social' auspices. Their role is educative as well as practical, and if social workers are uncertain about the nature of the tasks they are undertaking they will not obtain the degree of co-operation from the general public that is essential to the tasks they undertake. If social workers are not articulate about the needs they are trying to meet or the resources required to meet them, the work will not be supported.

This text attempts to help social workers to become more articulate and critical concerning the human purposes they are about. There are many reasons why social workers should encourage criticism of their competence and training. The task of serving and supporting clients and users of social service agencies places them in a critical situation. Many of their clients are deprived,

damaged or undergoing a period of loss and change and are particularly vulnerable to the power and influence of the helping
agency. Exploitation and manipulation, especially when it is con-
ceived in terms of the 'client's interest' can easily characterise
the solutions discussed, and laying down rules of procedure or
professional conduct may help but not wholly obviate this situation. Public criticism can help social work agencies to understand
how its users feel about the way the work is conducted, how rules
of procedure may themselves become manipulated or plainly
deficient. Without public criticism and accountability social work
stultifies. Every social worker should attempt to improve the
deficiencies of his organisation by arguing his case within the
context of his work through 'agency' pressure and application
through normal channels. When these fail the social worker
should bring to the attention of the public his limited resources
for the task to be done. Residential centres and fieldwork services
should not be manned by social workers silently colluding in an
inhuman process. All this involves social workers' understanding
a variety of concepts – need, equality, fraternity, justice, peace,
rationing, planning, as well as a range of sociological and psychological phenomena. We do not believe that any social work method
can be understood or applied outside the context of a range of
social concepts – the dimension of casework even with individuals
is a social dimension.

Our objective in writing this book is to contribute to the
student's understanding of the knowledge, values and beliefs that
social work impinges upon. Social workers must come to terms
with problems of knowledge implicit in their actions. We make no
excuse therefore for the academic content of this book, and if
clarity does not emerge it was certainly not through any intention
to mystify. We have pursued the academic in search of valid
practice. We do not presume that we have resolved the crucial
problems of knowledge and action, we simply offer a perspective,
a line of enquiry. Fundamental to this perspective is our belief
that the adoption of a 'helpful' role is beset with difficulty. Literature abounds with the acid rejection of the do-gooder and the
busybody – genuine caring is difficult to sustain in any society.
People who have demonstrated care have often been misunder-
stood at the best of times or destroyed at the worst. History offers
many examples. Social work is not an activity for those who can
persuade themselves easily of their general efficiency in the face
of multiple social problems. The smug sanctimoniousness of the

helper or the brisk certainty of the busybody are not proper models for social work – patience and rigour are more useful characteristics. This is not to suggest any detached attitude on our part. We hope that what we have already said makes it clear that 'getting the description (and justification) of social work right' is and ought to be a matter of passionate conviction.

> If the road I have shown to lead to this is very difficult it can yet be discovered. And clearly it must be very hard when it is so seldom found. For how could it be that it is neglected practically by all, if salvation were close at hand and could be found without difficulty? But all excellent things are as difficult as they are rare (Spinoza: *Ethics*).

The approach of this book

For many subjects it appears possible to produce one or more textbooks which outline the main features of an area of study and summarise the essential content under a limited number of sub-divisions. Such an undertaking in social work is much more difficult, at least at the present time, and there are obvious practical reasons why this should be so. It is far from easy to know what to exclude from a range of theories in a number of disciplines – psychology, sociology and even economics (ideas of costs, rationing and so on) and social philosophy. Legislation increases in scope and the social worker must at least know his or her way through and also around a growing number of acts and regulations. The scope of social work itself changes, so that residential work, for instance, now counts as a form of social work, whilst it remains unclear whether community work is part of social work or whether social work itself is best seen as part of community work. Finally, ways of doing social work or preferred models of practice change so quickly that several commentators speak of changes in fashion.

These difficulties in deciding what is inside and what is outside social work are obvious, but not less obstinate because of this. A further difficulty is, however, of more significance, and it is because of this that our book developed its present form. Previous books concerned with social work practice have attempted to indicate generally or in considerable detail what social workers should do. This is to put the cart before the horse. Prescribing social work techniques or analysing in minute detail what is called *the* social casework relationship are secondary matters. The primary question for the social worker is: What is it that I am doing when I practise social work?, rather than: How do I practise social work? Assuming the first question (what is it I am doing?) goes a long way to answering the second (how can it be done?). This is because achieving a description under which a set of activities (social work) is seen or establishing the reasons for doing these activities establishes a perspective which is crucial to action and which often justifies the action. If we know the perspective from which a social worker acts a great deal of the detail of his or her activity can be read off that position and a great deal concerning how the activity can be carried out.

Let us try to make this more concrete. What a social worker does can be described in a limitless number of ways. We could consider certain physiological processes at work as the social worker goes to visit an old person in an Old People's Home; we could describe bodily movements or we could answer the question, What is a social worker doing? by saying, 'He is interviewing or meeting an old person.' A more significant description, however, is to say something like 'He is trying to assess need or ascertain wishes or appraise the interests of a person'. If the social worker was trying to answer the question 'What are you doing in the case of that old man?' he could not with any conviction apply the 'Come and watch me doing ...' technique. He could not, in other words, say at any one point 'Come and watch me now at this minute trying to assess the need of a person'. Yet the reason for his action and very often the description under which his action is received by both the user of social work help and the social worker are central for the perspective of both social worker and client. What has to be done in detail are those things that count as assessing the needs (or wishes or interests) of a person.

We can perhaps summarise the difficulty in the idea of a textbook for social work by saying that it is simply not possible to put between two covers a compendium of what a social worker should know. It is, however, possible to describe and discuss what has to be grasped. It is with this end in view that this book has been written.

It examines ideas that have to be entertained and appreciated before social work can be intelligently grasped and effectively practised. It emphasises the critical appraisal of key concepts. In order to show that the concepts chosen are not arbitrary and in order to place the beginning of our discussion firmly within social work practice, we begin with what is usually called case material. It is somewhat unusual in that it is an account of experience of residential work and what is still termed field social work from the viewpoint of a resident. The account shows how firmly the main concepts from which social work is built up are embedded in a simple but articulate description of the experience of receiving social work help. We have in mind ideas such as need, emotion, respect, equality, friendship, justice, membership, community, human, and so on.

A residential centre for the physically handicapped

The following is a description of life in a hostel for eighteen men and women with varying degrees of disability. The writer was 24 when she entered the hostel. The account is given under sub-headings suggested by this user of residential and field social work.

Difficulties of regimentation

(a) *Direct conflict between individual needs and administrative framework* No one minds eating, bathing, getting up and going to bed at set times for most of the year – it is the *never* of watching of television after 9.30 p.m. – the *never* of returning later from a theatre, party, social gathering, etc. In the 'outside' world life after work does not start until 7.30–8.00 p.m. so that it was usually necessary to refuse invitations unless one could go through with the embarrassment of breaking up the gathering. There were 'special occasions', but the pleasant staff looked so dog-tired by the evening that to prevent them going off-duty at 10 seemed brutally caddish and the not-so-pleasant staff, also tired, were openly hostile.

I have enlarged on this because it seemed to me and my friends at the time, and to me now at a distance of four years, as by far the greatest single disadvantage of residential care. This limitation only affected those who needed help and we acknowledged our blessings when we learnt from two visitors, able wheelchair users, that where they lived all the residents, independent or not, had to be indoors and upstairs by 6.00 p.m. as the lift man went off-duty then. Fatuous and pathetic but perfectly authentic.

(b) *A strengthening of the isolating tendency* Every obviously disabled person is fighting, sometimes consciously often unconsciously, the concept that because of his physical disability he is a second-class human being. This latter statement will often shock and be violently repudiated by both able-bodied and disabled because our society makes strenuous and laudable efforts to deny its validity. But it is as strong as the concept of social colour and as deep-rooted, presumably, as prehistory. This is inflamed by residential care and shows itself in ways such as the following.

1 A fierce, disproportionate expression of independence – rudely rebuffing offers of help, etc.

2 The opposite – 'My individuality is lost in the group – I will assert it by demanding help.'

3 Division in the community – US . . . decent, sensible ready-to-make-the-best-of-it disabled, and THEM . . . unmentionably privileged on account of their unimpaired physique, lazy, insensitive, power-crazed staff. 'It's no good telling the welfare lady. She's very nice but she's really one of "them" and she'll betray you behind the shut door of the office. Anyway, she doesn't live here and she believes all they say. You'll only get yourself branded as a malcontent. . . .'

(I must emphasise and reiterate that it was in a newly formed hostel, founded and run on very liberal lines.)

I only had two contacts with visiting Welfare Officers which could qualify to be called confrontations. The first was in the early days when lip-service was still being paid to the idea that residents should and could (fantastic, revolutionary, dangerous notion) have a small share in running the hostel. I was chairman of the Residents' Meeting (which soon atrophied for lack of effective power to influence anything or anybody). We had one or two 'old hands', experienced opters-out, and I had been warned by the boss that they would find themselves moving on if they didn't co-operate. I passed this on in general terms at a meeting, with what I thought were rallying and encouraging comments. The response was a revelation. The cap had fitted the non-cooperator, X, who had written pathetically to the Welfare Officer complaining of victimisation and insecurity. The latter, whether seeing a vision of internal pressure gangs and rackets I never knew, arrived to pour out a storm of angry scorn over my head which mainly circulated around the two points that I had abused my great power and 'made X's life a hell for weeks', and that because of my public school education I was not worth 'the little finger of X'. It scarcely seemed a dignified or profitable position for either of us.

The other was a charming Officer who acted always on the principle that nothing must be individualised because it would lead to dangerous precedents and jealousy. So very little was ever accomplished. She drove me to hidden volcanic fury because she gave one the feeling that everything one said was a label enabling her to pigeonhole one according to type, and the name on the pigeonhole determined her response. It was like talking to a glamorised computer.

Now all this is trivial stuff, typical of the tea-cup storms in all communities, but it is responsible for unhappiness and a strengthening of the helpless sense of inferiority. Not only are you physically inferior but you are forced by that to be socially so. The repugnance we have for the very words and phrases demonstrates my point. I avoid the use of 'patient', 'Home', 'institutional care', 'matron', 'victim'. As the good lady said, 'Let us go and take one of the poor polios out from the home.' Anonymity added to social apartness and inferiority.

Residential care is a second-best as far as my experience goes. Though a tremendous, immeasurable advance on chronic wards it should be a stepping stone to integration 'outside'. An alternative is the experimental kind of amalgamated units. Sophisticated equipment can make this possible even for the very severely disabled.

Staff status needs raising enormously to attract a reasonable type. At present they may comprise men on the run from marital commitments, swindlers and tricksters (the same X was years later relieved gently of her £20 savings by a hard luck story followed by an offer of marriage from one of the latter), junkies, ESN types, grubby slatterns and many obviously in need of psychiatric help. This is grossly unfair on the many generous, patient and highly competent attendants.

4 (belatedly!) The 'opters-out', as X above. Usually strong characters with a lifetime of disability behind them. They form a fiercely preserved 'private life', no matter within what small confines, have their own rigid routine and, being convinced that they are different and separated from 'normal' people, refuse to be flexible or to 'co-operate' in a society. What profit can there be? And they might be imposed upon, lose what individuality they have managed to preserve.

5 The disabled vegetables. So brainwashed by physical disability that they are carried by the community, never needing to make a decision, increasingly incapable of any initiative, convinced that what 'They' say has cosmic backing – sort of extreme fatalists. (Actually, any initiative is hard to take in a community. There are so many interests to consider, so much consultation to be done that it's easier not to. The passionate, bursting energy to achieve is

very rare – I had to have sustained pushing from friends and relatives before eventually starting a course of study.)

(c) *Enervation* – as immediately above. Like hospitalisation, etc. As a foot may hurt for a while in a wrongly shaped shoe but end by being moulded so that it doesn't hurt – at the expense of a certain amount of deformity – so the personality may rage for a while against regimentation but changes to an acceptance of it as a habit of life and, sometimes, to a dependence upon it. Many of the disabled residents had led far more active lives before they came to the hostel – but how can they cook if the kitchen's barred, garden if there are no facilities, machine with no space, or take in the occasional private pupil for coaching if they are not allowed ever to monopolise a room for the purpose of earning money? Things improve all the time, but very slowly, and often bedevilled by the completely fallacious fear that arrangements for one to pursue an activity will make the others jealous. I never ran into this at all; rather the opposite, a vicarious pleasure in someone else's different activities and achievements and a wonderful and heart-warming willingness to help. I should never have been able to pursue my course without the tremendous help I received from other residents – or, indeed, accomplish any of the ordinary things of life, as for instance doing up Christmas presents and cards. I was one of the most favoured residents as I had a wonderful family and friends. I tended to go out more and have more visitors and I virtually monopolised the 'Quiet Room' for study but the others were always friendly and interested.

Advantages of regimentation

(a) A useful common denominator and communal factor in a community consisting of such varied people.
(b) A solid structure which gave one a measure of stability and security within which one could live one's own life without the nagging worries of 'being a burden' or of having to struggle beyond one's capabilities.

There was a considerable bond of kindness between residents – even the rows had to blow over for everyone had to go on living there; we couldn't, as somebody caustically put it, give in our notice. And there was a respect, which grew rather than diminished through the years, for residents who coped valiantly with their individual disabilities, a considerable tolerance and compassion. We had our different 'escapes': a session of heart-to-heart gossip, radio/television, gambling, smoking, going to the pub, reading, staring into the goldfish pond, falling in love, sitting on the telephone, writing angry letters, going out to work, having another illness, going for a ride in your own car, away on holiday (despite pressure on staff and accommodation, time away was beginning to be limited just before I left because local authorities aren't keen on paying for someone who's not there – as if they save somehow when they are! – but this may have altered).

Being fond of reading and talking I was well catered for. Also I had a family and friends who assured me, unspokenly, that I was a real person, and had my own valid individuality as a human being on the same plane as themselves. This was undergirded by fellowship with other residents and fine, sensitive friendship from members of a remarkable Friends' Association. Also, I had/have a religious faith which adds a new set of dimensions.

When I had repaired the communications bridge to X and convinced her that I was one of US and not a quisling in THEIR pay, we had a strong bond, later sharing a room with three others and then with each other. For many moons she devotedly did all my washing and mending and I listened to her side of the unfortunate and prolonged infatuation with the conman.

It all boils down to the old 'dignity of the human individual' – and the staffing difficulties, which are often pretty desperate. Having disposed of many old abuses don't let's fall into thinking that material benefits (important and pleasurable) compensate a disabled person for the not-quite-degradation of being labelled and segregated on account of the one thing which they fight to forget and surmount – a stigmatising and irrelevant physical inadequacy.

PS. We decided, at the hostel, that mixed degrees of disability were essential; that mixed ages and sexes were desirable; that mixed backgrounds were a good thing – more natural – but that the numbers should be ideally larger to enable people to find friends of like interests – otherwise small mixed groups of like interests.

I think I survived difficult moments with such dull mental tricks as: it'll all be the same in a hundred years' time; it doesn't really *matter*; this is good for the soul – make the most of it; she/he is a boorish pathetic clot, anyway; only another hour and I'll be in bed; I could always write to the *Daily Mirror*; what right have I to live anyway – I'd have been left to die in the Neolithic Age; it's much worse for old so-and-so; shut up doing mental harangues and say something – it'll speed the moment into the past . . . etc., etc.!

Another odd thought occurs to me to support the second-class human point. We always had the strong feeling that everything concerning life in the hostel was discussed by the resident Olympian gods – sometimes in consultation with visiting gods and goddesses – (like Odysseus and company, we didn't always consider that the deities filled their positions with wisdom, maturity or even an ordinary measure of sensitivity and benevolence). It was rather like being in the fourth form and seeing the staff file into the principal's study, occupying oneself with futile speculation, until suddenly new desks arrived or everybody was told they must eat a ration of cod liver oil and malt every day before breakfast. The visiting gods would chat pleasantly with us over tea, hiding their worried frowns, but we would rather have discussed steps to improve staff conditions, worried with them about the sewage problem, or the heating, or the best kind of new equipment.

Present state of social work theory and practice

The situations and the responses in this account appear reasonably simple to grasp. No corresponding simplicity is evident if we ask about the present condition of social work practice and theory. Social work presently suggests in fact a bewildering picture, especially to those in training for the occupation. As we have already noted, the so-called methods of social work are on the increase; not only are we now presented with the possibility of casework, groupwork, community work and residential social work, but particular approaches within each of these are sometimes accepted as dominant or even exclusive. Crisis intervention was in this position a short while ago, and a task-centred approach in casework and in groupwork now receives a great deal of attention. Within some of the methods it is possible to see the sustained development of a comparative theoretical approach, so that students can begin to choose in social casework, for instance, between the functional school, developed in America and emphasising personal will and the social work agency, and a behaviour therapy approach based on numerous experiments designed to test aspects of learning theory. Different theories are less well developed in residential work or community work, but different models have been proposed which claim the allegiance of social workers. If we glance at the theories social workers are urged to use in the description and explanation of human behaviour we discover a similar apparently ever-increasing range of choice – variations of psychoanalytic theory, systems theory, role theory, labelling theory, theory of anomie, and so on.

Some of these terms will be clarified later (either in the text or through the guidance to further reading at the end of each chapter) but at this point it is worth mentioning one of the ways in which social work writing and spoken discussion can make these or similar terms even more complicated. 'Theory' is quite often used in social work in an ambiguous way, referring as it does to at least three possibilities: theory about what constitutes or justifies social work, theory about how to do social work and theory in the sense of propositions from, say, the social sciences. In the theories just mentioned we can note an additional complication: 'theory' is sometimes used instead of 'concept'. So 'theory' has simply been added in the above list to the rich but contested concept of anomie (or 'normlessness') with its different roots in Marx and Durkheim. This is not a merely semantic point: 'concepts' are not the same as 'theories'; we cannot test concepts as we test theories; we expect different things from each of them. In this respect it is instructive to compare recent treatments of 'systems theory' in social work, some of which uses the concept 'system' throughout, but unlike others refer to none of the constituent elements of systems theory, such as feedback, homeostasis and so on. It is these elements that are combined to produce testable propositions.

Turning to the current scene of social work practice, the contemporary state of the art is well conveyed by the increasing use of a term we have already noted, 'battered social worker'. This is used to express uneasiness about the pressure of caseload size, exclusive reliance on the offer of first-aid work to social casualties, and persistent reference in the media to what appear to be the shortcomings of social work. More importantly in our view, it suggests a basic conceptual problem, how to describe and to realise the proper relationship of the social worker to 'society'. Social workers seem to experience increasing uncertainty about the place of social work in society. They believe that their work is somehow socially sanctioned, that the 'social' in their title refers to the auspices under which they work rather than to their field (working, as it were, with 'things social'). Yet 'society' seems often to deny them the resources they need and sometimes even under-standing. So they are criticised as ineffective, soft, do-gooders. They are also blamed for being extremely effective in a negative direction by keeping clients in their place through the moulding language of diagnosis and treatment if not by cruder forces.

Of course, it is not only because 'society' shows such contra-dictory attitudes that social workers seem at times uneasy about their own influence. They have sometimes been influential in movements to create important changes. Policy in relation to the removal of children from parents who were judged inadequate in certain respects has changed over the years, and this was partly due to child care lobbies, local and central, in which social workers played an important role. Such a policy is tested publicly from time to time, and cases are reported in which children either should have been removed from their parents or should not have been returned to their care. In such situations it is unhelpful for social workers to turn round and blame the social climate (for instance the expected behaviour of courts in relation to parental application) as if they themselves had had no part in the creation of the social weather. In fact, in this instance a belief in the value of a child's own home led to dogmatic assumptions about the evil of separation rather than a policy to be applied when certain con-ditions prevailed. Social workers allowed themselves to be guided by faith rather than an appreciation of what it is to carry out a policy. They had not attended sufficiently to social work as planning.

We have described the main problems of contemporary social work – uncertainty about method, about intellectual foundations and about social roles and function. We could add that further problems arise from a belief, sometimes expressed, sometimes half concealed, that in any case 'research' shows social work is of no use. It is into this complex and confused situation that we launch a new text for social work practice. The situation does not appear promising, to say the least. How can a textbook negotiate a reasonably confident way through such conflict and uncertainty? On the other hand, there seems to be ample warrant for a fresh approach which at least unravels some of the complexity and points the way to a reconsideration of the basic questions. We have no wish to add to the problems of social workers, but the main purpose of this book will have been achieved if we have helped to substitute for the present bewilderment an active sense of puzzlement that presses forward towards new solutions.

Social work 'theory': complex and complacent

We want to increase systematic curiosity about many of the 'solutions' available in the social work literature and about many of the prescriptions offered. Take, for example, a recent study (Reid and Shyne, 1972) which has, correctly in our view, been well received. An active sense of puzzlement would lead the reader to pause at the title, which refers to a task-centred approach in social casework, and to ask what could have happened in an activity as practical as social work that 'task-centred' has become the name for a distinctive approach. Turning to the content of the study we note the statement that 'the most distinguishing characteristic of casework, if indeed it has any, is its dual focus on psychological and social phemomena' (p. 30). Again, a sense of puzzlement would suggest to the reader questions concerning the force of 'if indeed it has any', and the implications for the practitioners of maintaining the dual focus described, particularly when, as the authors acknowledge, 'We have yet to develop an adequate body of theory that integrates these foci.' It is as if the authors are saying we know that people are called and call themselves caseworkers, and that they practise casework, but it may not be possible to pick casework out from whatever else exists and even if we could identify casework its special identity seems to be based on a present impossibility. This does not seem a very plausible position, but we would not wish the matter to be left as a demonstration of a difficulty. The way forward towards resolving the problem is partly through reconstructing what happened in the development of social work to produce this kind of tangle and partly in looking more closely at what social workers do. We intend in the course of this book to provide some conceptual tools that will enable the student to undertake these tasks.

We want to discuss the basic questions posed for practitioners which require answers before social work can be adequately grasped and intelligently practised. We believe that these basic questions have often been obscured in the past through two tendencies: premature theoretical integration and ingestion, and misplaced complexity. The integration and ingestion we refer to can be seen in the daily language of social work as well as in attempts to clothe the frame of social work in some new theoretical language. So, social work teachers refer to a student's ability to 'integrate theory and practice', but this confident shorthand conceals the fact that each of the terms used – integration, theory, practice – are problematic. Similarly, basic questions can be concealed by the present thrust towards new theory. Take, for example, 'systems theory' which, as we have already suggested, enjoys a current vogue. A recent discussion argues that such theory is compatible with, but gives greater breadth and scope to, the goals of social casework. It is suggested that the goal of self-fulfilment could be recast in systems terms as follows: 'to produce the change from an initial state to the goal state, to assist the client in maintaining a steady state (in dynamic relation to his environment) and to overcome what is impeding and to foster the attainment of that steady state . . .' (Stein in Strean, 1971, p. 51). What is gained by substituting this particular formulation for ordinary and reasonably well understood talk about helping people to overcome barriers to the realisation of their purposes?

Problems in unravelling social work are, in our opinion, 'solved' before they are well understood. Problems are also created by making social work over-complex. This is perhaps most noticeable in the field of social casework. Take, for instance, Hollis on diagnosis (1958, pp. 89–90). She argues that social caseworkers should be able

(1) to answer certain questions about the nature of the client's personality and the dynamics of his functioning;
(2) to understand something of the etiology of the client's behaviour;
(3) to answer certain questions about the significance of the problem for the client; and
(4) to classify his adjustment.

The third set of items at least looks reasonable, but consider what is required under just one of the other headings:

Concerning the nature of the client's personality and the dynamics of his functioning, we secure information on the following points:
a) What is the quality of his libidinal relationships? To what extent is he capable of warm object relationships? To what extent is he dependent, and to what extent is he narcissistic?
b) What is the nature of his sexual identifications? His attitude toward his own and the opposite sex? His specific sexual adjustment?
c) What is the quality of his aggressiveness? How extensive and how primitive are his hostilities? What direction do they take? How much of his aggression is channelized into problem-solving?
e) How well does his ego function in the following respects. How accurate are his reality perceptions? How accurate is his image of himself? What capacity does he show for self-criticism? How good is his judgement? How efficient and effective are his controls of his own behavior? What is his ability to secure reality

gratifications? How intelligent is he? How great is his anxiety, and
how does he handle it?
f) On what defenses does he characteristically rely?
g) What symptoms has he needed to develop?
h) What are his principal character traits?

We question how far these kinds of judgments can be made, the
persuasive way in which some of the questions are formulated
(what symptoms has he *needed* to develop?), and also, perhaps
more importantly, we ask what difference knowing all or most of
this would make to what a social worker actually did. This prescription prompts us to ask whether social work has not suffered,
like a character in a novel of de Vries, from 'acute diagnosis'.

It is important to note that we are not suggesting that the
approach adopted by Hollis should be dismissed. We believe we
have suggested ways in which it could be actively questioned.
Such questioning is not based on a crude assumption that social
work is 'simple'. It is our contention that social work has suffered
from *misplaced* complexity and from a rather heady optimism
concerning the likely returns from clinical omniscience. Social
work *is* complex, but the complexity of social work is to be found
not in esoteric theory, but in the undoubted complications sur-
rounding the use of 'simple' concepts such as 'friend', 'influence',
'plan', 'interest', 'wish', 'need', 'human', 'reasons for action', and
so on. In seeking to follow an approach based on simple and basic
ideas, we do not assume that social work can be blanched of all
theory and that thereby some kind of neutral, theory-free description is produced, but we do question the kind of very close relationship that has developed between one set of theories (psychoanalytic) and social work. This is not because we regard such theory
as providing no basis at all for social work understanding. As will
become apparent, we envisage social work as activity that can be
informed by a number of theoretical viewpoints, and psychoanalytic theory would be one of them. What we do criticise,
however, is the apparent merger of a practice (social work) with
a theoretical system (psychoanalytic theory) so that it becomes
difficult to see the procedures and objectives of the practice apart
from the theory: the theory that should inform the practice has
simply taken the practice over.

Possible criticism of our approach

It is perhaps at this point that the reader may begin to entertain some
misgivings about the usefulness of our approach. Puzzlement

sounds like a good name for a preoccupation that is basically academic, and the analysis of concepts, fascinating though it may be, tends to become an exercise that is all 'starting-point' and no arrival. Our reply to this would be twofold. In many respects 'theory' and 'practice' have been misused in social work: separated when their connectedness should have been recognised, and forced together (as in 'the integration of theory and practice') when their distinctive nature should have been upheld. We do not aim to present a book that is 'practical' in the sense that it offers a detailed blueprint of the series of actions a social worker should take when trying, for example, to help an old person to settle into a residential home or a group of mothers concerned to start a playgroup. Indeed, we believe that light is shed on the kind of activity social work is by considering that such a blueprint is not, as some have maintained, undesirable, but quite simply impossible. Detailed instructions cannot be issued to cover human interaction even in those comparatively simple situations. We aim to offer something that resembles a map rather than a blueprint.

Mapping the territory of social work and remarking some of its more important features and frontiers must involve an examination of the main concepts used in social work. 'Social work practice' is itself a concept, but the activity of social work involves concepts most of which are problematic – concepts like 'parenting', 'self-determination', 'love', 'authoritative intervention', to name but a few. We cannot intelligently discuss or practise social work without an understanding of such concepts. However, to admit that these central concepts are problematic and the proper subject for discussion is not to argue that such discussion must be endless. We want to raise many questions in the minds of students, but we would not be satisfied simply to have unsettled some convictions without putting anything in their place. What is put in their place will not be a list of formulae for the production of a good interview or a reliable relationship nor a prescription that theory x should be followed in all cases, but a conviction that social work is characteristically action by and for persons, action from certain perspectives.

By perspective we mean a basis from which action proceeds and in terms of which it is described and justified. Perspectives are made up of a number of key terms (human need and human purpose, for instance, fraternity or fellowship, membership of an organisation, suffering and intervention). These terms are explicitly or implicitly connected into clusters and sometimes these clusters are given the name 'ideology'. This term has been used in many different ways, sometimes to express false belief and at other times simply to refer to a set of beliefs actually held. It has been applied rather loosely to social work, and some of the main applications so far attempted will be discussed later (chapter 3). At this point we wish only to state and attempt to justify preference for the less emotive description 'perspective'. Ideologies tend to be described in a few, very persuasive terms. So Miller (1968) urges social workers to 'join with . . . clients in a search for a reaffirmation of their dignity. . . . Let us become mercenaries in their service – let us, in a word, become their advocates. . . . Let our clients use us . . . to argue their cause, to manœuvre, to obtain their rights and their justice, to move the immovable bureaucrats.' In this sweep of persuasion we are actively discouraged from remarking that mercenaries are not usually known for their advocacy, and that advocates help to achieve a justice that can only be common and not the property of any group. It may not be possible to describe exhaustively let alone analyse the constituent elements of a perspective, but we should not be arbitrarily halted in the task by a highly selected emotive description of some ideology.

This book also aims at trying to explore the significance of social work activity by examining related activities and relevant questions from other areas of work, practical and theoretical. Social work should be seen as more than a series of cases that illustrate but neither confirm nor deny particular theories. In our view recent British texts in social work have been either too parochial or too 'practical'. It is consequently often difficult to know what they are *saying*.

We wish to adopt the simple approach and to help to build a picture of a structure of social work, but this work of construction requires patience. We believe that the critical examination of language is crucial, but we want to base such examination on a few simple questions which are as close to practice as we can get. So this book is organised around a number of key questions which students must raise, consider and answer. Chapters will be devoted to the following: Is social work any use? What should a social worker know (short of 'everything')? What should a social worker be able to do? What beliefs are and can be upheld through social work? In trying to answer these questions we are addressing primarily students on social work training courses or those who already have some acquaintance with social work. We assume the

kind of introductory knowledge already available, from the literature or from a basis of acquaintance with social work. We try to
introduce social work students to a wide range of literature (not
all of which is academic). Again, the purpose is not to add to
bewilderment, but to attempt to move social work from reliance
on a basically verbal way of professional life. Much of 'practice
wisdom' is only passed on by word of mouth and hence is not
subject to public criticism, and much of what is written is clearly
professional talk simply transferred to paper. We believe that
social workers should be encouraged to appreciate literature that is
available and to establish some kind of critical dialogue with it.
That is why we have made liberal use both of quotation and of
critical comment upon the ideas others have expressed.

Value in not focussing on any one 'method'

This book is addressed to students of social work whatever method
they favour. We accept as possible and desirable a concept of
social work which embraces all the methods so far elaborated,
even though, as will become apparent, the idea of 'method' has not,
in our view, always been helpful in social work. So this is not a
specialised book for caseworkers.

There are, we believe, positive advantages in trying to bring
together each of the methods identified in the history of social
work. Discussion of social casework has advanced understanding
of the complexities of interaction between an individual client and
a social worker and between that couple (dyad) and the client's
family and social network. Such an understanding is used in any
social work. At times, however, the dyad became too private – and
in America some social workers became private practitioners – and
the counselling that was done in the name or under the guise of
social casework occupied an increasingly commanding position in the
hierarchy of value if not in the time of the social worker. Residential social work helps to remind social workers of their close concern
with the clients' problems of 'getting through the day' and of
choices clients have to make – of friends, solutions to difficulties
encountered in their social network and so on. It also suggests
that much social work interviewing takes place not in the highly
specialised area of the office but in the client's own life-space.
Residential social work cannot become precious because of the
social worker's involvement with the residents' daily life, and this
gives the work a realism that other methods occasionally seem to

desert. However, there is more to this involvement than healthy realism. It points to a creative flexibility of role (the person who has been engaging in therapeutic discussion of some kind becomes the person who helps other children as she cooks or is child-minding). By this we mean that a change of role may relieve other staff members who for good reason need to stay with a particular task (a child in a crisis of some kind) or may help the resident to realise certain feelings or ideas directly because of the change in role. The problems of integrating residential social work fully into the family of social work 'methods' have still to be resolved, but the resolution will help all social workers to see that social work is characteristically a matter of support and maintenance of milieux or the creation of new milieux on a permanent or temporary basis.

Social groupwork can indicate that much social work interviewing and other work is typically not on an individual basis, but revolves around meetings of families, or parts of families of clients, officials and so on. It also reveals the possibilities of the helpfulness, potential or actual, of others in the situation beside the social worker. This is a neglected aspect as far as social casework is concerned. Such helpfulness is, of course, one of the central dynamics of community work which also reminds us that much social work has always been concerned with discussion, negotiation and bargaining with officials in local and central government departments. Community work also demonstrates another general feature of social work – the difficulties in drawing a boundary closely around its practice. It has been suggested in relation to community work, for example, that people in many walks of life may practise it – planners, architects, doctors and so on. Yet such people are, of course, not professionally trained in social work. This possibility – that an aspect of the job of a doctor, nurse, even policeman could be called social work – fills some social workers with alarm. For them social work that is not the exclusive work of a fully trained professional specialist is not social work. It is our view that social work is not that sort of activity: its boundaries are loosely drawn and often permeable, and this is one of its chief advantages. This looseness of boundary constitutes one of the major challenges, if not one of the glories, of social work.

Our approach to social work is, as may be apparent already, inclusive and catholic. We do not believe that any one explanatory theory can be exclusively adopted. This is not to say that in social work 'anything goes'. Some such danger is perhaps implicit in an approach which questions received wisdom, and the solidarity and certainty reported by the use of terms such as 'professional', 'social work value system', 'diagnosis', 'treatment', 'theory' and 'practice'. The fact that these terms as commonly used do not work very well does not mean that social work necessarily is reduced to being a mere bundle of services (tied together, but by red tape). A case of partly mistaken identity does not rule out the possibility of a characteristic existence. Quite how the existence of social work coheres will, it is hoped, become apparent in the course of this book.

This book emphasises 'pluralism' in social work both in the sense that many different activities can count as social work, and that the problems facing social workers can be understood in different ways. Such an emphasis runs contrary to the strain within some social work writing towards the promotion of a single, unitary approach. Perlman, for example (1972, p. 209), believes that among the marks of a social caseworker should be found the ability 'to bear uncertainty and tolerate differences at the same time as he must act within one framework of thought and one style of action'. We believe that progress can be made in unravelling the identity of social work only once we have succeeded in disentangling the activity from debate and assertion concerning a number of crucial questions: for example its status as professional and the explanatory theory used by practitioners. Progress cannot be made if we simply *assume* at the outset the unitary nature of social work as a profession and of the theory that informs it, and then imagine that our deductions from the assumptions produce information about social work activity. As Titmuss (1970, p.14) stated,

> There cannot be one unambiguous goal for social work; human needs and desires are complex, interdependent, simultaneously rational and irrational, and often in conflict. Nor is there one unambiguous objective for the social services. It would be terrifying if there were and if we thought there could be.

Finally, it should perhaps be repeated that this book is not intended to contain all that a social worker should know or consider. Specialised works have been published, for example, on particular 'methods' of social work or on particular knowledge social workers should possess (e.g. law). One book cannot cover all the ground. It can, however, hope to trace a general layout, to plot a broad ground plan. We hope to sketch such a plan in a way that guides the beginning practitioner through a faithful exploration of the terms he uses and the questions he will and must ask. We have tried to indicate at the end of each chapter some further reading which will take the reader further in exploring and deciding on the questions we have raised in the main text. We hope both in the main chapters and the suggestions for reading that we have paid sufficient heed to an observation by Jenkins (1971), which social workers and social work teachers should mark: 'One can always talk. To talk relevantly in relation to actions actually required and required by the actualities of situations is quite another matter.'

Suggestions for further reading

We assume some prior acquaintance with social work, but some of the issues raised have been discussed in Timms (1970), which provides an introduction to social work. At this point definitions of social work do not matter (as will become clear, we think the search for definitions of social work has been exhausting and rather fruitless). Good descriptions of different theories in social casework can be found in Roberts and Nee (1970) and in Strean (1971).

These collections of essays succeed in conveying an informative picture of each of the theories, but the crucial connecting chapters are not very helpful, and it is clear that the basis for selection of the theories for detailed exposition requires justification – crisis theory, for example, is not a theory in the same sense as ego-psychology.

We have referred in the text to various explanatory theories. The following should be consulted.

On systems theory generally see Katz and Kahn (1969) and Forder (1976). Social work applications are considered in Vickery (1974) and Janchill (1969). The latter correctly notes that systems theory is not itself a body of knowledge, but a way of thinking, an analysis which accommodates knowledge from many sources. It is, we should also note, a way of thinking that can be interpreted conservatively or radically. In this it resembles social work itself.

Role theory suggests a further way of thinking, though some sociologists can find no use for the idea of role and there is no set of propositions about role that could be called 'theory'. The concept is, in our view, a fruitful one. Most of the difficulties in its use have been well discussed in Ruddock (1970). See also Olds (1962) and Biddle and Thomas (1966). It is in our view surprising that more attention has not been given in social work to the concept of network. No one speaks of 'network theory' – and for this we should be grateful – but the concept is capable of differential use: we can speak of the anchorage, density, range, etc., of network. See Clyde Mitchell (ed.) (1969). J. Shaw (1974) has reviewed the self theories of a number of theorists, including Maslow, Allport and Rogers, and suggested the bearing they may have on social work.

Labelling theory is a rather crude summary of a number of approaches that have in common an emphasis on the crucial nature of the processes whereby people are identified and, equally important, come to identify themselves as 'deviant' and different, as subject to differential treatment and respect. A good way of coming to grips with this 'theory' is to read Becker (1974). See also Case and Lingerfelt (1974).

'Theory of Anomie' is discussed by Hartman (1969), in an attempt to show how a sociological and a psychological version of anomie can be used.

Our approach depends to quite a large extent on raising conceptual issues. The discussion of concepts may present some initial difficulties and a good general introduction to such work can be found in Wilson (1963). One of the examples he uses for analysis has direct relevance to a problem in social work knowledge. He quotes Lawrence as follows (p. 25):

> To *know* a living thing is to kill it. . . . One should be sufficiently intelligent and interested to know a good deal *about* any person one comes into close contact with. . . . But to try to know any living being is to try to suck the life out of that being. Man does so horribly want to master the secret of life and of individuality *with his mind*. . . . Keep KNOWLEDGE for the world of matter, force, and function.

Social workers and others sometimes seem to feel that knowledge can be destructive. Wilson's discussion of the concept of knowledge is useful in itself but also because it forms part of a general view of working on concepts.

It is easy to find discussions of social work and 'society' which state a general argument that social workers must maintain a dual focus (yet another) on the individual and society, but work on developing this or any counter-argument has only developed slowly. Approaches through case example may be helpful. In terms of current practice the report on the Maria Colwell case provides a rich opportunity to see something of social work response to these questions. Historically, we can find studies that illuminate the relationship between social workers and society. See, for example, Platt (1969) who describes the humanitarian invention of juvenile delinquency in America in terms not of the liberation but of an effort to control the lives of lower-class urban adolescents. Social workers can begin to see some neglected aspects of their own relationship to society by studying historical accounts of social service development which do not assume a cumulative series of progressive movements towards enlightenment.

We have referred in the text to law. On this see Zander (1974) and McClean (1975). On the concept of friendship see Telfer (1970).

Taking bearings on social work

It is surprisingly difficult to define 'social work' or even to describe what social workers do. This is sometimes a subject for semi-humorous or rueful comment by social workers, but in this chapter we will try to go beyond any fatalistic acceptance of the difficulty, to do more than shrug intellectual shoulders.

How can we begin to grasp the sort of activity social work is? Three main ways have been used in social work in the past – the first is to follow the injunction 'do it and you will know what it is'; the second suggests that an historical approach would be illuminating, whilst the third relies on definitions and very brief descriptions. It is rarely that the actions of social workers have been examined. Apparently it is feared that the essence of social work will somehow slip through descriptions of discrete services given by social workers. It is in such a vein that a recent British attempt to define 'the inalienable element in social work' stated (BASW, 1973):

> We have deliberately not couched our definition in terms of what social workers do because this varies greatly with the agency and with the worker. Moreover other people – teachers, clergymen, politicians, civil servants and many more – do things which are very similar to those which social workers do.

It is perhaps because the group working on the definition turned away from any examination of what social workers do that they concluded with a description of 'the inalienable element' that whatever else it achieved hardly distinguished social work from the work of politicians and civil servants.

> The special function of social work, and its inalienable element, is to protect and promote the interests of the individual client or clients and to ensure that social technological changes serve and do not enslave the individual as a person in his own right.

33

Just do it

A trenchant example of this approach can be found in the advice of an anonymous contributor to the Charity Organisation Review in the early part of this century, 'If you want to train for social work find an A1 worker, work under her, live on the spot and read Balzac' (Anonymous, 1919). It is worth pursuing Balzac a little further to see how far such a no-nonsense approach takes us.

In the novel *The Fatal Skin*, Balzac refers to a M. Dacheux, the founder of some kind of charitable agency for the rescue of would-be suicides from the Seine. He is pictured 'in all his philanthropic panoply, raised up to set in motion those well-intentioned oars which so often crack the skull of drowning people unfortunate enough to rise to the surface' (p. 16). So, reading Balzac, whatever else it might achieve, would not always provide encouragement for those who would make a career of helping others. M. Dacheux's rescue work is not simply ineffective, however. It is fatally so, and similarly basic faults have been found by many others in those of their fellows who set out as a policy to help other people. Emerson, commenting on the motivation for such activity, said, 'Take egotism out, and you would castrate the benefactors.' Others have referred to the essential niggardliness of such: 'You find people ready enough to do the Samaritan without the oil and twopence' (Sydney Smith). M. Dacheux, like Lady Bountiful, is the fictional representative of a long and persisting tradition of downright doubt concerning the actual motivation and the real achievement of a policy of altruism. These doubts must be appreciated if social work is to be understood at least generally as a kind of altruism. There are a number of reasons why this is so. First, in looking at social work as an activity with a long history we should try to judge how far the verdict on altruists, enshrined in figures like Lady Bountiful, is based on a true picture of the altruistic enterprise. Is there something essentially inefficient or ludicrous in adopting a policy of helping others? Is it an activity that calls appropriately for an apologia of some kind or at least an apology? Second, the criticisms we have very briefly illustrated enable some important distinctions to be made between the offer of help, the effort to help and the outcome of the effort to help and to be helped. Quite often when attempts have been made to evaluate social work these distinctions have been ignored. Third, these simple distinctions enable us to see more clearly that the results of social work activity could, in certain circumstances, actually produce more harm than good. This outcome – as a report of the Edgbaston Mendicity Society 1871–2 suggested, how to help people without injuring them – has been insufficiently considered. A 'just do it and you will see' approach ignores this possibility and the whole issue of the importance of getting a description right. It also ignores the role of calculated risk-taking for both social worker and for client.

In order to illustrate the importance of risk-taking we have chosen another consumer account. This, of course, excludes the social worker's own account of what she did and why she did it, but it does show the risks the client experienced and also the risks the social worker had to take simply because she was a social worker. A 'just do it' approach characteristically ignores the contribution that consumer accounts can make to understanding the meaning of social work.

A medical social work client

I am a woman who for a long time was fed up with the world. Life to me was not worth living for, I didn't know what to make of it. I fell pregnant at the age of 16 years, which I told my boyfriend (who is now my husband). He wanted to marry me but I was against it, anyhow we got married. My first child – well life wasn't too bad but we still had our quarrels my husband and I, but life had to go on. I then had another two girls, after that life began to press me. I started to think a lot which made me irritable and depressed then my troubles began. I kept it inside me for a very long time till I could take no more. I got worse with life and so much wanted to do away with my kids and my husband. Depression grew worse and worse. I went to see a doctor to whom I tried to tell but I could not – I started to cry and get upset so he put me to a social worker. I took one look at her and thought I'm bloody sure I'm not speaking to her, who the hell is she? I'm not going to tell her anything. 'Come in and sit down', she said. I walked into the room and sat down watching every move she made. 'Can I help you?' she said. I started to think she's going to get me to talk, but she's had it, I don't even know her. My body, it shook as I looked around the room, I noticed the door, I thought you can run out of it, which would save me talking, for I didn't know how to take her. I just wanted to be left alone. The woman would tell me to relax and make myself comfortable – 'I want to help you'. God I would think go to hell, you're not getting me to talk, leave me alone. I don't even know you, why should I trust you. I kind of settled down a bit, but still aware of – hell how am I to start, my head it would go all funny and its tension would press hard. Why did I let myself in for this? Again she would say 'Let me help you to take this pressure off you'. I began to talk but still eyeing her up. It wasn't so bad I was asked if I would like to come back – I agreed. Weeks and weeks went by – in I would walk with a little confidence, there we would talk. Talking to her gave me a little strength. Gradually I would tell her what really got me down. I would go home, still I would sit and think, now you've done it, she'll tell what you've said and yet every time I came back to see her she made no difference to me, never pressed me. Often I would think now she's going to tell me how terrible I think you are, but she never. Yet I would tell how sick I am of life, get my kids away from me, I don't want them. This depression I would take would go up and then down. God how hard I tried to get rid of my family – to me they were the ones who were doing it – why don't they leave me alone. I want to be locked in a room all by myself. Always I would say to the social worker, I don't want them they're bloody pests. I'm better off without them. My youngest girl, she was a bit of a girl to cope with, she had a temper of her own. I lost control of myself one day. I took my child I battered her till she fell to the floor, I saw she did not move, I began to panic. God I cried what have I done. Everything went black before I realised what I did. I took a bottle of pills. I managed to get to my neighbour and tell her what I had done. She phoned for my doctor. I waited for I was so frightened. Get Miss X. I want to see her. Please get her. Doctor came with a nurse to take me to the hospital for disturbed people. The nurse took me in and along the corridor some – now I thought and turned to the nurse and shouted 'You're not putting me in this bloody place – it's a mad place'. I struggled to get myself free but it was no use. Once I reached the ward it looked pleasant enough. A few hours I was in, my social worker came. I looked at her and thought I needed you, but you weren't there. I don't want to be here I said to her. I don't like it. She tried to make me comfortable and tell me the rest would do me good. Well I listened to her and did what she said. Six weeks I was there getting better. My social worker came up as often as she could come. Soon I was to be released from hospital. I had to go back and forth to the hospital just to see how I was managing. Well there was days I would be fine, days when I would go low. This depression would always come back. I'm no better than I was when I first went in. I expected to forget everything and be cured I thought. Then my friend (social worker) would tell me it takes time my dear. My mind would ask do you know what you're talking about. I don't think you do. Back and forth I would go to keep my appointment at the hospital one day and then I would go the next day to see the social worker. This continued for a while then I got fed up running back and forth. I stopped going to the hospital, but kept going to the social worker as I relied on her. Yet there was days when I was so low I would go half way down to her then I would turn away. It's only me they're going to talk about, I'm fed up of it. I would come home get so upset that my family would get it – 'go to hell the lot of you, get out of my life,' I would shout; 'leave me alone, I hate the lot of you'. Often I would cry. I don't mean to say these things then I would go for a walk trying to ease my mind, but I would think – you're no good, how cruel can you be, the kids didn't ask to be born. 'Go and see your social worker' would run in my mind – somehow I'd phone her to tell her that I had a problem. 'Go home my dear, I shall be up,' and sure enough she'd come and we'd talk. It took me a long time to trust her for she had given me strength, my trust in her grew stronger – it was good for she really understood me and I her. Mind you things were good for a while then the off days would keep coming back again, trouble would start with me and my husband. We would shout at one another. My mind once more was twisted – so twisted that when I made my husband tea I would put Vim or peroxide in it, hoping it would do something to him. I sat down and watched him drink his cup of tea then waited but nothing happened, so the next day I did the same – by night he fell sick and came through for me to comfort him – when I saw him I gave him two codeine, which made him sleep. I went downstairs. Oh God, what have I done to him, he doesn't deserve this. I got frightened, please don't let me do these things. I need help I must go and see her, she will understand. The more I thought the more I was afraid. I went down – my friend (social worker) saw how distressed I was. 'Come in and tell me what has happened.' Well I said I have done an awful thing. I want to stop it. I don't know how I'm going to tell you, you might think, well, that's the limit, I don't want dealings with you now, I thought but I was so wrong. I looked at her. I didn't want to undo the work we both did together for I got my courage and strength by her understanding me. God knows I would never have done it by myself – to me it is good to have such a trusting friend. Nowadays I can get over my troubles which is a tremendous reward – yet I hang on to my social worker just in case I need her.

The one I thought who was just wasting my time was showing me how wonderful life really was. It is a good thing for someone else you can trust to help you with your burdens.

Definitions and brief descriptions

There is no shortage at all of statements, made with obvious informative intent and usually very deep seriousness, that begin, 'Social work is . . .' or 'Social work aims to . . .' or 'Social work is concerned with or for . . .'. We give now examples of some of these: an exhaustive list would be impossible, and in any case not worthwhile.

'The hallmark of the profession of social work must be its readiness to commit itself to meeting human need . . .' (Meyer, source untraced).

'Social work is a form of intervention which enhances, conserves and augments the means by which persons, individually and/or collectively, can resolve disruptions . . .' (Goldstein, 1973).

'Social work is a form of human activity in which certain members of society, paid or voluntary, intervene in the lives of others in order to produce change' (Haines, 1975, p. 1).

'Social work is concerned with the interaction between people and their social environment which affects the ability of people to accomplish their life tasks, alleviate distress, and realise their aspirations and values. The purpose of social work, therefore, is to (1) enhance the problem-solving and coping capacities of people, (2) link people with systems that provide them with resources, services, and opportunities, (3) promote the effective and humane operation of these systems, and (4) contribute to the development and improvement of social policy' (Pincus and Minahan, 1973, p. 9).

'Social work has inhabited an uncertain world, and always will. Its operational base is at the boundary of our knowledge of human behaviour. Its ethics are ambiguous and conceptions of its role and function fluctuate according to the demands made upon it by various groups and by the vicissitudes of the society within which it operates' (Fowler, 1975, p. 88).

'We have regarded as a social worker someone employed at the "consumer end" of a social service, who is in personal contact with those using it, and who is able to appreciate them in their family and social background. It is generally realised that much depends on the quality of the relationship that the social worker is able to establish with those he is concerned to help' (Rodgers and Dixon, 1960, p. 11).

'Social work aims to harness the potential in society towards solving its own problems. . . . It is concerned with bridging the gap between the individual and society, with supporting him when he is vulnerable and with striving to improve the quality of life by ensuring that human needs are not overlooked or over-ridden in this industrial society' (BASW, 1973).

This is a comparatively long list of examples of attempts to point the direction in which we should travel if we want to discover the sort of things social work is. It could be extended almost indefinitely, and a similarly lengthy list could be made of attempts to define what are recognised at various times as the methods of social work. Do these (and by implication) other definitions and descriptions help us to grasp the kind of thing social work is? A number of points will be made, to support our conclusion that the definitions and short descriptions offered are of limited usefulness.

1 The definitions and pronouncements sometimes succeed in pointing to a more general category about which something is known. For example, the first quotation (and many more that could have been included) states that social work is a profession, and this assertion tells us – in principle at least – something about social work because we have some knowledge of professions. It does not matter for the present that the assertion is extremely doubtful nor that for some social work students and social workers it would, if true, represent an undesirable state of affairs. But it does matter that social work is defined as a profession. Other suggestions, however, fail to do this. For example, to be told that as a social worker one ought to be ready to make a commitment to meeting human need conveys little by way of instruction. Commitment is in fact a term beloved of some social work teachers, who are anxious for students to demonstrate 'commitment to social work'. But this is only half an instruction. Commitment has to be *to* something: to a particular belief or set of beliefs (Trigg, 1973). Hence, commitment to social work entails conviction concerning certain beliefs about social work, which should be spelt out. It is not sufficient to talk simply of commitment to human need, or to social work.

2 Insufficient attention is paid to the differences between attempts to say what social work is and what it ought to be. The assertion which we have just presented concerning the professional nature of social work is better seen as a claim that social work

ought to be recognised as a profession. Similarly, to say that social work 'enhances, conserves and augments' is to describe very persuasively indeed. Whereas, we probably know where we are with the description 'its ethics are ambiguous'.

3 Certain terms emerge which must have a place in the attempt to say what social work is, 'human need', 'humane operation', 'personal', but the complexity of these terms is not recognised. They are, of course, not just complex but also contested. It is likely that people arguing about what counts as 'human' or 'personal' will not easily resolve any differences. This difficulty is shared with other activities, notably education. We can say easily enough what teachers do; we can describe their day's work in a number of ways, but it is by no means easy to say what 'education' is. Similarly, we can (but on the whole have not done so) describe what social workers do, but it is not easy to say what 'social work' is.

4 Many attempts to grasp social work take the form of definitions of 'social work' and produce highly abstract descriptions which succeed in conveying very little information. Typically, definitions talk of social work as activity 'concerned with' or activity with certain (vague and very long-term) aims. Each of these ways of talking has its own complexity. 'Concern', as Barry has noted (1964) is a slippery concept, and definitions of social work do not always distinguish between being concerned *at* (a state of affairs), *about* (an issue), *with* (an organisation) or *by* (in the sense of being affected by a policy). Hughes (1973) has distinguished three practical forms of concern, which he has called 'concern about', 'concern for' and 'concern with'. 'Concern about' refers to careful investigation; 'concern for' is the disposition to respond to need practically and with kindness (it might be described, says Hughes, 'as a primary sign of the acknowledgment of humanity of the person for whom you are concerned'); 'concern with' arises when we identify our interests with those who are not, at least initially, natural associates. These different senses of concern are important in identifying what social work writers may mean when they speak, for example, of social work's wholeness of concern with unmet need. 'Concern with' which is unaccompanied by 'concern about' can easily lead to the mutual floundering of social worker and client in a cause they have made their own. 'Concern about' can lead alone to the amassing of information and very little action. Talking of long-term aims, whether in terms of harnessing the potential of society or of helping people to enhance their coping capacities, distracts attention from the important consideration

that long-term aims are never realised. Hence, in trying to discover the nature of an activity it is more rewarding to describe short-term objectives.

5 Typically, definitions and descriptions are couched in terms that are themselves problematic. In the above list, for example, reference is made to the social worker's concern with 'bridging the gap between the individual and society', but what sort of gap is this and how would one know when the bridge had been completed and actually used for the work of crossing from one side to the other? This way of speaking which involves reference to 'the individual' and 'society' is to be found in much social work writing, but the result is often to prise a person from his social context and to personalise 'society'. Our grasp on each category slips as a result.

6 Definitions and descriptions should also be appreciated in full. As an illustration we will consider the statement from Haines's recent text already quoted – 'Social work is a form of human activity in which certain members of society, paid or voluntary, intervene in the lives of others in order to produce change.' Initially, this looks unexceptionable if uninformative, but it could perhaps be made to yield more information. It cannot be denied that social work is a human activity, but that it is 'a form' of such activity is not so easily acceptable: form implies shape, boundary and so on and it is precisely this that is often in doubt. Descriptions of social work should help us to see what is 'inside' and what is 'outside' the form, at least in a general way. In our view it is also important to appreciate that 'human activity' can be either descriptive (it's what people do) or evaluative (we may want to stress the 'human' and say not everything people do is human: a human activity is one that meets certain criteria, for example, human acts are characteristically rational). We believe that calling social work a form of human activity says a great deal, but this is perhaps because we take the words further than the author intends.

The author gives some account of the form of activity he has in mind: it is a form in which 'certain members of society, paid or voluntary' do certain things. We agree that the financial status of these members is irrelevant to the elucidation of what they do, just as we argue that the question of professional/lay status is irrelevant to this issue, but what is added to our understanding by describing these paid or voluntary men and women as 'members of society'? Again, we would suggest an interpretation since, as will become apparent, we believe that the 'social' in social work should be given a particular emphasis. We would suggest that social work activity is activity through which questions of membership of society reverberate: ways in which social workers and clients express different modes of social 'belonging' are at the centre of the description of social work and at the heart of social work activity. This is not to say that 'membership' is an easily understood notion or that questions about the terms on which people wish to belong can in practice be easily identified, let alone answered. It is to suggest that if 'members of society' is simply a complicated way of referring to 'people', then a good opportunity has been lost to get nearer to the core of social work.

Finally, we should note that Haines talks of social work under a particular, if general description. It is a form of activity in which certain people intervene in the lives of others.

'Intervention' can be used to describe a particular kind of activity directed at relationships suffering from particular kinds of harm. 'Intervention' can suggest a comparatively forceful effort. This becomes evident if we consider what 'non-intervention' means; it is not a complicated way of referring simply to abstinence from action; particular kinds of activity are ruled out. Yet 'intervention' has now become, without anyone remarking on it, a description for social work in general; reference is frequently made to strategies of intervention in social work and to levels of intervention. In one way this widespread use of 'intervention' may mark a positive change in social work language. 'To intervene' implies action directed towards particular objectives. Social work intervention is thus action instrumental towards particular objectives and not a benevolent but rather vague presence.

Such a positive change may not be purchased without cost, however. 'Intervention' can refer to a forceful effort directed towards two or more partners in some kind of conflict. Examples from social work activity seem to point to this as a possible meaning – intervention between a man and wife at physical blows, intervening in a situation in which a landlord is exploiting his tenant, intervening to prevent a mother assaulting her child. Social workers have intervened in these and other similar situations and the justification for such action is partly contained in the description of the situation – exploitation, the prevention of physical and mental harm. Yet not all actions by social workers are as forceful nor are they invariably directed towards situations in which one person is actually or potentially harming another. In other words 'intervention' may describe some social work activity but not all social work. This is of some importance, since intervention by a social worker may require justification over and above that required for social work in general. We seem in fact to be faced in the consideration of 'intervention' with a situation familiar in social work, namely a term that is used in both a strong and a weak sense. 'Intervention' can refer to a special kind of activity or simply, it seems, to any kind of activity. We hope that our brief discussion has at least indicated that the distinction between these two meanings is important.

The historical approach

Some writers are of the opinion that social work possesses the longest of possible roots and that identifying these will help us to say, in part at least, what social work is. We are told that social work owes something to the basic tenets of democracy or to what is described, somewhat breathlessly, as Christian-Greek-Roman civilisation. Distinct parallels have been drawn between the work of significant historical characters and modern social work (St Francis and the Franciscan ideas of Family Service Units) and attempts are made to link past achievements and ideas with the present. In our opinion, an historical approach is rewarding but only if two dangers can be avoided. First, history is often used in social work simply to vindicate the present. This occurs on a large and small scale, and is not just a recent development. So C. S. Loch simply dismissed centuries of thought and practice when he stated that 'to the theory of charity it might almost be said that since Aristotle and St Paul nothing has been added until we come to the economic and moral issues which Dr Chalmers explained and illustrated' (Loch, 1910, p. 197). On a small scale, article after article in the social work journals truncates history by referring briefly to a past in which we rather foolishly did x, whereas now we (more wisely) do y. A variation on this is to encapsulate history by referring to the time 'at which we came to see such and such'. So in a recent text Goldstein (1973) says of the period 1960–70 in social work, 'This decade built on the major efforts of the fifties and witnessed an evolving maturation and expansion of practice' (p. 47). Second, particular interpretations gain a mastery which is hard to shake. Two examples are of particular interest. First, the Webbs' crisp distinction between two traditions of giving. The first was identified with Roman Catholicism and stressed the benefits to the giver and the rather gratuitous and even haphazard nature of the activity. The second tradition, identified with Protestantism, saw giving (as in the giving of alms) as a rational activity directed towards the achievement of certain objectives in the receiver. This distinction has been persistently questioned by historians, but this questioning has not reached those concerned with the history of social work; the studies of Tierney (1959) or such detailed work as Pullan's on Renaissance Venice (1971) are ignored. Yet these works suggest strongly that talk of two rather monolithic traditions is misleading. Thus Pullan states:

> Medieval Catholicism has often been accused of encouraging haphazard and even actively pernicious charity by encouraging the giver to think only of the benefit to his own soul, and not of the effect of his alms on their recipient. Judging by later history, it is dangerous to assume that at any given time one can distinguish a single, unitary Catholic attitude to the problem of the poor – in the sixteenth century, the views of Mendicants in Flanders and Spain differed radically from those of Ignatius Loyola, of Italian Jesuits. . . . Then, at least, there was a wide spectrum of opinion among the Catholic clergy, with no clear consensus emerging (p. 199).

Now this may seem rather pedantic, but the historical judgment we have quoted serves a number of purposes: it has not been included as an esoteric decoration or an addendum of high culture. It has been used primarily as a way of illustrating the paucity of social work history, but it also suggests that apparently monolithic traditions can encompass a variety of strands. This is important for the contemporary practice of social work. First, social workers should not be encouraged to rest content with bland generalisations whether these are applied to the historical origins of social work or to matters of more immediate import. Second, a realisation of the non-monolithic nature of previous traditions suggests a possibly less anxious way of facing, perhaps embracing, the various factions within social work at present. This is not to approve of a pot-pourri approach – anything goes because everything goes in – it is to suggest that particular traditions can be articulated in a number of different ways. Some aspects at least of contemporary community work can be understood, for example, as developments of the lost tradition of the Settlement Movement. Third, the possibility of variety can alert us to the fact that a consideration of the motives for social work will lead to discussion of the place of Christian motives (amongst others) and, as we shall see, it would be wise to question the assumption that all Christian motives are of one piece.

The second example of the freezing of a particular historical interpretation comes from much more recent history: we refer to a period in the 1930s which has become known and accepted as 'the psychiatric deluge' (Woodroofe, 1963). It has been suggested that from about the 1930s social work in America was overwhelmed by the ideas and terminology of psychoanalysis: the sociological stirrings, which some claim are to be found in the classic breast of Mary Richmond, were stifled, and oedipal social-work man was born. The shorthand expression to cover this change is 'the psychiatric deluge'. Again, this is a historical judgment that requires criticism. In the original formulation, and even more in the frequent use of the term subsequently, we move uneasily between psychiatric, psychoanalytic and psychological – as if these were all the same. Moreover a detailed study of primary and secondary literature sources by Alexander (1972) suggests 'that, except in a few northeastern cities, Freudian theory was not well known to social workers. Its influence was limited to an élite few rather than to the main body of the profession.' Such an observation is of general as well as particular importance. It helps us to appreciate the gap that can often be found in the history of social work between the prescriptions of theory and the actualities of practice. It also suggests that a theory or set of theories can easily be applied crudely and dogmatically.

A combined approach

We have so far considered examples of three ways of attempting to take some bearings on social work. Each way has a particular advantage, though none alone is sufficiently able to suggest a rounded picture of social work. 'Doing social work' reminds us that social work is a practice and that a successful piece of social work is not concluded in the testing of a theory or the proving of some theorem. Yet the attempt to advocate a simple 'practical' approach – do it and you will see that it's just a matter of helping people – very soon breaks down. Theory used in social work may sometimes have seemed unhelpful to the social worker, but concepts are critically involved in the activity, since at least in part a description of social work has to be conveyed to those who are offered or would use the services of a social worker. In so far as social workers need to be explicit about their objectives and methods, about what is involved in social work as far as clients are concerned, it is clearly insufficient to say to a potential or actual user of social work: 'It's like riding a bicycle; I cannot tell you how, but I will run beside you until you catch on.' There are ideas, notions and assumptions that constitute the practice of social work, as well as ideas and theories which suggest ways in which the practice can be well executed.

The approach of short description and definition suggests elements that must find some place in a good description and they set before us an idea of the unitary nature of social work, even though a hold on this unity is somewhat difficult to sustain. On the whole, it is probably not sensible to spend much time on the comparisons of definitions of the term 'social work'. 'Social work' means many things to many different people and attempts to establish an agreed definition show all too often the marks of professional ambition and a short sequence of long words. Instead, we should try to build a picture of what social workers do, including what they believe in interaction with their clients.

An historical approach helps us to see some aspects of social work, but only some. It suggests that the problems facing social workers and their clients are partly new and in part old. In so far as they are old, then an historical approach indicates a number of different reasons. Care has to be taken, however, that an historical approach is not confined narrowly to 'the history of social work'. Social workers should always attempt to place clients in their context and, similarly, this should be their aim with the historical study of their own activity. It is somewhat surprising that whilst social history of the nineteenth century usually forms a part of the education of social workers the significant experiences of that era are not used by social workers as fully as they might be. A brief illustration may be helpful. Social work writers often assume and sometimes explicitly state that social work techniques or methods are based on scientific or theoretical advance, but this is to mistake the kind of thing a technique is. This mistake could perhaps have been avoided by attention to the technical developments of the Industrial Revolution. Hall (1974), for example, makes the following comment on the greatest of engineers: They '. . . inherited a sound though limited engineering tradition, and developed it much further, without borrowing from or themselves creating a rational science of structures' (p. 150). Technical advance in social work does not necessarily have to rely on previous theoretical advances.

Altruism under social auspices

How do we propose to bring together elements from the three approaches we have considered? We suggest that they cannot be integrated into a succinct definition of the term 'social worker', but that together they illuminate a great deal of the purposes and actions of social workers. We believe that this can be done by giving attention to the fact that both understanding, and also understanding social work, are best seen as a semi-philosophical enterprise. In our view action on behalf of others (altruism) is one of the general headings under which social work should be set, and the other refers to the social auspices under which altruism is carried on. The auspices refer to general social support for social work and to the form of work, the agency. Agencies, voluntary or statutory, offer a range of services (counselling and advice to individuals and groups, advocacy, milieux of different kinds) and social workers are responsible for 'administering' these services to persons and for creating, where necessary, new services. In offering and rendering one or more of these services social workers meet problems on which psychology and sociology throw varying degrees of light, but many of these problems require moral and/or political perspectives.

How then do we propose that social work should be delineated? We think it useful to take a historical viewpoint and to place social work within a general framework of altruism, action on behalf of another. Ideas of altruism can form a context for social work and are part of a tradition much longer than that of professional social work: such a context and tradition supply breadth and depth without hiding any of the major problems in the practice of social work. This is not to argue that any altruistic activity should be counted as social work, any more than, with reference to the earlier list, anything that contributes to the development and improvement of social policy or anyone employed at the consumer end of a social service could be counted as social work or as a social worker. What we suggest is that social work is seen as a type of altruism (rather than primarily as a profession, a form of therapy, or a kind of revolution). It is altruism that is systematic, self-conscious and practised under social auspices. Each of these qualifications presents problems, as we shall see, but none is in essential contradiction to the idea of altruism.

At first glance perhaps using 'altruism' seems to present no advance at all. Rosenham (1970) says correctly, 'Altruism, in its widest sense, describes a great variety of behaviour which ranges from doing small favours to saving lives in crises, from "doing good" to inordinate selflessness.' A recent collection of psychological studies suggested that two main meanings might be given to altruism. On the one hand, any behaviour which happens to benefit another is altruistic. On the other, it is motive which is crucial in identifying an action as altruistic. If an actor fails to respond with empathy to another he cannot be called altruistic. He must experience empathic pleasure as a result of behaving in a way that has consequence for another (Macaulay and Berkowitz, 1970).

Certainly behaviour that happens to be helpful can be connected with different motives, and it would be stretching altruism too much to include all of these in altruism. When we say social work is a kind of altruism we mean that social workers intend to help people who are strangers to them by offering and providing, in their interests, for their needs or in response to their wishes a range of services. These services were in the past offered by non-statutory agencies, but the state has come to take an increasing part. To place social work in the category of altruism under social auspices is to deny none of the problems faced in social work but to place them in a wider context. Altruists over the centuries have been asked such questions as: can anyone really help another; is not all action self-regarding, so that the offer is really a way of helping oneself or of controlling another in one's own interest; is our perception and imagination so limited that we cannot adequately grasp another's plight? How do we manage our own feelings in the face of distress we have to try to relieve? These questions, based on the tradition of altruism, seem to us more meaningful for social workers than issues usually presented half-dressed in the borrowed clothes of professionalism. Some aspects of professionalism, as we shall argue, constitute answers to only some of these questions, and they do not help in their formulation.

It seems that talking of altruism helps to bridge the gap between personal and professional relationships in a way that does justice to social work activity. To describe the relations of social workers and clients exclusively in either personal or professional terms is to lose something of the amalgam that can be found in social work. The contrast between the two approaches can be illustrated from Strawson's description of taking an objective attitude and taking what he calls a personal reactive one.

> To adopt the objective attitude to another human being is to see
> him, perhaps, as an object of social policy, as a subject for what, in

> a wide range of sense, might be called treatment; as something
> certainly to be taken account . . . of; to be managed or handled or
> cured or trained. . . . The objective attitude may be emotionally
> toned in many ways. . . . But it cannot include the range of reactive
> feelings and attitudes which belong to involvement or participation
> with others in inter-personal human relationships; it cannot include
> resentment, forgiveness, gratitude, anger or the sort of love which
> two adults can sometimes be said to feel reciprocally, for each
> other.

Social workers, as it seems to us, move in and out of objective and
personal reactive attitudes and are usefully identified with neither
position. This movement is well accommodated within the notion
of altruism.

Altruism also enables correct emphasis to be given to certain
important elements in social work. We shall mention just three of
these: the idea of a person, the notion of exploitation, and the
similarity and contrast between help and friendship.

Altruism requires logically that the altruist has and can use the
concept of a person to describe the object of concern and the
reason for the concern – I am concerned about X as a person, and it
is because he is a person that I am concerned. It is this centrality
of the notion of person that enables us to see that some of the
long-established criticisms of altruism have incorrectly described
altruism.

Altruism also rules out exploitation. Now exploitation is not the
most simple of ideas, but it can perhaps be agreed that it contains
three elements: use, harm and deceit. Exploitation refers to a
whole range of ways in which people can be used to their own
harm, even though they may not feel they are being harmed.
Characteristically those who are exploited do not realise that they
are being used. Some idea of the way exploitation as we have
described it may intrude into social work can be seen in Cohen's
(1975) recent reference to some radical critiques of social work.
They see, according to Cohen, human problems as 'not interesting
in themselves, but as signs of something else, such as the crisis in
the system: the solutions are not important in themselves unless
they help something else, that is, the working-class struggle'.
Altruists, because they are concerned with the needs, interests and
wishes of persons, cannot as altruists brush aside what is presented
as personal needs, interests, and wishes, and work on the 'real'
problems, whether these are those of the underlying neurosis or
a failure in consciousness. Altruists work within the bounds of
what is known; as altruists they cannot enrol those they help in

the Kingdom of God on earth without first showing them a constitution.

Altruism also suggests ways in which social work activity can be distinguished from friendship. Friendship itself has been insufficiently considered in social work writing, but following Telfer (1970) we may say that friendship is made up of shared activities (not just reciprocal service), the passions of friendship (such as affection), and the acknowledgment of a special relationship. Friendship depends not just on the performance of certain actions, but on their performance for particular reasons – out of friendship. This concern of affection which is one of the distinguishing marks of friendship is a concern for this other, particular individual. The concern of the altruist is also with the individual, but for each individual and not for one rather than others.

It may be objected that whilst 'altruism' helps us to shed light on the intentions of social workers, on their objectives and those of their clients, it distorts social work by reducing it to the small scale and the individual. This is where we should recall the second major element of our description, altruism under social auspices. Social work, in our view, is always bound up with social agencies. In so far as it is a profession, we would agree with the position of the Functionalists that it is a special kind of profession, namely an institutionalised one. In so far as it is a therapy, it is a special kind of therapy. In so far as it is a social movement its concern is with people as actual or potential users of social services.

Now it has been objected that an emphasis on the social agency produces an inevitably conservative bias. This is not so. It is true that some formulations of the connection between the social worker and society made through the agency are unsatisfactory, as we shall see, but that there is a connection is undeniable. As we have already said, 'social' in 'social worker' refers to this connection, but we do not take this to rule out critical activity in social work. Social work is often critical of social provision and current social beliefs and attitudes. Moreover, it helps users of social work towards an appreciation of their situation, a greater discrimination between their wishes, interests and needs, and a closer identification of their emotions. In this sense social work encourages the client to engage in work of appraisal (criticism) and in many cases to try to change his social situation. Social work is helpfully seen as critical (but not condemnatory) activity, and such a view can be contained and nourished within the perspectives of altruism.

Suggestions for Further Reading

We have not been able to trace any detailed accounts of doing social work from the point of view of the social worker. Some aspects of the stress and strain of doing social work have recently been studied by Mayer and Rosenblatt (1974). A novel by George Konrad, *The Case Worker*, can be read with profit. Those who advocate a 'just do it' approach seldom describe for the benefit of others just what they do.

Definitions of social work have not been reviewed, but some of the main definitions of social casework have been collected and, to an extent, assessed. See Bowers (1949), but there are definitions of other kinds than the kind he attempts; see Robinson for a useful discussion of these (1968). Readers will find it useful to collect and evaluate their own list of statements which begin 'Social work is . . .'.

We suggest that the history of social work has not received sufficient critical consideration. The best general history of social work available is Woodroofe (1963), though as the text indicates it is not completely satisfactory. Light is shed on the history of altruism mainly from studies of particular periods and localities. See also Seed (1973) for a brief but thoughtful introduction to the history of social work. On the tradition of the Settlement Movement see the essays in Addams *et al.* (1893). Psychologists have been studying the psychological sources of altruism and the situational determinants of acts of altruism. See Macaulay and Berkowitz (1970). Also Montefiore (1973) for a number of essays that have relevance for personal relations considered philosophically.

The best account of the significance of the social work agency is still to be found in writing of the functionalist school. See Smalley (1967). Writers in this school usually manage when writing about the agency to avoid the deep mystification that afflicts their treatment of 'the will' or the helping relationship. See, for example, Gilpin (1963). This is unfortunate since her topic (the relationship between theory and practice), to which we have referred very briefly in our discussion of the 'psychiatric deluge', receives very little consideration in social work writing.

Lubove (1965) has used the term 'professional altruist' to describe social work, but his book contains no detailed discussion of the concept of altruism.

Does social work work?

The significance of evaluative research

This chapter will be concerned with a number of related questions. We start by asking if social work works. This apparently simple question leads to a consideration of the possible meanings of social work for clients and for social work practitioners. In general in this chapter we are asking the question: Why social work – because it is an efficient instrument for achieving certain purposes, because of the meaning it conveys to clients, because of its bearing on the worker's sense of vocation? It may seem perverse to attempt to face questions concerning the effectiveness of social work so early in our text, particularly when, as we shall see, research into these questions cannot, at first glance, do very much to encourage the social worker. In our view, however, it is as well to face questions of effectiveness, and of the place of research in and into social work at the earliest possible moment. Such a judgment is based on three grounds. First, research and social work should go much more closely together, and this requires some change in both partners in the enterprise. As Davies (1974b) has remarked, 'Despite the steady proliferation of research literature, many practitioners find it difficult to make the link between what they read of research and what they do in their everyday work; indeed it cannot truly be argued that empirical studies have made much positive impact on the traditional pattern of diagnosis and treatment in casework.' Practitioners of social work tend not to look to empirical research for guidance on problems they encounter. Research workers should address themselves to these specific problems. Until quite recently they have tended to accept too readily the kinds of general description of social work given to them by the practitioners. Practitioners for their part have tended to accept too readily a distinction between producers of research and consumers, neglecting those elements of research activity that should be found in the practice of social work, for example in assessing local need.

Practitioners, in their turn, mistrust generalisations and general survey methods. A discussion of actual research studies will show, however, the value of the systematic study of the individual case. Howe (1974) has recently argued for a single-subject approach to the assessment of casework in a way that shows clearly the sort of relationship between practice and research that, in our opinion, should be encouraged. Howe believes that a number of requirements must be met if a single-subject approach is to be successfully pursued. For instance the caseworker-researcher must focus on simple, concrete description. He notes that social workers 'always work with events at this descriptive, observable level' but they 'may not order and structure abstractions from this level'.

Second, we think that gloom generated by most of the research reports is entirely misplaced. Some social work authorities have even suggested that evaluative studies in social work should cease. But how strange it would have been if social work activity could, on the basis of the first handful of studies in evaluation, have been shown to be entirely successful. An activity developed up to that point through the experience of practitioners, the work of clinicians and a large number of deductions from theory, would have been shown 'to have got it right' the first time. Social work could hardly have survived such unique and spectacular success. The fact that social workers have a long way to go in conceptualising and improving practice means that their activity falls into place as a normal and human one. As we try to evaluate social work we learn something that may increase our effectiveness and we certainly discover more about what social work is.

The third reason for discussing this topic now is connected with the reason just discussed. We believe that the research studies into the effectiveness of social work repay careful study. We should not be content to register a global and dismal impression that 'research shows social work does not work'. Rather we should learn to qualify initial impressions in the light of evidence collected from careful and wide reading. This approach to research suggests a possible model for at least some aspects of social work itself. As social workers we should learn to build up and to test over-all impressions through particular observations.

The contemporary social worker is perhaps less sure of the

answer to the question 'Is social work effective?' than social workers of an earlier age. Social caseworkers in the late nineteenth century often claimed dramatic and lasting improvements from comparatively simple changes. Simey (1960) called attention to similar claims made by voluntary Children's Societies in the same period.

> Unstable boys, cared for in a small Home in which they are given psychological treatment, become happy and responsive; none of them proves to be impossibly difficult or unmanageable. The ragged child wandering in the streets, son of a drunken mother, is adopted by a Canadian barrister. The girl who had been consistently and cruelly beaten by her father is terrified of men, but her confidence is won by a man on the staff of a Home after a single interview. And so forth and so on, unendingly (p. 28).

These and similar success stories were produced, partly at any rate, to raise funds to build more Homes or employ more social caseworkers. Doubts were raised from time to time, but these tended to be directed more towards caseworkers than residential staff. It was easier to deduce that residential social work worked from the fact that residential establishments simply existed. Criticism of social casework tended to be based on very general considerations—How could case-by-case treatment solve widespread social problems that required reform on a wide scale or revolution? Such criticism, applied to social work as a whole, has recently been revived.

The uncertainty of today's social worker seems to proceed from two sources: the supposed or actual results of empirical investigation, and the generally grounded criticism that social work because of its nature either achieves no results or very effectively achieves results that are the direct opposite to those explicitly intended—it intends to liberate but succeeds in dominating.

It is only comparatively recently that empirical investigation has attempted any assessment of the effectiveness of social work, and this has been mainly in the field of social casework. In residential settings attempts are now being made to describe and measure 'regimes' (Sinclair, 1971) and to measure and compare parts of organisations on particular scales (King, Raynes and Tizard, 1971). These are important research developments, but organisations always include staff who are not social workers, so it is not always the effectiveness of social work that is in question. Some kind of evaluative study is often built into new community work projects, even though there is disagreement about the justification for this. So we shall be able to make some reference to evaluative research into social work generally, even though the major work has been attempted in social casework.

First evaluative study

Probably the first significant attempt at an experimental test of the effectiveness of social casework was the study by Meyer *et al.*, published in 1965. Its importance, however, is not exhausted by its place in what has become a relatively long list of projects, so it is worth discussing in a little detail. The study attempted to approximate the model of the clinical trial. This imposes considerable demands when applied to social work. Briefly there are five crucial requirements: a reliable and valid measurement of conditions before and after 'the treatment'; random assignment of different treatments or treatment and non-treatment to an experimental and control group that are similar in all relevant respects; measurement of treatment dosage; establishment of criteria for success; and finally some means of connecting outcome to the treatments given. In social work each one of these requirements poses extremely difficult problems. Non-treatment of persons in apparent need for example as a part of the research activity presents an ethical problem. It is obvious that large numbers of people in apparent or real need do not receive help, appropriate or otherwise, but this is an entirely different situation from that in which service is withheld from a known group that must form part of the study. Even if this problem could be satisfactorily resolved, a severe practical difficulty remains. Meyer *et al.* frankly admitted that their experimental test 'was not one of provision of service *vs* withholding of service, but rather the known provision of service *vs* unknown experiences excluding these specific services' (p. 24). It is important to note these requirements since they should be met by any study that attempts to use a clinical model.

Another reason for discussing *Girls at Vocational High* concerns the difficulty of ensuring that it is social work that is being measured. This is clearly a crucial question. As Reid and Shyne (1969) correctly state, 'It does little good to state that treatment X had better results than treatment Y, if we cannot say of what the treatments consisted' (p. 55). Meyer *et al.* comment that in the initial plan for their project it was proposed that 'treatment' should be described more systematically than was the usual practice in the agency with which they were concerned. Such a description was not, however, proceeded with and the description, let alone measurement of the mixture of casework and groupwork offered, remains one of the weakest elements in their project. It is perhaps surprising that even a relatively small proportion of girls showed improvement after casework that, according to the girls' perspective, assumed they were 'crazy and otherwise invidiously identified' (p. 37) or a rather directionless course of groupwork. The researchers had in addition the problem of the lack of motivation in the girls studied, so that there is some doubt whether social work was actually delivered.

This study attracted a great deal of attention. According to one writer discussion of this research in America has been 'endless' (Hartman, 1971). Its major finding that the various measures adopted failed to succeed in preventing such occurrences as school drop-out, illegitimate pregnancy and so on conveyed a depressing message. It was also a message that could be and was exaggerated.

Those making the claims are not always the researchers, but considerable claims were made for this evaluative study. These claims had their source partly in the foreword to the book which started by asking 'Is social work on the wrong track?' and then adding that this question 'is neither asked nor answered' in the book. Some commentators seem hardly to have read beyond the first seven words and assumed that the results of the study (which require careful analysis) answered the question in the affirmative. This kind of interpretation evoked a defensive reaction from American social workers (Macdonald, 1966).

It is worth noting at least one of the ways in which the results were re-interpreted or rather explained away. One writer (Gyarfas, 1969) argued that generally the research tended to devalue the subjective aspects of the interaction between social workers and clients. It was suggested that casework theory would have provided a firm basis for the following time sequence to have been predicted in relation to the girls at Vocational High: a period of denial and rejection of the need for treatment; a period in which the existing problems were projected on to the school, the girls' families and so on; a gradual acceptance of a relationship with the social worker, a decrease of anxiety and a beginning in taking responsibility for the problems; and a beginning awareness of the possibility and the importance of choosing goals and working towards them. The writer suggests that a year for each of the four phases would not have been excessive. As a consequence it could have been predicted that in the length of time studied in the research the subjective changes implicit in the research's objective criterion (e.g. reduction in school drop-out) could not have been accomplished. These comments begin on what appears to be a promising track: what the interaction between social worker and client may mean. However, it soon becomes bogged down in the rut of a conventional (and controversial) account of social work from the point of view of the social worker, and of the social worker who adopts an exclusively psychodynamic perspective.

More recent studies

Since the publication of this study there have been a number of studies, mostly by American researchers. Goldberg *et al.*'s comparative study (1970) of the effectiveness of trained and untrained social workers in giving service to the old is the only British study. The American studies have been summarised and reviewed by Fischer (1973) who collected details of eleven research projects (from 1965 to 1970) and analysed not only their results but the characteristics of the populations studied, the method of selection, the theoretical orientation of the treatment offered, the major method employed, the length and amount of social work contact, how success or failure was defined (e.g. social work is effective if the treated group engages in less delinquency) and how the success was measured (e.g. number of court appearances). Fischer concluded his analysis by stating that the studies give no ground for thinking that social work results in a significant difference between contrast groups and groups receiving social work help. In addition, there is some evidence to suggest that some people who receive such help experience deterioration. This last opinion has, however, been criticised on the grounds that it is only a product of Fischer's own method of analysis (Hudson, 1974). A more extended analysis and commentary on research on evaluation in social work can be found in Mullen and Dumpson (1972).

The results of much of the research so far undertaken can most usefully be illustrated by brief references to a small American study, and Goldberg's work in the field of old people. The first illustrates the lack of positive result and the second a more positive outcome. The Chemung County Study (Brown, 1968) was conducted into two groups of fifty problem families: and the other studied in a comparative manner intensive casework by professionally trained social workers whose caseloads were reduced and who had access to more than the usual range of community services.

In the Chemung study casework was carried on for a median time of around 95 weeks and at the end of the study it was concluded that nothing much seemed to have happened in the cases given intensive casework that did not also happen in the control group. The former were slightly higher on most of the judgments of family functioning and of movement in social casework, but the differences were not statistically significant. Indeed, if in the case of one family there had been a lesser degree of movement the whole difference between the special group and the control group would have become indiscernible instead of being merely statistically non-significant.

Some aspects of this research will be discussed when we come to take an overall view of evaluative research (e.g. the failure to describe the casework help offered), but at this point we should note some implications of the last statement in the paragraph above. The results of the research seem to throw into relief one particular case which apparently showed movement against the trend. Social work will be impoverished if we do not attend with care to such individual instances, whether these are uncovered by particular research projects or through practical experience. One of the issues for social work revolves not around the desirability of a general survey as opposed to the intensive study of particular clinical instances but around the interplay between these two approaches, which are interdependent. Commenting on this possible significance of the individual case seen against a particular general background Robinson (1971) states that

> The non-significant results shown by individuals are important, in the same way as the results shown by individuals who respond against the general trend. The promiscuous adolescent who makes an unexpectedly good marriage, the chronic schizophrenic who has no further breakdown, the inadequate psychopath who holds down a steady job, and the many little successes where they were not expected, all are very appropriate foci for investigation.

He then adds a point which emphasises that this observation does not imply a responsibility just for the researcher, 'Here reporting by the social worker is more important than ever . . .'.

The Chemung study suggested that the workers involved felt that in some cases a great deal had been done. The earlier Cambridge–Somerville study (Witmer and Powers, 1951) reported that the counsellors concerned believed they had substantially helped two-thirds of the boys, and more than half the boys said in their final interview that they had been helped. It is one of the several positive aspects of Goldberg's study that it includes a chapter on consumer opinion (to which further reference will be made in the following section). This study, like the majority of research in the evaluation of social work, employed a contrast rather than a control group: in other words what was tested by the careful measures employed was not the effectiveness of social work help compared to no social work help, but the differential effects of two kinds of social work. In this respect it resembles the Chemung study.

In other respects, however, it differs significantly. Great attention is given, for example, to describing and measuring the help received and the help 'attempted but not received'. Such a distinction is quite crucial. The results of the study are also more encouraging. After the detailed study and assessment of 300 old people three of the general hypotheses (e.g. more clients in the special group will show positive changes in their social and medical condition than in the comparison group) were partially confirmed and five of the seven specific hypotheses (e.g. more people in the special than in the comparison group will develop interests and activities; will show an improvement in their attitudes to their present situation as measured by the attitude score).

Before we attempt to assess the value of the evaluations of social work so far undertaken we should refer to two other groups of work which, again, suggest more positive results. We refer to studies in marital counselling and to a number of studies which seem, in the view of Davies (1974b), to re-emphasise the importance of the individual worker.

Beck (1973) has reported on a critical examination of 32 controlled studies into the outcome of marital counselling. She notes that statistically significant positive gains have been reported in all but one of the 32 studies and that additional evidence of positive effects can be found in eight further studies where, however, control groups were not used. Such a result compares remarkably with what we have seen to be the general outcome of evaluative studies in social work. Beck appreciates the problem this poses and offers the following answers.

1 In the studies of marital counselling surveyed couples were actively seeking help or were willing to volunteer, whereas in some at least of the other studies, a casework package was thrust at the client.
2 The marital couples in the studies formed a relatively homogeneous client group.

3 The main problems were modifiable at least without drastic change in the wider social context, whereas some of the groups of social work clients studied suffered from material and social deprivation and had manifold problems, so that it was, to say the least, unlikely that intensive casework alone could produce much change.
4 The measures used to evaluate change were specific to the kinds of change that could be expected and to the problems that were given attention.
5 The measures were able to reflect relatively small changes.

Some of these answers reflect, in our view, an observation of major importance, namely that counselling for counsellors and for clients alike represents a comparatively clear method and procedure. Counselling, as we shall see, is one kind of activity in which social workers engage, but it is a special activity not to be confused with the whole of social work or even of casework.

Davies (1974b) has referred to 'a range of findings about the force of the worker's individuality'. He refers in particular to the Community Treatment Project in California (Palmer, 1973), which usually receives scant attention in this country, and to Sinclair's work on probation hostels (1971). The former emphasises the positive results to be obtained from the matching of client and social worker and argues that this variable is one of the most significant elements to be discovered in the course of the Project. Sinclair concentrates on the role of the warden in the success or otherwise of hostel regimes, but argues that this should not be seen in isolation. The warden's impact depends upon the nature of his relationship with the matron and on the climate current in the hostel. Sinclair's work is well worth detailed attention not only because it has general importance for residential social work, but also because it produces results from what appears to be unpromising and routine material.

Finally, reference should be made to some evaluations of community work projects. The theme of these evaluations makes in general terms somewhat depressing reading. Benington (1974), for example, concluded a discussion of one of the Community Development Projects by observing that 'self-help and community action within the neighbourhood may help to gain marginal improvements and some compensatory provision'. In fact some aspects of community work might be judged to be productive of a kind of harm. ' "Participation" can pre-empt real debate of issues, and co-opt possible conflicting interests.' Ashcroft and Jackson

(1974) concluded a study of adult education and social action with the appraisal: 'There is no doubt that we will leave Scotland Road in Liverpool much as we found it; a massive monument to an exploitative society . . .'. Community work projects are clearly very different from programmes of casework, but attempts to evaluate these different approaches have at least this 'finding' in common: they take us back to purposes and the connections between purposes and methods. If the purpose of community work is the destruction of a particular socio-economic system, then, almost all community work projects will be found wanting.

What can the student of social work derive from this evaluative research?

Certainly, no sense of self-satisfaction, but a number of important lessons not exhausted by the realisation that evaluative research is difficult and exacting. This means that we should give each study the credit at least of following with care its measures and definitions. It is important that in considering the results of research neither critics nor advocates rush to a premature and global impression – 'I always knew social work was useless' or 'I cannot accept that the results of something as personal or intangible as social work can be measured.'

A careful study of the research so far attempted suggests no evidence of the ability of social work to produce dramatic change, but the researchers help social workers not simply to be more modest but also to learn much more about social work. Perhaps Pringle was speaking just for himself when he suggested in the 1920s that social casework was the antidote to Bolshevism, but it is more likely that social workers either entertained great hopes of themselves or allowed others to do so. Following the series of research reports on effectiveness, it is much less easy to do this. It is also more likely that social workers will concentrate more on the careful delineation of the objectives. As Mullen and Dumpson have said (1972, p. 10) of many of the demonstration projects, they failed 'to reach their goals because the following question has been inadequately considered: on what basis and toward what end will who do what to whom, for how long, with what effect, at what cost, and with what benefits?'

One of the major results of the evaluative studies is to highlight two important questions for social workers: one concerns the nature of social work activity, and the second the kind of evaluative research that is most appropriate for social work. We shall consider each of these in turn.

We can find at least three issues of importance for the nature of social work activity that are illuminated by the research we have been considering: the problematic nature of social work; the place of the client in social work; the predominant focus of social work activity. These issues are, of course, interrelated.

We have already suggested that researchers have, on the whole, been rather 'charitable' to the language and explanations of social workers. ('Charitable' is a description used by Gellner (1970) to characterise the positive response of people seeking to understand a foreign custom and assuming that the foreigners' explanation of the custom will be directly informative.) Commenting on the thirteen evaluative studies which are the subject of Mullen and Dumpson's work, Breedlove suggests that

> The most striking observation to be made about these studies is that they took social work practice as a given entity instead of a problematic subject, needing investigation, specification, and conceptualization. Rhetoric to the contrary, there is no evidence that social work practice is as yet a fully formed, clearly specified, and unified set of procedures (Mullen and Dumpson, p. 60).

Such a conclusion is not depressing in any conclusive sense, but challenging.

Second, criticism of some of the researchers emphasises that social casework cannot be seen as a service on a collection of services that are simply left, as it were, at the client's door. Perlman (in Brown, 1968) has criticised the Chemung study, for example, because in her view the research design assumed that casework was an unvarying process guaranteed to give satisfaction regardless of the specific nature of the client, the problems, the agency's rules and resources and the guiding conceptions of the caseworkers themselves. Such an observation reminds us of the central place of the client in all social work, but it is unhelpful to suggest that we must simply accept as a matter of definition that casework is 'not a bundle of services that can be "given" or "done" to those who "need it" '. Because it may not be a bundle of services that can be given, it does not follow that it is not a bundle of services. Of course, neither does it follow that it is: it remains a subject for investigation.

The researchers of the past have usually concentrated on the social work treatment that has been, as it were, administered. As we read these studies, however, it becomes more clear that it is what happens 'outside' the treatment relationship that requires more extensive consideration. Davies (1969), in a study of probationers not so far mentioned, observes that

> The quality of the casework relationship was statistically associated with parental relations, father–son and mother–son relationship, the probationer's contemporary associations, the level of support he enjoyed at work, and his personality characteristics. Furthermore, the casework relationship is itself related to reconviction. Clearly then we have a vicious situation: bad social circumstances related to bad personality characteristics, both of which are linked with a bad treatment relationship, all in turn associated with a greater likelihood of failure (p. 121).

The direction in which this perspective will take us, if we let it, is clearly and explicitly stated in the first evaluation study we have mentioned in the chapter. *Girls at Vocational High* ends with the recommendation that social workers should give much more attention to the social context in which their clients live.

> Radical changes are infrequent; small and gradual changes are more common than dramatic ones in learning social behaviour. . . . Thus changes tend to reflect the proximate. . . . What is proximate for the kinds of girls in this project? Their families, their neighbourhoods, their friends, their schoolmates and teachers, their jobs and their employers. Is it not through these – in short, the social systems that contain these girls – that we may achieve changes? Should it not be with reference to these that we determine the proximate goals for change (p. 215)?

Such a perspective is, however, often ignored by social workers. They may, it is true, collect information on the environment, but this information makes little apparent impact on their 'treatment'. This is partly because some psychoanalytically orientated social workers adopt, through conviction or defensively, the stance of Miss Burke in *Mother and Son* (by Ivy Compton-Burnett). 'Miss Burke looked about her without curiosity. She seldom felt it, as she attached no importance to what she saw. She had learned that the setting of human experience was no key to itself.'

As we have seen, many of the studies undertaken so far have followed the experimental model as far as they could, but how far is this an appropriate model for social work? This question has been discussed by Marris (1974) with particular reference to community work projects. Marris distinguishes two kinds of research project, the reasonably rigorous conventional experiment of a very specific issue, and research into community action of a more diffuse kind. He gives as an instance of the first the negative income tax experiment in America. This was an instance in which 'government is already committed to a policy, and wants to know which alternative design for its implementation would be best'. Even in this situation, though procedures approximating to those of a scientific experiment can be used, the results of the experiment may be valuable chiefly as propaganda. This aspect applies even more to more diffuse programmes of community work with which we are familiar. In these situations, argues Marris, 'you have at the outset to take a stand on questions of value and belief, which commit you to more than the value of experimentation itself'. In research into the effectiveness of social work it seems that a number of approaches are possible and desirable as long as the questions being asked are clearly and sharply defined. The effectiveness of a programme (say of using highly trained personnel) is different from the effectiveness of a way of working and from the effectiveness of a particular social worker. We should seek to increase effectiveness in each of these meanings of the terms, but our methods of doing so will be different in each case.

Finally, we return to the conception of treatment often used in previous research. In social work it is not sufficient to say that treatment depends upon the client's co-operation with the social worker. In one sense the co-operation *is* the treatment. Such a perspective raises more questions concerning the appropriateness of the clinical trial model. Certainly, we cannot begin to test the effectiveness of social work until we can recognise social work, and recognition depends to a considerable extent on what social work means to clients. This aspect has slowly been given importance in the research we are discussing. It is interesting to see the way in which these research studies have changed in relation to the client perspective. Meyer *et al.* give very little attention to this problem beyond a general question concerning the amount of help their subjects might have received from parents, friends, a doctor, a social worker, etc. Reid and Shyne (1969) on the other hand, examine in more detail not only the clients' assessment of the helpfulness of the service but also their views on the components of the service. For example, clients reported their views on the facts that the worker gave little advice or talked little. (It is, of course, essential to know what clients mean by advice.) Yet if we are to become more sure of the meaning of social work before we start to measure it, the client perspective will have to take a much more central place in our research strategy.

To gain some idea of the clients' perspectives on social work we have to turn to a different collection of studies, ones not primarily associated with measuring the effectiveness of social work. They are important in our present argument, because the value of social work may lie more in the fact that it expresses a particular set of meanings for client (and social worker) than in its effectiveness measured by other means.

The meaning of social work to the social work client

Consideration of the possible meanings of social work to those who receive the attention if not the help of social workers is an important part of the main purpose of this chapter since it could be the case that social work worked in the client's estimation but not in the social worker's. Clients may have a very different idea to social workers about what it is for social work to work. Over the last seven or so years a number of studies have been undertaken in this country and America into the clients' perceptions of social work.

We will use these studies to illuminate approaches to a social worker and the client's view and assessment of the help offered. In the concluding part of this section we will comment on the status of consumer opinion in the social services.

The approach to help

It is difficult to distinguish clearly the paths along which people may travel or be sent before arriving at a social worker's office or a residential centre. Generally but crudely speaking, people may come on their own initiative, on the advice of friends or relatives or through referral by official sources. From studies of consumer opinion we can make two generalisations. First, no matter the source of referral it is safe to assume a considerable ignorance of social work and social workers. In Sainsbury's (1975) close study of 27 families helped by a Family Service Unit, for example, referral was inadequately performed in at least 12 families who had been left by the officials concerned wholly unaware of the function of FSU. A respondent in Reith's study (1975) said: 'I didn't know what they did. I heard this, that and the next thing from people and I just thought they would help me.' A study of just over 300 consumers of the services of a local authority department suggested a lesser degree of ignorance, however, since less than a third said that they did not know what to expect or that they did not expect any help (McKay *et al.*, 1973).

It appears that friends and relatives are often a source of information about social work, but – and this is the second generalisation – social workers often neglect to give this fact full value. We mean by this to draw attention to two matters. First, clients often come because of some defect or lack in their social network of help and support, and this influences what they expect from the social worker not simply at the beginning but also during the course of the contact. Second, the network often acts as a kind of Greek Chorus throughout the social work action commenting upon and sometimes – unlike a Chorus – influencing the outcome. At times the outcome is influenced through the client comparing (favourably or unfavourably) the help given by the social worker with that available in the non-professional network. Consider, for instance, the kind of expectation of social work that would be entertained by a client who said, 'I discussed it with that lady up the road, but I don't know if she understands right or not. She just agrees with you, kind of style. She just says "yes" and "no". She just took a load off my mind talking to her. That was all' (Reith, 1975).

Interestingly enough, when the power and influence of this network is explicitly recognised by social workers it sometimes becomes itself the object of treatment. Certainly, this is the finding of a study by Leichter and Mitchell (1967) which emphasised a conflict of value between clients who were deeply involved with their kin and social caseworkers who were trying to encourage independence. As the authors concluded, 'The finding that caseworkers or their clients differ in their experience and views about obligations towards kin poses questions of why restriction of kinship contact was so frequently sought in casework treatment. Is this a product of cultural assumptions or of scientific knowledge (p. 271)?'

Some of the ignorance of the possibly special functions of a social worker arises from the difficulty facing certain people of picking social workers out from the comparatively large number of 'officials' with whom they have contact because of their particular problem. Rees (1974) has drawn attention to this, quoting as one example a family with a mentally retarded girl.

We've had all sorts of contacts over the years. When it began it was really education. But when she got over the school age who did you turn to? Sometimes it's just been welfare or we've contacted centres for handicapped children. When we moved last time we didn't know who to turn to. A friend said the Red Cross ran a baby-sitting

service but it turned out they didn't. One day I was desperate and
I remember ringing people from one department to another about
an allowance. We rang one department and were referred to
another and another, no one knew. A health visitor said she would
look into the possibility of someone looking after Karen occasionally.
She never did find out but at least she wanted to help. We've not
really asked for much ever. Those who don't have a mentally
handicapped child don't appreciate how much you are tied. I didn't
know what the social worker was, I thought it was all security,
something for nothing and we didn't want that.

Clients come or are sent to agencies (and agencies include
residential establishments) with varying degrees of ignorance of
social work but, as the last quotation indicates, they come also
with certain expectations. Recent research suggests at least three
aspects of such expectations that shed light on what social work
means to the consumer. First, consumers often expect material
help, but social workers seem to assume that consumers look for
something more personal. Thus, in McKay's study (1973) the
majority of social workers thought that clients actually expected
most of all to be able to discuss personal problems and to receive
advice and sympathy; whereas less than 10 per cent of the clients
said that they expected that kind of help. This kind of finding says
nothing, of course, about what help clients should receive.

Second, potential consumers or actual users of social service
seem to have a poor view of the group or groups of people who
become the clients of social workers. To some, at any rate, such
people are at best to be described as desperate and at worst to be
categorised as scroungers. This is hardly a group which one would
seek to join with enthusiasm. Moreover, with agencies offering a
casework service it is comparatively rare for clients to meet others
being helped so that they can test out their picture of 'the typical
client'. In other situations clients are very quickly aware of
the other members of their group, for example in residential
centres.

Third, consumers who come to social work agencies for material
help of one kind or another do not expect a sympathetic reception.
Social workers are expected to be stern, strict and abrupt, and
rather inquisitorial. Thus, one of the clients of a voluntary society
said:

Well, I thought, honest to the Gospel, that she would check on
every part of my life – the ins and outs of everything. I thought
they'd pry – do I drink, do I smoke, how many women have I
divorced. . . . I imagined people coming to my address, saying, Does

he live here? Is the light off? Try the switches! . . . That was one of the things that stalled me off. I thought to myself, I can't go through all that – everyone's entitled to a bit of privacy (Mayer and Timms, 1970, p. 103).

The help itself

Consumer opinion has a great deal to say on the help given by social workers. At this point we will concentrate on what clients seem to value in social work, the frequent uncertainty and misinformation about whether one is or is not a client, and the possibility of a conflict of perspective on the part of the clients and of the social worker.

When users of social work are asked about the social workers they have encountered in their experience of the agency they tend to stress the personality characteristics of their social workers. In McKay's study clients valued an understanding and sympathetic person, a pleasing personality, with such skills as the ability to put people at their ease. Sainsbury's FSU clients stated preferences for social workers on the following attributes ranked in order of frequency with which they were mentioned: informality (homely, easy to talk to); getting close enough for honest discussions; patience; equal caring for everyone in the family; politeness. Similarly in Butrym's study of (what were) almoners, a patient said, 'She is a friend to you there. Almoners feel more for you than doctors and nurses. Doctors and nurses know how you feel from your charts, but the almoner knows how you feel personally' (Butrym, 1968).

But we should not rush to assume that here, unlike anywhere else, love is enough. This for two reasons. First, the FWA study (Mayer and Timms, 1970) noted that clients often expect a negative reaction, and the positive response to the social worker's non-condemnatory approach is largely a contrast effect, i.e. things are good because they are not as bad as the client initially feared. Second, clients also expect from social workers some expertise. In Goldberg's study (1970, p. 193) of social service for the old, for example,

> The old people rejected a rather impersonal services-orientated approach, as well as a very personal one which did not heed their practical needs. Their comments also showed how important a consistent willingness to help in any situation was to them and how much security they derived from knowing exactly where to turn in time of need, confident that a response would be forthcoming.

In the FWA study clients stressed their expectation of concrete advice. Take, for example, the case of Mrs Farrell who said:

> I can easily tell you what I thought it would be like going to the agency. I would bare my soul and my reactions to what my husband did and said. I would hold nothing back, like I do with the neighbours. I would tell the lady all the nasty things that I did back to Brian, and I thought she would say, 'If you didn't say this or react like that, Brian wouldn't react like he does.' As for Brian, I was hoping that they would tell him, 'Well, if you didn't treat Mary like that, she wouldn't lose her temper and scream and go into hysterics.' I would have helped build something out of the marriage if the woman had said, 'You shouldn't have said that' or 'You shouldn't have done that' or 'I think your marriage would work if you didn't do that, Mary, or if you didn't do that, Brian' (Mayer and Timms, 1970, p. 67).

It seems, then, that the initial contact between client and social worker can constitute an important experience. What happens after that, however, can vary considerably, and sometimes clients can be mistaken or in doubt about the social agency's continuing interest. For example, in McKay's study two-thirds of those who thought they were 'closed' were in fact, as far as the agency was concerned, on the active list, and one-tenth of those who thought they were 'active' had been closed. Jones's (1975) study of people who had ceased to foster children found that a substantial proportion of the ex-foster parents were not aware they were ex- in status. Among ex-foster mothers 20 per cent thought they were current and 15 per cent were not sure. Among ex-foster fathers 33 per cent thought they were current and 20 per cent were not sure. So, there seem to be questions around 'Am I/am I not still an object of concern to the agency?'

Difference of opinion between social worker and client about the closed or open status of a case is a possibility that should be recognised. This, however, does not exhaust the ways in which clients and social workers may disagree. Beck and Jones (1974) have drawn attention to the pervasive disagreements that can occur between client and social worker 'in the definition of what the problem was, the kind of help needed, the treatment approach that was appropriate, the level of satisfaction in the counsellor–client relationship, the reason for termination and the evaluation of outcomes'. It is, of course, possible to treat each of these disagreements in a discrete manner, investigating in turn the definition of the problem, the evaluation of outcome and so on. It is important for the social work practitioner to be aware of each different aspect, but it is also important to consider that the aspects are in fact linked and that what is at issue is the difference between two distinct perspectives on social work help, its process, objectives and outcome.

One example of this possible clash in perspectives can be found in Mayer and Timms (1970). Their study suggests that a number of clients came to social work with a particular perspective on help. They expected that the social worker would make some sense of the situation, discover the basic fault (usually, this meant judging who was to blame) and then take active steps to rectify the situation. (Take, for example, Mrs Farrell's ideas on this question, already quoted.)

Social workers on the other hand approached the problem differently, in an explorative, rather passive manner, implying, if not stating, that the problem was somehow 'within' the personality of the client. As one client said of her social worker,

> She was more like a person that was going into you mentally. I can't explain it. She kept asking me about my background and all that – about things that were bothering me when I was a young girl. But that's got nothing to do with what's going on now. Well, that wasn't going to solve my problems, was it? I mean it's now. I'm grown up now (p. 71).

Now the research we have been quoting can only be seen as suggestive, but what it suggests is of some importance. We have to consider that 'helping', its processes, objectives and so on, is not the same for everyone: that there are significant differences between perspectives on help and that these reflect other differences between people (perhaps differences of social class, region and so on); and that unless social workers are alive to this possibility they will assume a general agreement on these matters with their clients which could be the basis of a great deal of misunderstanding. We should also note that when such a clash in perspective occurs, it can lead easily to even further complications. The client when confronted by unexpected and strange behaviour on the part of the social worker may try to find an explanation. The explanations may further estrange them from the social worker. So, in the study we have been discussing 'some clients reasoned that their workers were simply not interested in them and therefore not overly anxious to help them'. Mrs A. came to this conclusion, remarking:

> Once I got talking to the social worker, I felt at ease, but then I realised that she wasn't entering into what I was saying at all. And I

thought, you are not really listening to me. You are not really
interested. She just wasn't giving me an answer or any advice at
all. . . . She just kept saying 'Yes, yes' in a quiet sort of way and
nodding her head and would I like to come back and that sort of
thing (p. 73).

Other clients concluded that the workers did not understand
their difficulties and therefore failed to deal with the problems
effectively and realistically.

Mrs K., for example, thought the worker did not really grasp
the terrible effect of her husband's gambling on the family. Mrs W.,
whose husband evidenced symptoms of mental illness, commented that no matter how she put her case she felt the social worker
did not understand what it was to live with a man like her husband.

Significance of consumer research

First, the term itself – consumer of social work. Mary Richmond
once observed that those whom social workers help are called by
many names. Any humour was unintentional, but it is true that
users of social service have been termed – at different times –
supplicants, applicants, clients, and now consumers. Objections
can be – have been – made to each of these, but for the present
purposes it is sufficient to note that each of these terms calls
attention to a significant shift in the relationship between those
providing and those using a social service. Take, for example, the
following use of the term 'supplicant' in an eighteenth-century
sermon: 'While you demand . . . we refuse; when you begin to
supplicate, from that moment, we bestow. While you continue to
lift the sword to our throats, so long we repel your threatenings
with disdain – but condescend to supplicate, and you receive.'
'Client' seems to mark an improvement on 'supplicant', but what
of 'consumer'? This term seems to lead us into a particular kind
of world which stresses demand and goods, as well as market and
consumption. Some aspects of such a world are to be welcomed –
the stress on consumer preference and the consumer knowing
what he or she wants. However, as we shall see, social work cannot
be seen simply and exhaustively in terms of 'giving people what
they want', and, in so far as participation describes the part played
by 'the client' one is perhaps led to see the client as 'member'
rather than consumer.

Second, and our first point already touched on this – what is the
main lesson to be drawn from the study of the client as consumer?

There are two distinct answers to this and the difference between them is the difference between two views of social work. Consumer views can be interpreted as useful reminders of good practice, as tactical information that will enable the social worker better to deploy his or her forces. Or 'the-client-as-consumer' can be seen as a way of coming to grips with the meaning of social work. A patient's opinion about the delivery of medical services will not usually be able to say much that is authoritative about the content of medical treatment. Customer opinion about products can usually be taken to be sovereign. Somewhere between patient and customer is the consumer of social work. Social workers are not, in our view, social doctors. Rather they are deeply involved in the area of planning with people so that they can better meet their needs, attain their goals, serve their interests. In this kind of enterprise seeking consumer opinion is not a frill, not a public relations exercise; it is the heart of the matter.

We have been concerned in this chapter with the light even existing consumer studies can shed on the meaning and the process of social work. It is a matter of debate whether the consumer studies so far undertaken constitute a sufficiently firm basis for changing social policy. Shaw (1975) has suggested that studies of consumer preference should meet a number of criteria before they can serve such a purpose. There should not, in Shaw's view, be any other significant groups of consumer whose viewpoints differ from those in any sample studied; consumer opinions should be relatively permanent and must rest upon informed consideration of the possible range of alternative ways of dealing with the problem. These criteria are important and it would certainly be against the spirit of this book to underestimate 'the real diversity of preference' among consumers (Shaw, 1975).

The significance of social work to the social worker

If we are in comparative ignorance concerning the views of the clients of social work – and we have no systematic study of the views of clients who have been in residential care, or in groups in the community run by social workers – our lack of knowledge about social workers is almost complete. Yet our training arrangements and our elaborate beliefs and procedures concerning the supervision of students and, sometimes, of beginning social workers suggest that social work as a career has deep personal significance.

It is certainly the case that social work is exceptionally demanding. As Wasserman (1970) says

> The professional social worker must be able to fulfil the roles of wise judge, loving parents, firm advocate, and patient friend. His intellectual and emotional resources are constantly being tested: he must be able to respond in a humane manner to a diversity of troubled, often difficult, people. The fate of children and families often hangs on the correctness of the professional social worker's judgements and decisions.

What does a social worker rely on to maintain his choice of career in such a context?

Answers to such a question can only be speculative at the moment, but we will discuss briefly the motivation for social work, since it is motivation and re-motivation in the course of training that receive most attention in informal discussion. Prins (1974) has recently suggested that the following motives may be influential in the choice of a career in social work: a creative impulse; curiosity about the lives of others; the need to make restitution for early destructive phantasies; the need to express the great mother complex; the altruistic motive. Explicitly Prins draws attention to something quite fundamental to his whole discussion, namely the assumption that social work is not a job just like any other. But he gives no indication of what 'a job just like any other' is like. Certainly, we do not show much interest in motives if someone announces his intention of becoming a doctor, a nurse, a postman, language expert and so on. So, asking for someone's motive in becoming a social worker suggests that the questioner is unsure, requires something to be justified.

Yet the object of justification changes as the face of social work changes. What motivated middle-class women to persist in offering their services to the male-dominated social work world of the mid-nineteenth century – 'I have hardly a hope', said Octavia Hill of one of the early COS committees, 'that they will place me on the committee; I shall try boldly but I think no ladies will be admitted' (Barnett, 1918, pp. 27–8) – will probably differ from what motivated those working-class women who were recruited to psychiatric social work in the 1930s in Britain. Similarly, curiosity about the reasons prompting a very small proportion of men to choose psychiatric social work before the Second World War might be justified, but not about the reasons why men now choose to enter an occupation with a clear and well-rewarded career structure.

So, the search for motivation must take account of the changing historical nature of social work. It must also acknowledge that at any one time people see and experience a number of 'social works'. As Pearson has argued (1975),

> To read the literature of social work one would imagine that social workers are essentially unlike other men, that they are men who have been reared in a moral–political vacuum, and that their decision to earn a living in social work is not in any way informed by the ideological contours of social welfare.

He identifies three ideological positions in relation to social work: Christian, humanist and radical. We should also note, however, that each position may in turn cover a number of differing perspectives which have implications for the meaning social work may have for the practitioner.

Take, for instance, Christianity. It is often supposed that Christianity, having supplied the original licence for the practice of social work, continues to be most congruent with the main tenets of social work. Yet this is to assume that differing traditions in Christianity produce no similar reverberations within social work. So Shaw comments from a fundamentalist position in the following manner on the Thomistic view that because man, any man, is worthy of salvation in the eyes of God, so in the eyes of the social caseworker he is worthy of courtesy and understanding:

> But nowhere in Scripture is redemption portrayed as grounded in the (hidden) worth of the individual. The necessity of redemption is grounded rather in God's sovereign good pleasure. And it is not inherently necessary to that love which God necessarily and eternally is, that He should set such love as results in redemption upon men and women who are deserving only of His wrath.
>
> Such biblical teaching as this should lead us to question the appropriateness of notions such as acceptance.

Such discussion of motivation as has reached the printed page has not been very useful to the social worker. It has been characterised, as we have seen, by an individualistic emphasis which has emphasised motive as 'push' rather than as 'the reason why'. It has encouraged social workers to mistrust their intention to do good, and the development of a climate in which difficulties are traced to some psychological difficulty in the individual practitioner. Mayer and Rosenblatt's pioneering work into sources of stress among student practitioners (1974) yields the following typical examples of this tendency from statements by individual social workers:

> My difficulties were due to the fact that I was emotionally immature.
> I could not get in touch with the client's feelings because I was too involved in the suppression of my own.
> I allowed the client to become too dependent on me. This was not in the client's best interest but fulfilled my own needs of being the client's saviour.

The students in the study appeared to have unrealistically high standards, but blamed themselves when they encountered difficulties in developing the right level of relationship with their clients or in accomplishing treatment objectives with the limited resources at their disposal.

Social work seems to carry considerable meaning for social workers, but we should recognise that a range of meanings are legitimate. We should not seek to canonise only one. So far we have looked at these meanings in a very general way: for example, social work is meaningful as one kind of religious vocation. It is, however, possible to suggest a rather lower level of analysis which indicates differences between workers that are productive of different styles of working or of different treatment policies. We refer to the growing interest in ideologies of social work. 'Ideology' is a very complex term but it is used increasingly to refer to an interconnected set of assumptions and feelings which together constitute a kind of outlook on the world. These assumptions are spelt out with difficulty and are basic, that is, they are not susceptible of proof. The existence of different ideologies has recently been suggested to account for differences of behaviour in the social services and in social work. So, in the field of blind welfare a distinction has been made between the restorative approach, which aims to establish the blind person in increasing independence, from the accommodative approach, which seeks to place the blind in controlled environments and to increase their dependency on specialised welfare agencies. We shall refer later to Miller and Gwynne's (1972) distinction between a warehousing view and a horticultural view of residential care. Cypher (1973) has referred briefly to four possible orientations – Therapist, Traditionalist, Reformist and Activist, whilst Smith and Harris (1972) discuss different ideologies of need. Rein (1970) has constructed a fourfold typology of social work ideologies based on attitudes to standards of behaviour (acceptance or challenge) and the target of theories of social change (the individual or social conditions). This produces four orientations: traditional casework, radical casework, community sociotherapy, radical social policy, though it seems from Rein's article that the last may not be a form of social work.

These studies suggest that it is fruitful to search for the particular image of activity that expresses the meaning of social work for the practitioner. We should, however, note three things. Not any ideology can serve as the basis for social work activity: ideologies that sanction exploitation, that cannot be counted as human—such ideologies, as will become clear in the course of this book, are incompatible with social work. Second, ideologies are basic and cannot be exhaustively reduced to testable hypotheses, though they contain such hypotheses. They cannot be seen, as Rein seems to suggest, as temporary aids dispensable when a scientific theory of social change has been created. Third, they are described frequently through the use of one or two ideas only – it is for this reason among others that we earlier stated a preference for the term perspective which could be said to do much of the work done by 'ideology'. Such a restriction is limiting and moreover tends to exaggerate the extent to which social workers hold to only one ideology and hold to it consistently. As Smith and Harris have observed in a neglected footnote, 'Multiple ideologies are clearly possible.'

Suggestions for further reading

We have given directly or indirectly in the text the main evaluative studies in social work. Further detailed discussion of *Girls at Vocational High* can be found in Macdonald (1966). Some students will wish to set the discussion in a wider context, and will want to consider evaluative work in other areas. For a useful summary of such work in psychotherapy see Carkhuff and Truax (1967). We believe, however, that a study in depth and in detail of one of the studies is preferable to a brisk survey of the whole field. The kinds of question to be asked of each study can be found in the text and in Plowman (1969).

It would be unfortunate if readers were to carry away an impression that evaluation in the strict sense attempted in most of the studies is the only kind of research that social workers should learn about. Davies (1974b) has reviewed recent social work research using a threefold classification: administrative (what is the status quo?), exploratory (what related factors impinge upon the status quo?), theoretical (what is the status quo within the context of a predetermined theoretical framework?)

It is sometimes objected that research is not worth very serious attention by social workers, at least in its present state of development. It is suggested that research tools are as yet too crude to capture the nuance of relationship and the subtlety of interaction that is at the heart of social work. We would not wish to exaggerate the efficiency of research methods in these areas, but some promising work has been done, for instance in the measurement of family relationships. See Brown and Rutter (1966).

Those interested in learning more of the statistical methods that might be used should read Philip, McCulloch and Smith (1975). Such methods do not suffer any change when they pass into the hands of social workers, but it is useful to see them illustrated by examples that are intelligible to social workers.

The text has referred to the main studies of client opinion. Studies of social workers are less easy to find. Schmidt (1969) concludes that 'Clients placed more value on achieving concrete behavioural changes, whereas workers tended to emphasize more abstract, psychological goals.' See, however, Pins (1963) for a general study of American and Canadian social work students and why they chose social work.

What should a social worker be able to do?

Talking of methods of practice

One answer to the question which heads this chapter is to say that there really is no problem: a social worker must be able to practise one or more of the methods of social work. Social work is commonly divided into a number of methods and using any one is usually counted as 'doing social work', though no single method can stand for the whole of social work. In this way of thinking it is not possible to be doing social work unless one is practising one of the methods. How has this come about?

The first 'method' to be, as it were, baptised was that of social casework, but this started life much more as a general way of approaching a problem. Casework was the name given to a case-by-case approach; and method was the name given to carrying out whatever seemed appropriate in the individualised situation. Social casework was simply individualised social work activity: it was directed at a particular situation and was undertaken in a particular spirit; that is, something was done for *individuals* recognised as such. Gradually, ideas of therapy were injected into this approach and a 'method' of treatment was devised which had to contain under the rubric of method all that a caseworker had previously done as simply appropriate to particular situations. Once this new method had been accepted it was impossible for other approaches to gain acceptance except under the mantle of 'method'. Therapy, or as we would prefer to say counselling, took over the casework method, so that everything had to have a justification as contributing to or being part of 'treatment' (in a strong medical sense). Method took over in social work as a dominant concept and everything had to be justified as part of some method of treatment or other.

83

How many methods are said to comprise social work? The answer will depend on the period at which the question is directed. At the height of the influence of the COS the reply to the question would have been in the singular: social casework. Four or five years ago three methods would perhaps have been quoted: casework, groupwork and community work or community development. Now residential social work would be added. Of course, valuation of these methods would have been different at different periods: casework, for example, is said to suffer a current eclipse, but in the ensuing and very patchy darkness it is difficult to see which if any of the other methods is in the ascendant. Recently, discussion of the details of each method has tended to give way to the idea of multi-method practice, but in so far as this is seen as a combination of methods or simply as the ability of the practitioner to choose the most appropriate method of help for the particular client or clients, it is clear that the concept of 'method' is still dominant.

In our view the influence of 'method' has not been beneficial to the development of social work. Indeed it is because we take this view that this book has its present form. We believe that talk of method has not enabled social workers to clarify at whom the method is directed or in what it consists. In saying this we assume that method means more than 'being methodical' (as, for example, in the collection of information) and that 'a method is not something literally present to hand or something possessed and used as a chattel . . .' (Buchler, 1961, p. 95). If the concept of method is applied to the supposed recipients of social work or to the activities of social workers we believe that it works rather ineffectively.

Take the recipients first. Social casework is sometimes described as a method of working with individuals, but how can it accommodate work with families? – and families in some ways (though only in some ways) resemble the groups who might be said to qualify for the method of groupwork. If groupwork is the method of work used with groups, can we say that community work is the method of work used on communities and residential work the method used on those in certain institutions? Probably not, since a community (say contrasted with a series of networks) is very much less easy to pick out than a family or individual, and those in residential work seem to use, in so far as they use methods, a combination of the other three.

To suggest that the methods of social work are directed at systems of different kinds (from society down to the defensive systems used by individuals) offers too wide a target for any 'method'.

But what after all constitutes the methods so far identified in social work? Hollis has identified for social casework a number of procedures, but a satisfactory answer to our question cannot be found in listing a number of procedures. The procedures must hang together in a particular way: they cannot simply co-exist as items on a list, rather they must cohere as a method coheres. How do the constituent parts of a method go together? To answer this question we have to move outside social work. In the case of this term, as in so many of what could be called the constituent terms of social work (like treatment, technique, relationship and so on), social workers have been frustrated in their attempts to develop understanding because they have been confined to a purely domestic language. Some notion of what counts as a method can be found in a recent discussion in what seems a field of learning remote from social work, theology. (Unkind critics of both theology and social work language sometimes doubt that the distance is significant.) As Lonergan (1972, p. 4) puts it:

> There is method, then, where there are distinct operations, where each operation is related to the other, where the set of relations forms a pattern, where the pattern is described as the right way of doing the job, where the operations in accord with the pattern may be repeated indefinitely, and where the fruits of such repetition are, not repetitions, but cumulative and progressive.

If we apply this set of criteria to the 'method' of casework, group-work, residential work and so on it becomes evident that they do not stand up as methods. It is extremely difficult to separate services (say of counselling from advice, of treatment in a residential centre from the course of daily living and so on) let alone the methods by which the services are administered. It is difficult to describe distinct operations and to relate them to each other as operations. Arguments about what counts as 'the right way of doing the job' are endless and extremely difficult to settle in a satisfactory manner.

A further problem arises if we ask what in general terms are these methods of? Obviously they are methods used by social workers, but characteristically they are seen as methods of treatment. The question to be posed, then, is what we think of descriptions of casework, residential work, and so on as methods of treatment. It seems to us that social workers in fieldwork or in residential work do very many things, and that it is over-persuasive to assume that these activities all form part of a particular method of treatment. Much of social work 'method' passes for treatment only in the very wide kind of sense given to medical treatment to be found in the 1959 Mental Health Act, where medical treatment is defined as including not only nursing but also care and training under medical supervision. Social workers, more frequently than perhaps is appreciated, work to facilitate others to help their clients. Social workers thus attempt to help foster parents, relatives, teachers, neighbours and others to help direct clients. It would be strange to describe this part of their work as the treating of foster parents, etc., or of the social workers' clients.

Rules

So, we do not believe that it is very helpful to answer the question, what should social workers be able to do, by saying that they should be able to practise one or more of the different methods of social work. We think that what social workers do slips through talk of 'method' in any strong sense of that term. It does not follow from this, however, that we are, as it were, left helpless in the face of the problem: we are not thereby reduced to saying to each social work student 'do your own thing as long as you don't call it a method'. On the contrary, we believe that the directions in which a social worker can be required to develop ability can be stated fairly simply and that some general rules can be devised to guide the activities in which he should engage. Now talk of rules is not usually congenial to a social work audience. Social work writing shows quite a suspicion of rules.

Take, as an example of this, the treatment of rules in a book on financial help in social work:

> Case work is individualised, and each family's circumstances and personalities are different, so that assessments of the need for discretion for each family are different too. It would therefore be inappropriate for caseworkers to depend upon *inflexible* rules. . . . The only possible method of work relies on the workers' on-the-spot assessment . . . there are no rules of thumb to be applied (Heywood and Allen, 1971, p. 11) (italics added).

Comment of this kind suggests an inadequate grasp of what constitutes 'following a rule'. Rule-following cannot be excluded from social work; even such activities as using a concept involve rule-following. A great deal of social work involves the use of concepts and hence following rules for the correct use of the concept, but such rules are not automatically to be classified as inflexible: they are often like rules of thumb which can only be used flexibly – that is what rules of thumb are like.

It is sometimes difficult to specify these rules in social work because different 'games' can be played. To speak, for example, about community work is not as such to give any information concerning the model of practice being used. So, a model of locality development might emphasise the social worker's tasks as co-ordinator, teacher of ways of solving problems, and catalyst, whereas a social action model would stress his role as agitator, partisan and activist. The rules for what counts as teaching and what constitutes good teaching are clearly very different from the rules that constitute partisan activity and a good partisanship.

The approach we adopt, in keeping with the spirit of this book, is to try to state simply what in our view social workers should be able to do, and to suggest some very general rules for performing the activities well. The temptation is, of course, to produce an extremely long list in the endeavour to leave nothing out. We suggest that the following selection highlights most of the activities social workers should be able to perform.

1 To conduct interviews with individuals or groups who often face and experience loss and change.
2 To plan and to help others to plan on a basis of the understanding of situations.
3 To offer and to support the delivery of a range of personal services including non-directive and directive counselling to individuals and groups and advocacy.
4 To know, use and criticise the policy of the agency.
5 To record.

It is not easy in social work to separate in any rigid way knowledge, action and value. In the above list we have concentrated on action, but it will be apparent already that the list entails knowledge (in the sense of knowhow) and values (we describe the services to be offered as personal). Knowledge and values will be dealt with in a later section of this book, however, and as far as possible we shall in this section consider separately the activity of a social worker.

One further general point should be made before we consider each of the above requirements in more detail. Talk of action, activity, doing may suggest that we see social work exclusively as (to adopt a sixteenth-century phrase used to describe Christianity) 'a busie practice'. We have no desire to underplay the importance of a social worker's receptivity or of the provision for some clients

of an unhurried pace of work and a quiet place for reflective discussion. What is experienced as an urgent crisis does not always
respond to a desperately assembled battery of tactics. Yet, in our
view, sufficient emphasis is not always given to social *work*.
Reflective discussion has to be worked at and worked for. The
acceptance much valued in social work texts is often taken to
sanction simple recognition and reception of what an individual
client or group is expressing, whereas acceptance should describe
the active search to discover *the point* someone's (initially strange)
behaviour has. Similarly, collaborating with clients or with others
on his or her behalf involves a great deal of quite complicated work.
'The problem of collaboration grows out of the same social processes of conflict, stereotyping and centrifugal forces which inhere
in and divide nations and communities' (Bennis, 1971).

Conducting interviews with individuals or groups who are often facing loss or change

Social workers spend a great deal of time talking and listening to
other people talk. They talk to clients, to officials in various departments, to the relatives of clients, the colleagues in their own
occupation, to doctors, health visitors and so on. They listen to these
and others talking to them. They talk and they listen because they
are persuading, developing their grasp of a situation, seeking information, or trying to achieve a number of other objectives. Their
conversation and their listening are purposive. We suggest that
much of the skill required can be captured if we think in terms of
the social worker as someone who is good at conducting interviews.

Such an approach will not be universally accepted. Interviewing
is not directly taught on many social work courses: much of the
relevant material is gloriously assumed into talk about 'the
relationship' which can become mystifying, especially if it is the
relationship that is the focus of discussion. There are perhaps three
main obstacles to the acceptance of the social worker as someone
skilled in interviewing: it may seem to narrow social work, or to
fail to describe it or actually to distort it. These objections can be
met. We are not suggesting that interviewing is all there is to
social work or that understanding and skill in interviewing is all
that is required to make a social worker. It is obvious that it
would be stretching the normal meaning of 'interview' too far to
say it describes all social work activity, but it does provide a
starting-point which is connected to a large body of research and

experience. Perhaps 'interview' conveys an impression of formality which is at odds with many situations found in community work or residential social work. Yet interviews do not have to be formal; they can be either formal or informal, and meetings between social workers and those they are seeking to help, however they arise, should always be turned to some purpose. Some fear that teaching interviewing will inculcate manipulation and a rather dry pre-occupation with techniques. There are problems around control, around questions like 'Is the social worker always interviewing?' (i.e. in charge of the interview), but these are not problems speci-ally arising from the concept 'interview': they are problems in social work.

In our view interviewing skill is based upon a number of abilities. The most important of these are: appreciating the process of interviews; managing in the interaction; taking responsibility for the conduct of the meeting.

The process of the interview

It is possible to talk mystically about process (whether this is the so-called helping process as interpreted by the functional school of social work in America or the process of the interview). The main point in using the term is to draw attention to the desirability of regarding each interview or sequence of interviews as consisting, quite simply, of beginnings–middles–ends. Each phase has special characteristics and these can be best discussed in terms of the typical problems posed.

Beginnings We have already had some indication of the kind of knowledge and expectation with which potential clients may approach an agency. There is perhaps in social work a tendency to undervalue the significance of 'what a person brings' to the agency, whether this is the office of a fieldworker or a residential centre. It seems to be assumed that the agency is so powerful that some kind of completely new beginning is possible. Sometimes this assumption derives additional strength from particular theories that social workers espouse. Thus, the absolutist concept of the 'total institution' underplays the continuing importance of what people bring, partly because institutions are seen as either 'total' or 'non-total' and there is apparently no way of measuring degrees of 'totality'.

'What people come (or are sent) with' is, of course a crude

abbreviation. We use it to refer not to 'the whole person', in the sense of 'everything about him' or the sum total of his experience but to certain elements in his experience that have relevance for the work to be done. People come (or are sent) with a problem in ordinary living; they have some kind of knowledge and expectation of the help they may receive; they come from a particular environment, and this environment continues to exert influence during their contact with the social worker. The social worker in the beginning phase of an interview should be alert to and should attend to the problems about beginning that a client may have as he also begins to explore the extent and nature of the problem.

Exploring the problem is undertaken partly by use of written material (e.g. referral material) and observation and partly through the use of direct questions. Social workers seem sometimes to avoid direct questions, possibly on the grounds that they are obtrusive. As Kadushin has noted (1972), 'Questioning is a much abused art. It appears to be very difficult for interviewers to ask a clear, unequivocal, understandable question and then be quiet long enough to give the interviewee an unhampered, uninterrupted opportunity to answer' (p. 157). He gives the following examples of this difficulty:

> A worker discussing choice of substitute-care placement with a 15-year-old girl at a child welfare agency.
> 'We wouldn't want to, uh, move you, and if things, you didn't get along there and it, uh, there were too many problems, you know, then it would be a . . . then what would we do?'
> A worker discussing marriage planning with a 17-year-old girl in a group foster home.
> 'What kinds of thing do you think, uh, do you think a person should be, like you know what kinds of things do you think a person should be ready about before they get married? Like what kinds of things about themselves should be ready?'
> A social worker in a divorce-court setting, interviewing a 40-year-old male with regard to a possible reconciliation.
> 'What do you think, what do you suppose she wants to do, like why do you suppose she's acting the way she does?'

Social workers, then, should place more emphasis on the results of questioning (particularly in the beginning phases), but there is one question that should be avoided. This is the question in the form 'Why did you/what made you, do such and such a thing?' Kadushin (1972, p. 163), says of this type of question that 'It asks for a degree of insight and understanding which, if possessed by the interviewee in the first place, would have obviated the necessity of coming to the agency.' This question provides the opening gambit for many a residential social worker faced by a sudden crisis caused by the behaviour of a resident.

When we first mentioned interviewing we also referred in very general terms to the kind of people the social worker interviews, namely those suffering or about to suffer some serious loss or change. It is true that many clients come to agencies knowing what service they require and are either unaffected by crisis or else coping very well with it. We must not assume that because people are put in touch with or put themselves in touch with a social worker they necessarily share common characteristics. None the less, many deeply troubled people will come to social workers, who must appreciate the effects their difficulties are having on the way in which they are trying to make contact with the agency.

We have already seen that some kind of stigma appears to be attached to approaching a social work agency. This is perhaps less true of the community worker who works on a detached basis 'in the community', but generally speaking social workers should be aware of the social meaning of contact with a social worker. They should also acknowledge that their interview is not the only or necessarily the most important part of the client's beginning with the agency. A new resident in a home has to undergo a long process of induction into a whole set of new experiences, and learning to relate to other residents is probably more important at the beginning phase than learning to relate to the social worker. Again, clients coming to the Social Services Department of a local authority may well encounter a reception process in the hands of receptionists. The environment at reception can do much to help or hinder the client in his attempts to tell his story. Hall's (1974) recent sensitive study of reception in four departments contains some vivid examples of what can happen in the beginning phase of contact. One receptionist, for instance, called across a crowded room, 'When did your wife leave you, Mr —?' Hall comments that 'This lack of confidentiality could be seen to produce anxiety and distress for a sizeable proportion of the clients interviewed' (p. 62). As a general summary he quotes approvingly Bessell's view (1971, p. 70) that 'in many cases, what happens before a client sees the social worker will not only determine the outcome of the interview but whether the client will even be admitted to see a social worker and if he does, whether he will return'. Such a view gives, in our opinion, altogether too much weight to 'what happens before', but it does draw attention to factors outside the interview which exercise a powerful influence and which also, it must be noted, are at least in principle, capable of control by the agency itself.

We may say that the beginning phase ends when contact, to use a phrase of Rees (1974), becomes contract. Making effective contact involves, as we have briefly indicated, a series of quite complex operations, but even established contact does not by itself lead to some kind of conscious agreement about the basis for future work and the problems that will be worked on. Indeed, at certain times in the history of social work contract was left so implicit that it was non-existent. Establishing a contract is difficult because it involves some kind of joint decision between client and social worker and this means that the social worker must have come to terms with one of the most vexing questions in social work, which can be put simply as 'does social work deal with the problem as presented?'.

Some aspects of this question will be considered when, later in this book, we discuss the concepts of need, wish and interest. What we should note at this stage is the importance for the social worker of settling for himself the picture he has of how he should be attempting to understand what is often called the presenting problem or the presenting symptom. As a social worker listens, asks, questions and observes, should he or she picture himself or herself as attending to what is really being said, trying to get behind appearances or to plumb unexpected depths? Each of these pictures contains a different set of possibilities for the social worker in action – as we suggested social work can be seen as a series of actions guided by certain dominant pictures. In our view, the major rule to be followed has been simply stated in an altogether different context – only connect. Past and present, one aspect and another of a problem, are not connected as symptoms are connected to illness or as what is hidden to what can be seen, but they are connected in ways in which what is implicit can become explicit. Alternatively, one rule of the first phase can be stated in the following terms: do not draw the boundaries (around client or problem) too tightly.

The middle phase   In so far as social work is concerned much more has been written about 'beginnings' than about 'middles'. This perhaps indicates the rather undramatic nature of the middle phase – middle age tends not to receive much attention in courses or books on human growth and development. It is also a fact, of course, that many clients do not progress beyond the first one or two contacts with the social worker, so that they never enter the phase of post-contact work. When we come to consider the place of knowledge in social work we shall emphasise the importance of knowing and acting on this sort of knowledge about social service users.

It seems that the middle phase of an interview or series of interviews can be seen in terms of sustaining the work, rethinking issues and problems, and using resources to help in the accomplishment of objectives. We can illustrate the demands of this phase on the worker by looking at a classification of verbal comments made by social workers conducting groups. Parsloe (1971) has suggested a sevenfold classification: caretaking remarks, concerned with the actual running of the group; cohesion remarks, to create identification and interaction between group members; holding reality or remarks 'which seemed to show the group discrepancies between the concept of reality being established by the group or one of its members and those more generally held outside the group'; steering remarks, to lead the group towards an important topic; educative remarks; explanatory remarks, which are similar to the educative but are directed at particular group members; finally, remarks which have as their purpose dealing with the group leader's feelings – as Parsloe remarks: 'At times a leader needs to reclaim leadership or express hostility in order to get back into a more objective position.' This simple but illuminating classification can be applied to social work action in general, and in particular to the middle phases of the interview. It does not seem to matter whether the social worker is in contact with one individual, a dyad or a group.

But the middle phase of an interview poses questions about the order and frequency of the social worker's comment and about the purposes of the meeting. The tasks in this phase falling to the social worker are partly to check that the objectives established earlier are still feasible and that some progress is being made in the direction of their realisation – steering, explanatory and educative remarks will probably predominate. The tasks also include the mobilisation of resources and, again, checking that these continue to be available and are actually being used and are having the kind of impact that was envisaged.

Much of this phase of an interview or sequence of interviews will revolve around sustaining the work agreed on or actually started in the beginning phase. It has to do with sustaining hope that something can be accomplished. Part of this hopefulness comes from the social worker's own ability to escape from an exclusive emphasis on what is wrong or has gone wrong with the situation facing the client or client group. It does seem to be much easier to see and describe what is pathological than what is healthy. Social workers in the past have been encouraged to assess the ego strengths and ego weaknesses of their clients, but it is usually the weaknesses that have predominated. Even the research studies that social workers might use follow similar tendencies. It is surely overstretching the bounds of credulity to suggest that residential centres of the social services invariably produce institutional pathology of one kind or another.

This is not, of course, to encourage euphoria or a return to the semi-miraculous gloss which, as we have already seen, was at one time frequently to be found in social work. It is to suggest that social workers should give more attention to sustaining a realistic hope. This has more to do with their confidence in 'knowing their way' in and around interviews and with their previous acquaintance with problems than with anything they may say directly. We said earlier that those who use social work services are a very heterogeneous group, but we qualified this by suggesting that the possibility of some kind of stigma being attached to receiving such service may be one characteristic that users share. We wish now to suggest a second characteristic which may be shared by users of social work services: we refer to the description that headed the section on interviewing – conducting interviews with individuals or groups who are often facing loss or change. We appreciate that some people facing loss or change may be helped by the provision of information, but that many facing such a crisis require in those who would help them an understanding of the psychological and social restructuring that is demanded by the processes of loss or change. The basis of such understanding will be considered when we turn to the knowledge social workers require, but it is important to note at this stage in our argument that loss and change can be experienced by individuals (a child leaving his own home and going to live in a residential centre), by groups (loss of members or a change of leader) or by 'communities' (residents of a particular road being rehoused). Understanding of loss or change is brought to bear characteristically in the middle and end phases of contact.

So far we have considered the social worker as conducting an interview or a series of interviews which together constitute the work or a phase of work. An interview or a series of interviews can be seen as following the process we are describing, but the idea of the middle phase of the interview or series seems to offer some problems when applied to residential work. There may be a middle phase, but how can it be recognised when it is seldom easy to predict the length of time any particular person may be in residential care? Beginnings and endings can be recognised with relative ease by all concerned.

The difficulty is fairly easily surmounted by conceiving of the middle as the time when the main work is done, but recognising that the work is not accomplished all at once. The middle phase can then be seen as divided into a number of different but connected tasks. Can we see what such tasks might be? The most fruitful source is, in our view, ideas concerning stages in the development of groups rather than any ideas concerning phases in individual treatment. Various suggestions have been outlined for conceptualising stages in group development, but one of the potentially most useful is that offered by Garland *et al.* (1972) who identify five stages or 'problem levels through which members and groups as a whole pass in the course of their development . . .: (1) pre-affiliation, (2) power and control, (3) intimacy, (4) differentiation, and (5) separation' (p. 29). These are called stages of 'growth', but this seems over-persuasive, since the stages of development could occur without the permanent beneficial achievements implied by 'growth'. None the less, the characterisation is useful in specifying certain tasks or problems to be overcome and also in reminding us that though we are in this sub-section immediately concerned with the middle or work phase, aspects of beginnings and endings are also likely to occur. In social work it is seldom possible to say that the problems, say of the beginning phase, have been completely dealt with. Fresh beginnings emerge (someone from 'outside' joins a group which is already well established), and endings are rehearsed; people return to particular themes as they enter a new phase of development or their milieux change.

This very brief discussion of the middle phase suggests a number of rules, but perhaps the most important can be given in the simple injunction – check. Make sure of certain basic facts – that you and your client are still together, that other resources are being used in a productive manner, that new work is taken on only if old work has been finished or if the new work is compatible with the old.

The ending phase This phase seems to present some difficulty to social workers, whether we are concerned with one meeting or a sequence. As far as we can see, the main problems can be grouped around the meaning of the contact or contacts to social worker and client. Closure of a case, the ending of a contact through human decision or through contingency (as in death in hospital or old people's home), raises questions about the purpose and achievement of the contact and about the feelings of the people involved. It is perhaps because these questions are sometimes very difficult to answer that in a number of situations users of social work services are unsure whether or not they are 'closed' and social workers postpone closure or mishandle the ending of what has become a relationship.

To end a meeting or a series of meetings implies that some work has been accomplished. It may be that what has been achieved is a decision that nothing more can be or is to be attempted, or a decision that some other agency or a course of action not involving the present agency should be tried. Whatever the achievement it implies that a goal has been set and approximated. Both these implications are severely testing for the social worker, who usually receives from the literature only the most general advice concerning goals, and little or nothing to suggest what approximation to goals can count as a good reason for termination. These failures are underlined by Bywaters (1975) who quotes Hollis's statement on goals: 'Improvement in communication is often a specific goal of treatment. . . . Common objectives are the modification of perceptions of others or of self, greater self-regard and greater self-confidence, a firmer sense of personal identity. . . .' It is not that such goals are necessarily irrelevant or incongruent with the rather humble technology social workers have at their disposal, but that, as Bywaters adds, 'The social worker needs to decide how much "improvement", how much "modification", how much "greater self-regard" imply that the contact should come to an end.'

Endings or closures are also avoided because they cannot be timed and decided entirely on the basis of the individual client's need and because of the feelings termination and consequent separation evoke. Bywaters argues that the closure decision should be seen as a rationing decision (the idea of rationing is discussed later) in so far as the social worker and the agency have other clients and new clients, and time given to one client cannot be given to another. It seems to us that decisions on closure are frequently adversely affected by one of the strongest implicit assumptions in contemporary social work practice, namely that social workers are fundamentally engaged in a kind of private practice in which, if only it were possible, unlimited time could be spent on unravelling and perhaps even solving an endless series of problems.

Certainly social workers are encouraged to see more than the problem presented, and we have suggested that boundaries around client and problem should not be tightly drawn. So, it is perhaps scarcely surprising that social workers fail to end an interview or a case well because of the feeling that there was so much more to do and even that more might have been accomplished, given more time. Feelings of affection are also involved as social workers consider the possibility of ending a positive relationship or feelings of guilt as they look forward with relief to the end of an unwelcome contact.

The main rule that should govern 'endings' can be stated as follows: interviews that are well begun have already solved at least part of the problem of ending, but consider also the feelings that are to be evoked in social worker and client. Remember also that it is social work that is involved (and therefore an agency rather than therapy on a private practice basis).

Managing in the interaction and taking responsibility

We have already touched on this group of issues and suggested at least that we do not see social work in terms of well-conducted meetings without specific content taking place in some kind of vacuum. We want now, however, to bring these issues to the forefront of attention and ask questions about the overall role of social workers in the interview.

By calling the meetings of social worker and client 'interviews' we have perhaps been taken as implying that social workers conduct interviews or that they are characteristically to be seen as interviewing people, as subjecting others to a process. This would be an incorrect impression, and we have deliberately headed this sub-section as managing *in* rather than the management *of* inter-action. We believe that a social work interview should avoid both of the following extremes. It should not be a meeting in which the client talks and receives virtually no response which can guide him and no expression that he can criticise or test out for himself. It should not, in other words, be a meeting on which the social worker has no grasp and for which he takes no responsibility. On the other hand, social work interviews should not be set in a direction by the social worker and kept unswervingly on course, taking no account at all of the client's views or behaviour.

We believe, then, that the social worker should be pursuing certain broad purposes and should acknowledge responsibility for so doing and for his part in the interview. This stems partly from the fact that social work can aim to accomplish only a certain range of objectives. As Brager and Specht (1973, p. 89) have argued in relation to the community worker, 'In deciding what information to seek (he cannot speak to everyone), or how to explain himself (he cannot say everything) . . . [he] must have purposes and direction.'

What should a social worker be able to manage in the interaction? He or she should certainly be able to manage their responses to different kinds of people and to people expressing different kinds of emotion and cognitive belief. This does not imply a rigid control so that the worker behaves like a kind of automaton: we are speaking after all of management. Nor do we envisage a situation in which schooled responses never break down. What we believe a social worker should be able to do is to acknowledge 'instinctive' response, but to learn from it for the benefit of the client. We have all learned, for example, a range of responses to a situation in which we meet a stranger, a stranger of particular characteristics (blind, deaf, disabled, black and so on). We have as social workers to be able to recall this so that we can empathise with clients who report such responses in others, but we have also to have negotiated our way to a new position from which we can move more positively towards the stranger.

There are moments when the social worker's attention to making considered responses weakens. This is perhaps particularly true in residential work in which the social worker is protected hardly at all by the structure of the formal interview or even the four walls of on office. When this happens, and a social worker loses his or her temper or simply stops listening or observing, it is sometimes said that the social worker is behaving like a human being. This implies a puzzling contrast with behaviour at the other times. Because a social worker is not responding immediately 'as the feeling takes him' we should not say he is not behaving like a human being. We shall note later some of the requirements of counselling and will refer to the importance of 'authenticity'. This is a crucial idea for social work as a whole, but it does not imply that the only way in which a social worker can express his or her 'real' self is by saying or expressing what first comes to mind.

Social workers should strive towards honest responses, but the responses are of one person trying to help another. We shall have to return to this subject when we consider knowledge, since it has been argued that a social worker's self-knowledge is a necessary basis for social work activity of any kind.

A social worker must be able to conduct an interview, but in such a way that the participation of the other person is encouraged and maintained. He should be able to facilitate the start and the conclusion of interviews and he should take responsibility for their general direction. This does not mean that he has a clear and detached view of the objective of each meeting and has his hand on the controls continuously adjusting the interview as it threatens to divert from the carefully plotted course. But it does mean that he has responsibility to see that a rough course is charted and that within broad limits it is maintained. It does not mean that he is always anxiously asking 'who is in control of this interview' or always seeking to assert control. He takes responsibility more for ensuring that certain processes take place (such as reflection, consideration of all possibilities) than for any particular outcome of the processes or the interview itself. He also has to acknowledge and work with the fact that on occasions he cannot reach agreement with the client about what should be done or even about the ways in which a problem should be viewed and considered. In such situations a way forward is sometimes found through a bargaining process and the management of this process lies with the social worker.

The interview, however, should not be seen as a meeting in which necessarily all the work is done nor as a meeting which is somehow insulated from the outside world. Interviews take place in a context provided by the client's own world and by those parts of the world of welfare that are or become relevant to the problem. This is so whether the client is an individual, a family or a group. The social worker has the responsibility for ensuring that, figuratively speaking, necessary elements in these worlds are present in the interview and that when appropriate to the understanding or solution of a problem they are recognised. This responsibility, like the others, does not have to be discharged only by or through the social worker. After all, one of the main objectives of social work is the recognition and encouragement of the efforts people make to solve their problems. The attempt to discern the worker's part in and responsibility for the interview should not be exaggerated into a takeover bid.

To plan and help others to plan, on the basis of situations that are understood

Planning is, in our view, insufficiently considered in social work, whether we are discussing working with individuals or groups, and whether these individuals or groups are living in Homes, with their own families or on their own. It has ceased to be a dominant element mainly because 'planning with people' can easily be overtaken by planning for them, or, more simply, planning them, and because planners are not therapists. We believe that planning should be seen as a major element in social work. We believe that agencies, milieux and the use of personal and social resources should be planned, and that planning should be a joint venture between social workers and their clients. Talk of planning conveys no necessary impression of omniscience or of rigid control to achieve some kind of utopia: one of the most interesting of recent perspectives on planning extols the science of muddling through (Hirschman and Lindblom, 1969). We think that clients and social workers should do more to muddle through. Hitherto social workers seem to have been so preoccupied with understanding a situation that they have not been free enough to do much to change it. This is not to say that attempts to understand people and their situations should be abandoned; the attempt to understand so that an appropriate remedy can be found and used is an essential part of social work. We do, however, question the form this understanding should take and we would argue that in many instances diagnostic elaboration has outstripped 'treatment'.

Social caseworkers have produced increasingly elaborate diagnostic schemes, and we quoted at some length from part of one of these in the first chapter. Groupworkers and community workers and those in residential work have not apparently felt that they required the equivalent in their work. In our view an adequate understanding can be built up with the client on the basis of answers to a few important questions. What purpose or purposes is the client and/or group seeking to achieve? What resources have they or can they mobilise to achieve them? What prevents the purpose or purposes from being achieved? This list of simple questions has at least one advantage over previous formulations; it takes as central the notion of the human actor, a person who can frame and carry out projects rather than an organism acted upon and determined by material or emotional forces. Such a notion can in fact be found in much psychoanalytic work where analysis eventually reveals human purposive behaviour at work rather than random, meaningless, 'odd' behaviour that simply 'happens'. Social workers (and others) have been prevented from seeing this rational model because they have often been over-impressed by the other model available in psychoanalytic theory. This is a model which stresses man as pushed, pulled and ultimately determined by forces beyond his control. Inside Freud there was a little Skinner trying to escape.

The kinds of question we think require an answer in order that social worker and client or clients may say they have understood a situation are more simple and more basic than those usually posed, but they are, of course, not without their own complexity. We should not, for instance, follow the example of certain theorists of organisations and assume that people are always seeking to achieve one overall purpose or that people do not characteristically entertain conflicting or contradictory purposes. Neither can we escape valuation since we are describing purposes as human: not everything someone wants to do can be described as an attempt to fulfil a *human* purpose. We have also to acknowledge that factors preventing the realisation of purposes are often to be found in the personality of clients or in the environment that encompasses both social worker and client. The environment has persistently eluded the social worker – a major point to which we shall return when we discuss knowledge in social work.

As situations are gradually understood plans begin to evolve. What are some of the most important ingredients of social work planning? Social workers need a knowledge of available resources, to be able to use their accumulated experience and knowledge of the length of time social worker and client will be in contact. They also require to decide which factors in the situations are, to use the terms of de Jouvenel, masterable and which dominant, and what will count as failure of the plan. We shall say a little more about each of these ingredients.

The phrase 'available resources' draws attention to the necessity of testing that resources can actually be relied on (i.e. they are available), and also to a considerable range of sources of help. Resources are to be found within the agency (we shall consider these separately), in other agencies, in the informal social network of which the client is a part, or in powers or potentiality that can be summoned by the client or clients, for example his or her own hopefulness. Resources are usually seen as clear in scope and measurable in quantity but social workers should also appreciate that just as their work with clients can create a new resource, so other resources can be created through the combination of a group of clients or clients and those not initially in touch with the agency. Sometimes in planning social workers adopt what may be called an idealistic solution; so social workers suggest that for example a particular child really needs a foster home which will last, will survive very severe testing out, and will also cater for his brother. In our view planning more usefully proceeds in a more negative manner. Instead of saying what an ideal situation is, it is better to think in terms of what the worst outcome would be and to plan realistically to avoid this. Appreciation that resources can be created helps us to avoid situations in which extant facilities actually dictate what will happen.

Social workers acquire a great deal of experience, but there are problems in bringing this to bear on particular problems. On the one hand, it is sometimes assumed that the social worker should become a *tabula rasa* on which each client or group of clients can imprint the fine detail of their own individuality. This is, of course, an impossibility, but the assumption does discount the value to the client of the accumulated experience of the worker. Another working assumption also interferes from time to time with the use of experience, and this is the view that social work is essentially a kind of private practice. Such a view can take hold of social work in any setting and it leads to the non-use of the experience of the agency. Finally, experience is often left, as it were, lying around; it is not gathered up for use. One way in which it can be collected into a usable form is through the predictive study: for example, in the field of foster-home breakdown and regarding the decision of unmarried mothers to keep or to part with their babies. Such studies have not been systematically developed or used in social work, even though all concerned need as much help as they can obtain to ensure that good decisions are made in these (and other) areas. The material for predictive study comes from the social worker's and the client's experience. The resultant predictive tables cannot decide for us, but they can provide material that will inform the decision (Parker, 1966), always provided the studies are repeated at regular intervals.

Social work help cannot usually produce results quickly, though we have sometimes been lulled into rather trance-like and rather fruitless work by the assumption that social work should itself produce growth, and human growth takes a long, a very long time.

It seems that one important piece of information required in social work planning is a reasonably reliable prediction of the length of time social agency and client will be in contact. One way to solve this problem is, of course, not to predict but to decide, and this planned use of a particular period of time has always been a central feature of the functionalist position, whether the social work 'method' involved was casework, groupwork, administration or research.

The terms 'dominating' and 'masterable' of de Jouvenel have been used by Parker (1971) in a stimulating study of planning in child care, but they can be applied generally in social work: they make sense to both social worker and client. Obviously, judgments about what to take as given and what to attempt to change are not made once and for all: changes in the situation, even a change of social worker may mean that certain features become modifiable. At certain times, of course, social workers have taken a general view that certain aspects of a situation are more modifiable by the means they have at their disposal. Thus 'attitudes' have been seen as the focus of the efforts of social workers, even though research suggests both that attitudes are extremely difficult to change and also that their relationship to actual behaviour is extremely complex (e.g. see Blumer, 1955).

Social workers have to make plans in conditions of considerable uncertainty; plans are formulated slowly and with difficulty. In these circumstances it is not surprising that when plans are made they are sometimes made to last. By this we mean that it is sometimes difficult to say of a plan what would count as evidence that the plan is not working and that, therefore, some new plan is required.

One serious problem here is the force that social workers tend to give to some of the theories that direct their own planning efforts. Take, for example, the view, previously mentioned, that children are more likely to thrive, psychologically and physically, if they are with their natural parents. In many cases following this assumption will produce beneficial results, but how much distress has to be shown by a child in contact with his or her natural parents before it can be decided that in this particular case the 'theory' is overridden? The difficulty of this question is increased because of the (correct) assumption that painfulness to some degree is inevitable. It can happen, of course, that the 'theory' is held invincibly and that it is followed no matter what the consequences. In this situation, of course, we are in the realms of dogma, not theory. Social workers, in our view, should not be encouraged to plan on a basis of such complete conviction.

'Planning' seems to imply control by the social workers. It implies control of some kind, but we do not have to think of this as control exercised by the social worker. Sometimes the resources required for a fruitful outcome are outside the separate control of client or social worker, and sometimes outside their combined control. Yet if we concentrate exclusively or even primarily on these situations we neglect other situations in which, with imagination, something can be achieved. We refer here especially to residential provision, in which it really is not beyond the wit and resource of social workers to devise and plan the provision of helpful milieux. Such mileux cannot be planned in very great detail. It seems to us that planning reception facilities in a social work agency, for example, should not be based on detailed predictions concerning any particular aspect of the milieu. So, to take a minor example, it is unhelpful to suggest, as Kadushin (p. 117) that 'Pictures in the interview room should be neutral and calming in their effect. A picture of, for instance, Michelangelo's Moses is likely to excite guilt and anxiety. . . .' Yet because such detailed planning is dubious, there is no reason to abandon planning altogether.

To offer and to support the delivery of a range of personal services

It is difficult to suggest an exhaustive list of personal services but it would include treatment in the strong sense of the term, as well as advice and guidance, advocacy, mobilising material and psychological resources, planning and helping people to use different kinds of milieu. We do not intend to examine each of these in detail, but we shall raise some general considerations.

These services are offered through social work agencies and are characterised by the fact that they are administered by persons for the benefit of persons. Services called 'personal' are not just services given to individuals or groups of individuals: they are services which involve respect for the dignity of persons and the recognition of personal rights (for example, confidentiality). Respect for persons is a complex notion, but one element which has direct relevance for the social worker can be found in an analysis of what it is to respect a person by Williams (1962). He states that 'each man is owed an effort of identification: . . . he should not be regarded as the surface to which a certain label can be applied, but one should try to see the world (including the label) from his point of view'. It follows from this that personal services cannot be given in a routine way or on a 'wholesale' basis: they must be tailored in important ways to meet the particular situation. The fact that the services given by social workers are personal yields, therefore, some rules about how the services are given.

Attempting to see the social worker as capable of offering and helping in the actual delivery of services is not the usual way in which social work is viewed. More commonly social work is seen as a kind of treatment, and everything a social worker does has to be justified as either a form of treatment or as contributing to treatment objectives. So financial assistance, which we would describe as a service, has been viewed as a treatment tool or as a contribution to casework objectives. In other words 'treatment', which in our vocabulary would be counted as a particular service or a group of services, has been stretched to cover all services. This has meant that descriptions of some services have been distorted. However, in avoiding the dangers of what we might call creeping treatment, we must take care not to deny that treatment has a place in social work nor should we deprive the non-treatment services of the characteristics they enjoyed when they were called treatment. These characteristics are, in our view, preserved under the description 'personal'.

Our possible objection to separating out the services in the way we suggest is that such an approach to social work may seem to threaten if not to destroy the relationship between social worker and client which has received so much attention in the literature. Certainly some clients in the studies of consumer opinion have spoken highly of the qualities of the social workers they have known and have valued their relationship with them. We would not want to question this fact or undermine the achievement, but we do want 'the relationship' placed in perspective. The perspective is different according to kind of service and type of client. We mean by this that a relationship of trust, a relationship in which persons can meet to transact the business of welfare, is a necessary means whereby all the services can be delivered, but that special considerations apply where treatment in a strict sense is used. This is particularly so in the case of non-directive counselling and therapeutic groups. All services run the risk that they may evoke intense reactions in certain clients. A service of advice and guidance offered by a probation officer, for example, may produce such a negative response that the officer will begin to ask questions about whom he may be standing in for in his relationship with his client. His task in such a situation, however, is to try to remove any obstacles that may stand in the way of his client perceiving or using the service of advice and guidance he is trying to offer.

In speaking of social workers as offering services we may be giving the impression that services are always, as it were, things given to clients. Sometimes, of course, they are – material help of different kinds – but characteristically a social worker is a middleman, a broker, who helps people to identify sources of direct help and to use them. In the immediate past social workers have perhaps over-emphasised the value of professional help, tending to exaggerate what could be accomplished, say in a series of weekly interviews of forty minutes' duration. Thinking more widely than this does not detract from the value of social work. Rather it constitutes a challenge to the worker as someone who can help to connect or to reconnect clients with their own social network or with the network of social services help.

When all or most of what social workers did was assumed to qualify in one way or another as treatment, it seemed logical to assume that all social work activity should meet at least the basic requirements of treatment. So 'advice' tended to be ruled out or devalued as an appropriate technique for beginning students or mentally subnormal clients, and social workers adopted a rather passive stance in relation to all their work. We should recognise now that social workers perform many tasks, and it is idle to pretend that all their work can be based on the assumption that all the people coming to (or sent to) social workers are just like people who freely enter treatment. So, in our short list of services we referred to advice and guidance, and we would separately identify non-directive counselling as a service offered to some clients only. Non-directive counselling is not a synonym for social work.

To know, use and criticise the policy of the agency

Critics of some recent developments in social work (Wootton, 1959) have argued that a perfectly sound and proper role for the social worker can be found in guiding people through the labyrinthine ways of the modern social service world. We agree with the importance this gives to knowledge of social services, but we would expand the suggested role to include criticism of the employing agency and of social policy in general. Such criticism must be informed, and this adds importance to recording, which we shall consider briefly in the next section.

Criticism will be informed, then, by the social worker's actual experience with clients, but it will also be informed through good knowledge of and a secure grasp of the policies of the worker's own agency. Agencies are sometimes reluctant to do the work that results in any declared policy. It is feared perhaps that policies may be defined too closely or carried out with extreme rigidity; that they will provoke criticism, since a policy is by definition not secret. Yet workers and clients should know what agency policies are, at least in relation to the services offered. Such knowledge is required because the client should know the sort of service offered and the conditions under which the offer is made and the service delivered. He should know this whether he is a voluntary or an involuntary client. The worker should know because he must try to engage the client not first and foremost in a relationship but in the work of orientation of the services offered so that these can be explored and used for the client's benefit. To leave policies implied, to offer help (apparently endless) to people in all kinds of (unspecified) conditions is to give neither client nor worker sufficient upon which to work.

To emphasise policies – and we refer here to something more than statements of very general aim – is not to suggest, much less to indicate, a world fixed for ever in a particular fashion. Policies become outdated, fail to cover new situations, are not effective. It is the social worker's responsibility to seek clarification of existing policies and to argue for changes and additions where these appear necessary.

Criticism of the policy of the social work agency – and indeed of social provision in general – is a crucial aspect of social work activity. We say this for two main reasons. Social work is a critical activity, as we have already suggested, and it is especially important to a view of social work as altruism that emphasis is given to resources. Without resources the concern of altruism becomes a mockery, without agency policies and practices to mediate and distribute the resources, the otherwise boundless project of altruism becomes unbearable. An illustration of the central importance of resources can be found in Bayley's study (1973) of mentally handicapped people in Sheffield. This questions the extent to which the available services were meeting the basic needs of these people and their families, that is, needs connected with the daily grind. Bayley argues that the social workers carried an unrealistic burden because the well-being of the family depended on aspects of daily living. 'It is true that the social workers could have known more about what services and aids were available, but basically they were in as impossible a position here as they were with the lack of day care for the very severely disabled' (p. 309). To remain in positions of impossibility renders service to no one.

It is important for social workers to note and to act on situations. A general illustration may clarify what we have in mind. In discussing residential provision with those who may require it, sooner or perhaps later, social workers would wish to adopt a certain rhythm of purposive work which encouraged forward planning, consideration of alternatives, taking the line necessary for a human decision and taking time into account. Such a way of working is completely undermined if resources are so scarce that admission (say to an old people's residential home) is only on grounds of emergency and crisis.

To record

This is not an activity of the same order as the others we have discussed. It is in fact a second-order activity, dependent on the original observation, plan, discussion, treatment or advocacy. It is treated by many social workers as not merely second-order but second-class. It is one of the most dispensable activities in the social work repertoire. We believe that this should not be so. The information that social workers collect has importance in reaching decisions about the appropriateness and effectiveness of the services being given. To leave such information in the worker's head is to run the considerable risk that it will not be used. Social workers certainly know much more about their clients than they record.

We earlier stressed the importance of planning, and recording plays a crucial part in the development and assessment of plans. Unless plans are recorded we can always, as Parker (1971) has reminded us, be persuaded that things fell out exactly in the way we had expected, that the outcome, which was in fact fortuitous, was as planned.

These and other reasons, which constitute quite powerful arguments, do not seem to be very persuasive. The 'theory' of recording, which often takes the form of simple exhortation, is very much at odds with the paucity of recording practice. Why is this so? Partly, social workers take refuge in the indefinite and there is no doubt that recording an appraisal, indicating an objective that is feasible, involves some risk-taking. Yet it is also the case that social workers are given insufficient help on what they should observe and on which of their many observations should be recorded. There is evidence to suggest that social workers come to decisions on a proportion only of the information they collect. This is hardly surprising in view of the severe limitations on the amount of information human beings can handle.

Finally, social workers are unsure about the kind of recording they should use. For a long time one particular mode of recording (process recording) was dominant in social work. This proved a valuable device for training, but insufficient attention has been given to exploring and teaching other forms of recording more compatible with the demands of day-to-day practice and also with other 'methods' of social work. It is clear that the meaningful recording even of an interview between two people is a complex task. The complexity of recording interaction in a group, say, of eight people or of the series of interviews and group meetings that constitute a piece of community work is overwhelming. Various attempts have been made to cope with the problems and, as Murray Cox (1973) has said in relation to group recording, 'These tend to fall between the extremes of being either so complicated that a staff team consisting of therapist, critic, interactionist and verbatim reporter is necessary, or so simple that little information is forthcoming re the group as a whole. . . .' His own group-therapy-interaction chronogram solves some of the major problems in relation to groups that have therapeutic intention, but could also be adopted to other kinds of group where the social worker requires to understand the interaction of group members. Much more experimentation is needed into methods of recording critical incidents in a way that does not lose important elements of the process. The present state of theory and practice in relation to recording has recently been summarised elsewhere by one of the authors (N. Timms, 1972). In this section we wish only to emphasise its crucial importance.

A recent illustration of the crucial disadvantages of the poor use of case records can be found in a study of children in residential care who wait for a foster or an adoptive family (Rowe and Lambert, 1973, p. 93). The authors refer to observations of the way in which agency records are used in reviews of children in care.

> Even when agencies had carefully devised proformas for reviews or summaries, these were often completed in such a routine way that they were relatively useless. It was clear that previous reports had not always been read, the same comments and recommendations being made time after time.

Suggestions for further reading

In the text we have questioned the value of the idea of methods of social work, but of course a great deal of the literature of social work admits no such questioning. There are a number of works devoted to various methods, but the majority have been written about social casework. Gordon Hamilton (1940) wrote the first text on social casework (diagnosis and treatment), though Mary Richmond (1917) on diagnosis is earlier and still worth reading – it is not, incidentally, a text that encourages a sociological perspective. This is often stated, but Richmond encourages rather the legal notions of evidence and semi-judicial decisions. Hamilton's approach is rather piecemeal and it is difficult to see a distinctive point of view. Perlman (1957) and Hollis (1964), on the other hand, have a distinctive point of view that informs the whole text. Comparative studies of casework have already been mentioned.

Groupwork has received less systematic attention, but students will be able to grasp something of groupwork as a method from Davies (1975).

Community work can be approached through Baldock (1974), and Jones and Mayo (1974, 1975) give good examples of community work and pinpoint some of the most important issues in its practice. Beedell (1970) offers a convincing and imaginative text in residential work with children; his work can be applied to other groups. See also Berry (1975).

Those interested in multi-methods should look at approaches to social work which encourage action at the appropriate level, e.g. Goldstein (1973) and Pincus and Minahan (1973). Reference should also be made to the more direct consideration of the methods that are to be 'integrated'; see Baker (1975). Turning now to our suggestions concerning what social workers should be able to do, it will by now be obvious that we have not been able in the text to discuss each suggestion exhaustively. On interviewing we suggest in order of complexity of material and breadth of coverage de Schweinitz and de Schweinitz (1962), Garrett (1942) and Kadushin (1972). The last-named contains a very good bibliography. In the text we described those for whom social workers conduct interviews as suffering from loss and change. Those wishing to take this description further should read Marris (1974). For the application of an interactionist approach to the social work interview (beginning–middle–end) see Fitzjohn (1974) and Kuhn (1962). In the interview we see the social worker as noting, standing in for or referring to significant others. On this see Nurse (1973). On 'beginnings' see Rosenblatt (1962).

Hopefulness and hope in general have been neglected in social work and in therapy. See, however, the study by Smale (1976).

On planning, see Parker's (1971) excellent and comparatively brief book. Planning is, as we have argued, a general aspect of social work, but it has been accepted most clearly in community work. In such a context the planning is unmistakably participative. See Rees (1973). Kahn (1973) argues more generally for a social policy basis for social work practice. See also Specht (1968).

Obviously prediction must play a central part in planning. Very few studies have been made of this area. Parker (1966) is well worth reading. Planning can be on different scales – planning an individual's return from a mental hospital to 'the community', planning new programmes in residential or day care with residents and clients, helping residents in a particular locality to plan resistance to the plans of others. On the wider scale see Dennis (1970), and Gilbert and Specht (1974).

The range of personal services is, as we have said in the text, extensive. Counselling can be studied in a number of texts, e.g. Carkhuff (1969) and Carkhuff and Truax (1967). The latter book identifies three crucial elements in counselling of a psychotherapeutic nature – empathy, genuineness and non-possessive warmth. These elements have also been emphasised by Rogers (1942). They are also important in social work, but of course this does not make social work into a kind of counselling. In addition, we should not see counselling only in terms of service to individuals or couples. See Muro and Freeman (1969) on group counselling.

It is one of the major arguments of our approach that social work should be distinguished from counselling and that social workers should be seen as offering a range of services. On financial help, for example, see Greve (1969) and Heywood. A group of services can be offered to or on behalf of children: fostering, residential and day care, adoption and so on. See Timms (1962),

Winnicott (1964), George (1970), Holman (1973, 1975), Raynor (1970) and Tod (1968, 1971).

We have also argued that our emphasis on the agency and its services is not inevitably conservative: new services can be and are developed. An example of such a service is advocacy. See Brager (1968) and Riley (1974). For a useful introduction to day care services see CCETSW, Paper 12 (1975).

It is possible to identify services of directive counselling and advisory services. The former are best illustrated in the work of the probation officer; see King (1969). Advice has had a poor press in relation to social work, but see Reid and Shapiro (1969), for what clients think of advice. For an amusing and pointed account of the way to give advice though claiming not to, see chapter VII of Jane Austen's *Emma*. It is not without interest that Ryle (1968) suggests that this novel might have been called 'Influence and Interference', since it is concerned with the distinction 'between proper and improper solicitude and unsolicitude about the destinies and welfares of others'.

In the text we identified one important implication of describing these services as 'personal'. Of course, there are many others. Lukes (1973), for example, suggests that three capacities 'belong' to the idea of a person: for autonomous choice and action, for engaging in valued activities and relations, for self-development. So that if services are *personal*, it could be argued, those who administer them are logically involved in treating those who receive them as (actually or potentially) autonomous, as requiring privacy, as capable of self-development. Of course, these terms themselves require analysis, but at least we can begin to see in which direction we are travelling. For a useful account of some of the problems in 'self-development' see Neilsen (1976).

What should a social worker know? Some general considerations

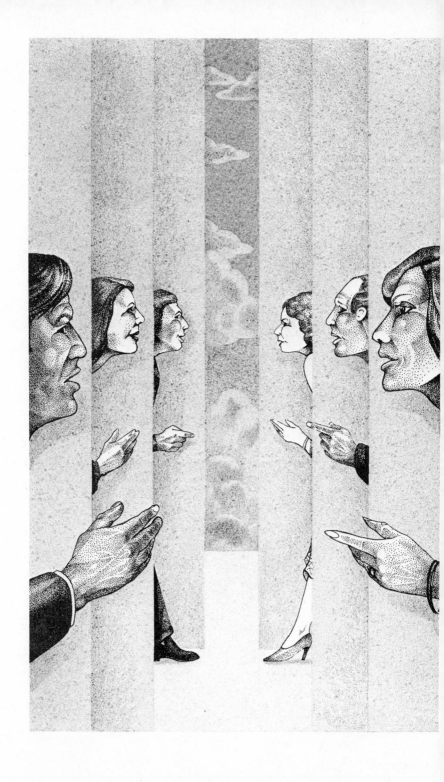

The basic issue to be confronted in this chapter arises from an apparent contradiction. On the one hand, modern social work writing seems to emphasise the valuable part 'knowledge' plays or ought to play in social work. (The distinction between the part knowledge actually plays and the part it ought to play is quite critical.) On the other hand, 'knowledge' in social work is so hedged around with qualification (you don't really know social work unless or until you do it) or the application of knowledge is so beset by hesitation that a position of downright scepticism at least looms on the horizon. This contradiction between confidently asserted hope and actual doubt requires unravelling and studying. We believe that some basic distinctions between kinds of knowledge aid the unravelling and the further study, and this chapter will be concerned with exploring the contradiction and presenting the distinction.

Knowledge valued in social work

Knowledge has been valued in social work for three main reasons. It has been seen as the only way in which social work could become scientific. Knowledge or the acquisition of a body of knowledge also provides the sharpest distinction between the professional and the layman. Knowledge for this purpose does not, of course, have to be scientific, but its possession must make a difference to what a person does. Finally, knowledge has been seen as a means of increasing the effectiveness of social work.

It is not easy to see precisely the point at which modern social work begins, but at least one important indication of change seems to be connected with emphasis on scientific knowledge. This in itself constitutes a development spread over a century or so. The Society for Bettering the Condition of the Poor, for example, issued in 1796 a circular in which it posed the question, 'Joint labours have produced inventions etc., in other fields; why not in the *science* of promoting welfare?' (italics added.) A later report urged that 'the inquiry into all that concerns the Poor . . . (should become) . . . a SCIENCE' (Poynter, 1969, pp. 91, 93). It was, however, in the middle of the nineteenth century that the most vigorous attempts were made to turn benevolence into a scientific activity. C. S. Loch, for instance, believed that good social work consisted in the recognition of, and the adaptation to, the laws of social life. This thrust towards the scientific has continued to the present, though its influence has been somewhat fitful. So Karpf (1931), in one of the very few attempts to discover the knowledge social workers actually use, sets out as an objective the development of

> the kind of knowledge which the chemist uses in the analysis and synthesis of the substances with which he works; the kind of knowledge which the engineer uses in constructing buildings, bridges, and tunnels, and which enables him to say definitely that they are safe; the kind of knowledge, even, which the orator uses in consciously and deliberately swaying and influencing his audience (p. viii).

Karpf also mentions the kind of knowledge the physician uses in the diagnosis and treatment of illness, and this model has often been adopted by social work theorists. We should, however, note the different kinds of applied scientist the social worker has been expected to become. A social engineer resembles but is also different from a social chemist (and both resemble in no obvious way the orator who seems very much the odd man out in Karpf's list).

More sophisticated and thorough attempts to encourage social work to move in the direction of a scientifically based therapy (behaviour modification) are to be found in the work of Thomas (1970) in America and Jehu (1967, 1972) in Britain.

The second source of the value placed on knowledge is to be found in the conviction that an occupation without a firm basis in specialised knowledge cannot be regarded as a profession. Cockerill *et al.*, for example, some years ago (1952) emphasised

> the necessity for establishing a theoretical base (for social work) since it is recognised that all professional practice proceeds from a set of clear principles and concepts about human beings and their needs which are consciously held, teachable as such, and which constitute the logical justification for the practice.

Since then there has been a strong and growing tendency to stress what has come to be called the knowledge base of social work.

This base is required in order that the professional character of social work may be more secure.

Third, social workers have become more aware of the resource of knowledge as a means of helping. They often seem to believe that if only the knowledge of psychology or sociology could be more extensively tapped then their clients would be helped more speedily or more effectively. There is, according to this perspective, an abundance of knowledge 'outside' and 'inside' social work if only it could be harnessed. Goldstein (1973) captures this view when he asserts

> There is no shortage of knowledge; the proliferation of research findings, the ascendancy (and frequently the decline) of schools and cults of practice and the significant theories, conceptualisation, and constructs generated by the social and behavioural sciences leave the practitioner, teacher and learner in a quandary about what to select from this vast array of information and how it should be related and arranged (p. xi).

Similarly, Jones (Jones and Mayo, 1974, p. 215) has referred to 'an excess of potentially useful material'.

This view of knowledge as an actual or potential resource has led to a number of attempts to delineate the areas in which social workers should be knowledgeable. Bartlett (1958), for example, has argued that the practice of social work is guided by knowledge of the following:

(i) Human development and behaviour characterised by emphasis on the wholeness of the individual and the reciprocal influences of man and his total environment;
(ii) the psychology of giving and taking help;
(iii) ways in which people communicate with one another;
(iv) group processes;
(v) the meaning and effect of cultural heritage;
(vi) relationships;
(vii) the community, its internal processes, modes of development and change;
(viii) the social services.

Some of these specific items will be considered later, but it will be obvious from the list Bartlett has compiled that ideas about the knowledge required must be closely bound up with views of society as well as a view of social work. To assume that communities have 'internal processes' or that 'cultural heritage' rather than social structure are worth studying is to adopt a particular view of society.

So far we have viewed the high value placed on knowledge in

social work, suggesting that this stems from three sources. It will also have become apparent that the consideration of knowledge in social work raises problems. Distinctions are not always made or maintained between the various meanings of 'social work knowledge': reference is intended sometimes to knowledge which social workers use to describe or explain human behaviour (knowledge, for instance, of sociology or psychology), sometimes to knowledge which describes or justifies social work, sometimes to knowledge which increases the effectiveness of social work. There is, moreover, the problem of the selection of knowledge, and of the precise contribution knowledge makes to informed social work and social workers who are knowing. Sometimes the treatment of social work knowledge may remind us of Locke's observation that 'The floating of other men's opinions in our brains makes us not one jot the more knowing . . .' (*Essay on Human Understanding*). It is hoped that the way in which social work has been considered in this book confirms the significance of these problems and also points in the direction of this solution.

These problems arise for those already convinced of the value of knowledge in social work, but, as was suggested at the beginning of this chapter, there is within social work considerable doubt or even ambivalence concerning the part knowledge should play. We have described this as a straining after scepticism and we shall now consider this in more detail.

Doubts about knowledge

So far we have suggested a high value for the knowledge base of social work, but, despite the continuing emphasis on theoretical knowledge, there is detectable in social work a considerable scepticism concerning the place of generalisations and the validity of knowledge that does not proceed from direct practical experience in helping individual people. Olive Stevenson (1973) has invoked the distinction between 'heart' knowledge and 'head' knowledge and it could be said that many social workers tend to favour knowledge arising from the first source. Sometimes such knowledge seems to be quite simply intuited without any prior intimation at all: it just, as it were, appears. Goldstein, for example, writes of 'those personal attributes that have to do with the capability for feeling and sensing, for "knowing" in internal ways the inner state of others at times without the benefit of specific clues' (p. 64). It is, of course, difficult to conceive of knowledge in the face of complete deprivation of any specific clues, and one is led to the conclusion that the intuition referred to by Goldstein and many others is expected to do too much. As Gellner (1974, p. 95) has observed in relation to intuition in general: 'Intuition is required to be a something which is simultaneously *both* the evidence, in the sense of initial conditions of an inference *and* the guarantee of the legitimacy of the inference from the evidence.' Other social workers distinguish between intellectual or theoretical 'knowing' and real or emotional 'knowing' and give primacy to the latter. It is common for social work teachers to refer to 'intellectualisation' to describe situations in which students pretend to an (intellectual) understanding. The teachers are seldom explicit about ways of telling the difference between false and true understanding, even though their use of 'intellectualisation' commits them to such a distinction. Indeed it is one of the charges of the modern critic of social work education that questions posing intellectually demanding responses are systematically translated into simple matters of feeling. Thus Deacon and Bartley, commenting on a particular project in social work education say,

> If heated political debate did occur, it would somehow be miraculously ended by a statement like 'It's good that we have expressed our feelings on this issue.' The ideas and criticisms expressed are not regarded as having importance for an analysis of the problems, nor for action proposals, but only in so far as they modify or clarify the relationship between the members of the group (H. Jones, ed., p. 78).

We do not, incidentally, believe that emotion is a simple concept (see next chapter) but we are convinced that in relation to knowledge social workers use a very over-simplified version of 'feeling'.

Turning to the actual use of knowledge by social workers, two main findings should be noted. First, it seems that social workers, in both Britain and America, do not regard a continuing use of research writing as essential to their practice and its development. Moreover, as Meyer *et al.* (1964, p. 253) have pointed out, 'The bulk of professional writing reports conclusions illustrated by cases rather than systematic research or practice procedures.' In a situation in which 'the particular rather than the general, the unique case rather than the accumulation of cases, the expressive description rather than the standardized report have received attention', it is difficult to see how practitioners could systematically relate particular groups of cases to the literature. Second, social workers seem to have preferred ways of working which respond little to the differences in the various kinds of clientele with whom they come into contact. So, for example, Meyer *et al.* (1964), report very little relationship between the background characteristics of clients and the way in which caseworkers report their activity in the first interview. It is perhaps arguable that activities in first interviews ought not to vary in very noticeable ways, but a differential approach is so highly commended in the literature that some differences might justifiably have been expected. If social workers do not respond with the differentiation upheld in the literature and if social work can be carried on in this way, then there is clearly little incentive to acquire more knowledge or remodel existing knowledge once a preferred way of working has been established.

The incentive to acquire more knowledge can also be discouraged by unrealistic descriptions of social work. Confident assertions of what social work is which fall short of reality actually encourage scepticism: because too much is expected of knowledge then, it seems easily to be assumed, knowledge can do little or nothing. A good example of lack of realism can be found in Hollis (1964), who refers to casework as 'a science in that it is a body of systematized knowledge based upon observation, study, and experimentation' (p. 265), or as a 'scientifically disciplined therapeutic model' (p. 267), but even if we assume these two formulations mean the same, wider reference to the question of what it is to be scientific indicates the unreality of the claim. Hollis has joined together elements that exist only in their separateness. There has been some, mainly unsystematic, observation by social caseworkers, who have also conducted some studies, but in individual cases or very short series. There has been very little that could count as experimentation. Whatever observing, studying, 'experimenting' has been done, it is implausible to suggest that these three activities can collectively provide a 'body of systematized knowledge'.

We want to suggest that progress can be made in solving the problems identified in the first section and in resolving the apparent contradiction outlined in this, by forming an idea of what 'knowledge' is and applying a relatively simple distinction between different kinds of knowledge. Problems about the constituents of knowledge and of the logical and substantive differences between different kinds of knowledge have, of course, occupied philosophers over the centuries, but it is possible to select from the vast expanse of theorising about knowledge certain features that are of immediate help in unravelling some of the problems of knowledge in social work. We shall first discuss 'knowledge' and kinds of knowledge before examining an area of knowledge particularly valued by the modern social worker, namely self-knowledge.

What is knowledge?

Briefly, we can say that a social worker knows something if three conditions are fulfilled: what is known is true, the social worker believes or is certain that it is true, and has adequate evidence or good reason for so believing. Knowledge is true belief properly evidenced. For social work the most important condition, in our view, is the last – What is the evidence? or What are the grounds for believing something is true? It is at this point that we need to refer to differences between kinds of knowledge, since such differences would point to different areas in which the relevant evidence would be sought. Again briefly, it is possible to distinguish between three broad kinds of knowledge – knowledge that something is the case (that people coming into residential care typically experience a certain range of emotions and problems; that a certain kind of marital role segregation tends to be associated with social networks of a particular quality, and so on); knowledge by acquaintance (a social worker could be said to know particular clients, to know a district 'like the back of his hand') and, finally, what a person knows when he knows how to do something (this can be called 'knowhow', as long as we are clear that we refer to knowing how to do something and not merely being able to do something).

Now this simple threefold distinction enables us to see that social work requires each of the different kinds of knowledge and that the differences cannot in some way be reduced so that 'social work knowledge' can be made to refer to only one kind of knowledge. It helps to show the different contributions that can be expected from knowledge of different kinds and how a knowing and knowledgeable social worker might be recognised as a person with three different abilities. Each kind of knowledge could obviously be discussed at length, but at this stage we think it important from the point of view of social work to concentrate on issues concerning evidence.

Evidence

We have already seen the problem concerning intuition, when social workers claim to know without, as Goldstein argued, 'the benefit of specific clues'. Another problem concerns the apparent decision to rule out in advance certain kinds of evidence. A position on a particular section of the knowledge base of social work is taken and held despite, it seems, whatever future evidence may suggest. We can see one example of this invincible selection in the list already quoted from Bartlett. The list refers to knowledge of human development characterised by emphasis on the wholeness of the individual and the reciprocal influences of man and his total environment. What, however, happens to evidence that questions these assumptions? The influence of man and his environment cannot always be shown to be reciprocal, and belief in the wholeness of man must face and deal with the contrary evidence, especially evidence supporting the idea of man as in a state of basic conflict.

A more striking example is to be found in the treatment Hollis (1964) gives to the contribution of sociology to social work. She argues that 'sociological data amplify the rich understanding of the internal dynamics of the personality developed by the Freudian school of thought; they do not replace it' (p. 11). (The data in question arise from sociological study of the varying content of beliefs, values and expectations of different ethnic groups and social classes.) Later the 'insights' of the sociologists are said to constitute '*additions* to the knowledge of the inner life of the child uncovered by Freud' (p. 11) (italics not original). But what do we recommend if sociological data question the meaning of the psychological, and how rational is a commitment to 'the Freudian school' without at least some examination of what can be and has been established on the evidence? It is no substitute to talk of Freud's discoveries or of what, very generally, practice has shown to be true.

Some idea of the way in which questions of evidence are avoided can be gained from a recent comparative study of the theories of social casework. In a discussion of the contribution of psychoanalysis and ego psychology Wood states (1971, p. 47) that

Some of the operational concepts of psychoanalytic personality theory have received so much empirical confirmation that they are generally used as if they were indeed established 'laws of the mind'.

Brenner considers two such fundamental hypotheses: the principle
of psychic determination, or causality; and the proposition that
*consciousness is an exception rather than a regular attribute of psychic
processes.* The first principle holds that in mental functioning,
nothing happens randomly or by choice. . . . The second hypothesis
holds that unconscious mental processes are of great significance and
frequently in normal as well as in abnormal functioning.

The problems here are twofold. First, a glossing over of the question of what could count as empirical confirmation of such principles or hypotheses: what evidence would lead us to support
or deny the principle of psychic determination; how would we
deal, for instance, with the description – He cannot help it, it's his
character? Second, the formulation of these principles or hypotheses changes as they are applied to social work. So, the principle
concerning the place of unconscious mental processes in functioning is formulated in the following way: 'Virtually all caseworkers
now contend that there exists a part of the mind that cannot be
reached directly, but can only be viewed as it is expressed through
its "derivatives" in overt behaviour' (p. 48). But, of course,
virtually no caseworker would be foolish enough to agree to such
a dubious contention. The 'unconscious' cannot be well appreciated
as 'a part of the mind': we can say with some justification that
there are various processes, and some can reasonably be described as 'unconscious', but they cannot be located. This may
appear to be a purely verbal point: it could be argued that the
acknowledgment of 'unconscious' processes is the important point
and that precisely how these processes are described (as, for
example, located in some place or other) is of secondary significance. Such a view undervalues the practical importance of the
way in which we envisage unconscious (or conscious) behaviour
and respond to it. Are we to picture the 'unconscious' as a kind of
inaccessible place from which heavily disguised messengers are
dispatched, or as a hidden feature of ordinary behaviour, or as a
man whose presence is crudely betrayed and portrayed by his
movements behind a curtain? Each of these different pictures has
different implications for the social worker's response. Our
preference would be for the second view, and we would agree with
Dilman (1959) that 'The statement about unconscious envy is a
statement about what can be seen in the same way that the snake
hidden in, but not behind, the bush is seen.'

Two further problems concerning evidence arise in social work,
particularly it seems at the present time. The first is connected

with the contemporary profusion of models and theories for social work and amounts to an argument that talk of evidence is an easy product of a consensual view of social work in general and of knowledge in particular. Leonard (1975) in a useful classification of forms of explanation in social work states

> Not only are rival and conflicting explanations of human behaviour and structure explored in social work education but many of these different perspectives are based on different criteria of explanation itself. In other words, the answer to the question 'What shall we count as evidence?' is itself subject to dispute. . . .

But, as the article goes on to demonstrate, it is in fact possible for people who use different explanatory frameworks to talk to one another (even if according to the article this possibility is confined to Marxists' sociological understanding and even valuing the findings of non-Marxists). If genuine conversation is possible then it is also possible to agree on what counts as evidence for a viewpoint and even to agree on what counts as good evidence. One does not have to adopt a viewpoint as one's own to be able to see what counts as evidence for it or against it.

The second problem of the two just mentioned concerns the impossibility of agreement. It seems that, at least in certain circumstances, there is simply no way of deciding between two appraisals of 'the same' situation. A good example of this can be obtained from the official report on the Maria Colwell case. The basis of the difference between the majority and the minority reports is to be found in different readings of Maria's early life. The detail does not concern us here, but what is of direct relevance is the statement in the minority report concerning the status of the difference between the readings. 'As a social worker,' says the author of the minority report, 'my education and experience has taught me that in such matters, there is no one truth: in considering the subtleties of human emotions everyone is subjective. One's feelings, attitudes and experience colour one's perceptions.' Yet if this is a true generalisation of our understanding of a case it would mean that comparison and disagreement are both impossible: there is nothing in common between two completely subjective appraisals. This is *not* to say that there is one completely true understanding of a situation, but it is to argue for the possibility of meaningful discussion at least of some aspects. As we shall see when we discuss the concept of 'emotion', it is possible to establish certain criteria for the use of 'fear', 'shame', and so on.

In fact, the minority report suggests that some explanations offered by the majority are not acceptable. 'The idea that [Mrs K] wanted Maria home to be a drudge is implausible . . . if Mrs K's intention had been to use her in this way, why not one of the older and more capable children?' We would suggest that discussion could fruitfully have continued with the attempt to agree, on the concept of 'drudge' and to ask, for example, whether 'drudges' are typically chosen for their capability. In other words, Maria's comparative lack of capability may have fitted her for the role of drudge in Mrs K's eyes. We do not doubt that perceptions can be coloured by feelings, attitudes, and experience, but this way of talking seems to acknowledge that to some degree perceptions 'exist' at least to an extent, apart from any 'colouring'. We do not expect agreement on the appraisal of complex human situations to be easy or that it can usually be extensive. We do argue for the possibility of some agreement.

This issue of the extent to which evidence can count between rival appraisals is of fundamental significance. If social workers are inevitably bound in by their subjective understanding of the subtleties of feeling there is no way of choosing between accounts and no way of improving one's understanding. We would be left with a group of people (social workers) who, relying on only personal insight, would be unable to converse on their understanding. There could be no possibility of transmitting systematic knowledge through training. A warning concerning the grave consequences of such an inability is to be found in Hegel's observation (quoted in Plant, 1973, p. 145) that

> Those who invoke feeling as their oracle are finished with anyone who does not agree: they have to own that they have nothing further to say to anyone who does not feel the same in his heart – in other words they trample under foot the roots of humanity. For it is the nature of humanity to struggle for agreement with others, and humanity exists only in the accomplished community of consciousness.

Self-knowledge

Self-knowledge has been stressed as a desirable objective in social work education for several decades. Historically, the objective arose from the attempt to establish the persuasive description of social work as a treatment or a kind of therapy. In psychoanalysis the self-knowledge of the analyst, acquired through his own analysis, is essential. A weaker version of this was adopted for social work: early psychiatric social workers argued for or against the desirability of a personal analysis at least for some kinds of social work. Because of the origin of the desire for self-knowledge in social work, a particular aspect of such knowledge has been emphasised, namely, factors in his or her early relationships that made work with particular groups of clients difficult or seductively easy. Self-knowledge has continued to figure as a major prerequisite in social casework, but is much less emphasised in other 'methods'. This is, in our opinion, a mistake. Social work, however it is subdivided, requires self-knowledge on the part of the social worker. We say this because social work, whatever else it is, is essentially a non-exploitive activity. Yet social workers characteristically work in intimate relations with clients and self-knowledge is one important way, though not the only one, in preserving such relations from being exploited. Self-knowledge does not, of course, guarantee this: it guarantees no special form of action, but it does provide a good basis for action.

In agreeing with earlier workers who have valued self-knowledge in a social worker, we do not wish also to express agreement with the focus of that knowledge. We believe that the boundaries of self-knowledge have in the past been too narrowly drawn. Self-knowledge in social workers must take cognisance of all the main factors that 'place' an individual in the world. These factors are social quite as much as they are psychological.

But how is this self-knowledge acquired? This is a complicated question: the problems of the knowledge of ourselves and of others have attracted a great deal of philosophical consideration. Some would argue that we come to know ourselves in ways completely different from the ways in which we come to know others and others know us. This difference is extended and consolidated by the fact that – according to one view – we are the only authority about our own minds. The position we would support is one in which self-knowledge can be attained in a number of ways. We would agree that in coming to know ourselves we do not habitually rely on observing our own behaviour and extracting clues. This is the method on which we rely for our knowledge of others. In knowing ourselves – what we will do, for instance, at some time in the future – we call not upon observation but upon what we have already formed an intention to do, upon the purposes we have decided to try to achieve, and so on. In this sense, knowing ourselves is different from knowing others. Yet it seems that at times we do develop knowledge of ourselves from observation, from, as it were, catching ourselves in a particular action or evincing a certain opinion. Sometimes in social work this observation comes directly from others, either through supervision of work during training or through formal or informal discussion of work.

We would make two further points. First, it looks as if self-knowledge (or insight into oneself) involves something more than acquaintance with parts or aspects of the self that are not readily acknowledged. Self-knowledge seems to involve in addition a kind of acceptance of what is known. Hamlyn (1970) has suggested that for a man to have self-knowledge involves his recognition not only that he is a person of a certain kind but also that he is just that person and not another. If this is so, then clearly the development of self-knowledge in social workers serves not simply as a protection for client and social worker, it also provides a model for the social worker's behaviour towards the client.

The second point is simply to observe that the process and the product of self-knowledge should not be considered in too precious a light. Nott (1970) has argued that 'we learn ourselves as we learn anything else; like any other kind of learning it is a process, and if during the process we look at the process we lose the trick . . .' (p. 209). At first sight this looks plausible, but reflection indicates that we can learn to look at many kinds of process in which we are participating without losing the trick. Not every kind of learning is like learning to ride a bicycle.

Consideration of self-knowledge enables us to summarise the main argument of this chapter, which has attempted to deal with some important general considerations in relation to knowledge in social work. Self-knowledge in social work has been valued highly, but sometimes it has seemed to be almost the only kind of knowledge sufficient for effective social work. This particular preference for knowledge of a single subject matter illustrates the more general problem posed by those who adopt entrenched positions concerning the superior performance to be gained from psychological or sociological theories. The value given to self-knowledge also illustrates preferences for a particular way of knowing, that of personal experience of a kind that cannot easily be described. That which is elusive, that which is of the finest nuance, that which can only be 'experienced' has always held a considerable attraction for social workers. Yet, as we have seen in relation to self-knowledge, there are different routes to knowledge and different aspects of behaviour that have to be known. Sometimes we know something because we – and only we – know we have decided something. On other occasions we know because we have seen something; sometimes, as Scheler (1954, p. 10) stated in a book on human sympathy which should receive more attention on social work courses, 'It is *in* the blush that we perceive the shame, in the laughter joy. . . . In the sight of the clasped hands . . . the "please" is given exactly as the physical object is.'

Above all self-knowledge has to be worked for, and in this again it resembles knowledge of other kinds. To claim knowledge is to claim conviction based on certain evidence. Sometimes this evidence will be of a scientific kind (the evidence of certain pieces of research), sometimes it will be of a different nature (surely that did not amount to a decision?). In stressing the role of evidence we are also emphasising the public character of social work and the responsibility of the social worker to test for himself and for those he would help what can successfully claim – at least for the present – to be known. Social workers may be tempted to follow the current fashionable belief in the relativity of knowledge. According to this belief there are no generally agreed ways of testing the truth of a statement: what is true for you with your perspective is not necessarily true for me. Yet knowing more about who holds a particular position or about the situation he or she may be in will only help us to see more clearly what is being asserted. Whether a proposition or a theory is true must be determined independently of who proposed it or under what circumstances.

Suggestions for further reading

Bartlett (1958) has probably made the most important contribution to considerations of 'the knowledge base' of social work; an essay by H. Meyer *et al.* (1968) discusses the criteria that should be used in the selection of social work knowledge. Most of this chapter, however, is taken up with more general considerations of knowledge. These can be usefully followed up in a number of texts, but we would refer readers particularly to Hamlyn (1970) and the succinct statement by Pears (1972). See Kassman (1973) for a clear statement of the relation between knowledge and belief – Kassman's view is different from that adopted in this chapter.

There is a great deal to be gleaned on insight in Winnicott (1964) and Jehu (1972): it does not make any difference that the insight or self-knowledge discussed refers sometimes to the worker's insight and sometimes to the developments of insight in the client as a direct objective of social work. Iris Murdoch (1969) has some interesting comments on the drawbacks and delusions of self-knowledge. 'Know thyself' is, of course, not a modern injunction. For some illustration of medieval usage see Morris (1972).

The distinction between 'head' knowledge and 'heart' knowledge mentioned in the text is, of course, an old one, probably deriving from romanticism. The literature on romanticism is almost of infinite dimensions, but readers may like to refer to Mencher (1964). This is not a completely satisfactory account of the influence of romanticism on social work, but at least it is a praiseworthy attempt to set social work in the wider context of a social movement.

Social work knowledge— some neglected key concepts

Social work literature abounds in concepts, so much so that the state of social work has been characterised as one of 'conceptual affluence and propositional poverty' (Timms, 1971). In the inflationary and largely uncritical production of concepts two crucial questions were submerged; what is involved in grasping and using these concepts, and whether we can identify any group of concepts that hold the key to social work. In so far as any critical purpose was entertained in the literature it usually took the form of the brief and unhelpful injunction to take care or be precise in the use of terms.

Now, social workers consciously employ a considerable number of concepts, as we have already seen – treatment, case, diagnosis and so on. Each of these would repay attention, but in our view some only appear to raise problematic issues, whilst some of the key concepts are scarcely recognised as such. As an example of concepts that may appear to raise important issues let us take 'community' and 'community work'. It is clear that definitions of 'community' abound, and it is probable that new ones will be produced, but progress in distilling the concept of 'community work' does not depend on first of all unravelling 'community'. It is possible to make some simple distinctions which help to clarify the objectives of community work. So 'community' can refer to a particular target for work (the local slum) or to a range of resources which have to be tapped if the work is to succeed (community relations). This distinction can be made relatively easily, and is not less important for that, but we can make it without bothering greatly over the concept of community. Assumptions that sometimes accompany community work (e.g. that it is the community, however defined, that suffers from a particular disturbance and it is in the community alone that the remedy can be found) belong more to the concept of 'therapy' than to 'community'.

'Relationship', again, is a much used concept in all forms of social work, and it is obviously used to cover a range of meanings. Reid and Shyne (1972), have recently suggested that 'it is a word whose usefulness has been fatally impaired by the variety of vague and ambiguous (and we would add, ambitious) meanings that it has accrued in over a half-century of treatment literature'. They say that it may be used 'to describe the sum total of events that occur between practitioner and client; or it may refer to certain qualities of these interactions, particularly of the attitudinal and emotional variety'. It seems to us, however, that the concept has not been fatally abused, and that as long as social workers remain aware of the various different uses of the term it can continue to be useful.

Most of the concepts used in social work would repay scrutiny and thought, but not all of them raise serious problems. Some concepts, however, are both complex and neglected. Of these we have selected for discussion the following: understanding in social work; emotion; needs–wants–interests; power; equality. These concepts are not all considered at equal length and it is obvious that all that can be attempted here is an introductory or purely illustrative treatment. This chapter will seem to be over-ambitious in objective and highly compressed in content, but it will have achieved its major goal if it is seen as an important sign-post pointing towards two crucial areas of thought hitherto neglected, wholly or in part, in social work education: political philosophy and philosophy of mind. We wish to say that there are certain key concepts which a student must be able to handle if he is to be a social worker. In the past concepts have often been used simply as embroidery on the opaque surface of social work, but concepts should be used to do spade work. Such an approach may help to reassure those who otherwise might misinterpret our emphasis on the conceptual equipment of the social worker, and judge it as an attempt to 'intellectualise' social work. Putting their response crudely, they could be imagined to say, 'What's the use of having all these concepts intellectually when there is no guarantee that they will be used appropriately – and with feeling?' This would be a misleading and uneconomic way of responding. Rather than assume two levels of appreciation, 'knowing the concept' and feeling right about it, we would argue that we are concerned simply with the use of concepts. If a social worker was acting inappropriately in a situation involving anger, for example, we think it is more helpful to state, as the most likely possibility, that his grasp of 'anger' is deficient rather than that he has the concept intellectually but cannot apply it emotionally.

Understanding in social work

'Understanding' features largely in the activity of social workers and in the writings on social work. 'I understand or I am trying to understand how you feel about X'; 'social workers should try to understand the social context of their clients' lives.' Or a supervisor may ask a student, 'What is your understanding of the case?' The assumption that understanding people is difficult forms one of the assumptions that distinguish modern social work from earlier benevolence. But how do social workers understand, and what general difficulties does striving for such understanding meet?

What sort of an achievement is understanding in social work? Before answering this question it is worth underlining the assumption that this question makes. Understanding is the result of activity. As Oakeshott (1975) has said, 'understanding as an engagement is an exertion' (p. 1). The social worker is not the more or less passive recipient of material that somehow or other falls into place, so that the social worker goes on collecting increasing amounts of data in the hope that at a certain time the accumulation will point in the right direction and tell people what to do. Nor is the social worker sifting rather aimlessly through a pile of facts, as one might search a heap of buttons, in the hope of finding the single fact that illuminates the whole problem. Both these notions have been canvassed from time to time in social work, but neither suggests a coherent account of understanding. For some kind of description is inherent in 'understanding' and we cannot respond to the bare instruction 'just describe a situation'. We discern certain features in the situation from a particular point of view. We must select aspects of a situation because of the infinite variety of possible aspects of the world, and we select so that our understanding is not a mere heap of disconnected statements. 'Point of view' is a rather wide expression: it could refer to a theoretical position (e.g. psychodynamic), a particular theory being used or a social role being played. At this stage, however, it is not necessary to disentangle these meanings.

So what sort of work is understanding? Perhaps the best way

to begin is by discussing two of the many different ways in which we try to understand. We speak of poetic understanding, of how an engineer would understand, or understanding as a doctor, historian, scientist and so on. We cannot discuss each of these, but believe that historical and scientific understanding offer as good a beginning and a contrast as any other two.

Some would say that social workers should aim at becoming members of a scientific profession because they should understand situations by applying science. This is attractive partly because for some this is the only way to be rational. Yet it is clear that scientific activity is only one way of being rational and that it has no monopoly even if it has great prestige.

Now it is perhaps heartening to realise that it is not too easy to say with confidence how scientists do understand. For example, Karl Popper's notion that scientists are always testing by attempting to discover what would refute their theory has to be contrasted with Kuhn's much more mundane view of normal science (that is science between intellectual revolutions) as puzzle-solving in the sense of crossword puzzle solving, i.e. the solutions are always in principle available. The fact that basic disagreement about the nature of scientific understanding is possible helps us to see that problems of what it is to understand are not confined to understanding in social work. It is also heartening that different interpretations of scientific understanding can be compared and contrasted, and criticism and argument can lead to modification – this is the case in the Popper–Kuhn debate (Lakatos and Musgrave, 1965). It may be difficult for one person to support both positions – logically and psychologically difficult – but each side is engaged on a single enterprise; they both wish to elucidate the nature of scientific understanding, and they talk to each other. This is the model of controversy from which social work could derive great benefit.

Fortunately, for our purpose we do not need to follow the discussion in detail. For the purpose of making a contrast between scientific and historical understanding it is sufficient to refer to Popper's early treatment of scientific exploration (1952, vol. II, p. 262). Popper maintains that to give a causal explanation (to understand in that sense) requires the combination of two different kinds of statements pertaining to the special case in question. Popper illustrates this by analysing the fact that a thread capable of carrying only a one-pound weight broke when a weight of two pounds was attached. The explanation of the thread breaking

consists of a universal statement – whenever a certain
undergoes a tension exceeding a certain maximum tension
is characteristic of that thread, it will break. The explanati
consists of specific statements – for the thread in questio ...
characteristic maximum tension is one pound and the weight in
fact attached was two pounds. Popper goes on to argue that some
disciplines are more interested in the universal statements and
others in the statements concerning the specific situation. Physics,
biology and sociology are offered as examples of the first, and
history of the second.

Now the fact that history is included in this account of scientific
explanation demonstrates one important assumption, i.e. that all
forms of explanation share, though to different degrees, the same
features. This assumption has been questioned by many of those
who have been interested in elucidating the special character of
historical explanation. Some of these who have rejected what has
come to be called 'the covering law' model have approached the
position of intuitive understanding close to that illustrated earlier
in this book from Goldstein. Others have insisted on the patient
work of reconstruction so that the ideas of significant figures in the
past can be rethought. Gallie (1964) has produced an alternative
account of historical explanation which emphasises the central
importance of telling a story. He argues that the conclusion of a
story is essentially a different kind of conclusion from that which
is synonymous with 'statement proved' or 'result deduced or
predicted'. Explanations are required in history to remove obstacles to the flow of the narrative and are often concerned with
demonstrating the rationality of action hitherto concealed in
puzzles.

We believe that it is important to grasp the social work claim
'to understand' and that even this very brief reference to other
models of understanding can illuminate the problems. First, it
does seem surprising that social work writers have made no
reference at all to the considerable body of work carried out on
exploring the nature of historical explanation. Even such an early
and comparatively crude concept as 'the social history' of an
individual ought to have at least suggested this as a likely avenue
for exploration. Instead, treatment of social work understanding
has been pivoted exclusively around 'science' and 'art', with little
attempt to explore either as a way of understanding with its own
perspectives.

Second, scientists and (some) historians argue over whether or not the human nature of what is to be understood creates a crucial distinction between modes of understanding. For some there is only one way to explain and it matters nothing what it is that has to be explained. Others recognise one way of understanding people and another way of understanding things. As far as social work is concerned we should note a simple, possible distinction between explanation and understanding, and suggest that both are required. What do we mean by this?

Often in social work, as in ordinary social living, description of a fairly simple kind conveys sufficient understanding: a person intends to find work, someone is grieving over a loss or fighting an injustice or having difficulty making up their mind. We understand because we see – and sometimes it is like seeing – that a person's behaviour is appropriate in the light of his beliefs about a particular situation. Sometimes this understanding can only be achieved by an imaginative effort, but this is by no means always the case. This imaginative effort is often called empathy and it is characteristically required to convey understanding, even though, as we have just stated, it is not always required for the achievement of understanding.

Sometimes, however, social workers look beyond the human actor, his beliefs, intentions and so on. They use, even if they do not produce, something approaching a general law or a regularity of some kind, to account for human action in particular instances. For example, they seek an explanation of why a man has come to entertain such self-defeating purposes, of why his learned responses preclude or severely restrict choice, of why he can apparently only entertain objectives of such a short term that they hardly count as objectives at all. In the development of social work it has sometimes been assumed that only this type of explanation was desirable and social workers have accordingly been inveterately suspicious of appearances, convinced apostles of the laws now of economic progress, now of the unconscious mind. Our account of 'social work understanding' separates understanding, empathy and explanation, and suggests a particular role for each. Usually it will be sufficient to appreciate human action as appropriate in the light of certain beliefs. Sometimes this appreciation cannot be attained without the empathy more usually required in conveying understanding, but understanding without any extra imaginative effort is quite possible. Yet understanding even when accompanied by empathy is not always enough: sometimes we require the kind of explanation involved in saying 'But don't you see how he has come to entertain such an intention?'

Emotion

Social workers frequently talk generally of 'feelings' and they often refer to particular emotions, such as guilt, fear, shame and so on. Yet the concept of emotion is given little or no attention. It is as if emotions could be directly and easily known and presented problems of handling rather than understanding: emotions can, with training, be identified successfully underneath the words used; social workers can be helped to deal with feelings of hostility. In our view, this approach is an over-simplification, and we want to make three points in support of our contention. The first simply draws attention to the ways in which social workers talk about emotions. They may see themselves as directly concerned with the concrete expression of emotions, but they often describe emotions in an elaborate and rather abstract way. So Leichter and Mitchell (1967) argue that whilst the caseworkers in their study placed high value on the recognition and expression of what they called 'true' feelings, their records reporting on the expression of these feelings tended to use generalised and neutral terms. 'When a caseworker speaks of "angry verbalisation", a client speaks of "emotional outpourings", "animosity", "giving it to them", "disparaging remarks" . . .' (p. 248).

Second, we believe that clients often require help in the identification of their emotions. This requirement has been well described and its relative importance assessed by a character (Bradley) in Iris Murdoch's novel *The Black Prince*. Bradley at one point asks 'What emotion had so invaded me? Fear? It is sometimes curiously difficult to name the emotion from which one suffers. The naming of it is sometimes unimportant, sometimes crucial. Hatred?'

Third, identifying these emotions undoubtedly requires observation, but not observation directed exclusively at various kinds of bodily movements. Emotions can and should be distinguished from moods or feelings (and from tics and bodily itches) through what is termed their intentionality and through what Wilson (1973) has described as their cognitive core. The 'intentionality' of emotions draws attention to the fact that emotions have an object or are directed towards an object: we are always frightened of something, shamed about something. The cognitive element in emotions concerns the fact that emotions are closely connected with judgments or appraisals of different kinds. Fear, for example, is connected to the judgment that a situation is dangerous; pride to the judgment that something worthwhile has been achieved. So it is not always a straightforward matter for social workers to be sure that they are faced with a particular emotion. As Melden (1969) has observed in relation to anger, 'We need to know a good deal about the people involved. Their social relations with one another, their habits, and their practices, to which rules of behaviour of various sorts are relevant, in order to ascertain whether in any given situation we have a case of anger.' This is, of course, far removed from the exhaustive technical diagnosis used earlier in this book as an illustration of the misplaced complexity of contemporary social work.

Needs–wants–interests

Social workers are people who try to help others, but how do they help or try to help, and what do they help people to do? We have already discussed the first question when we examined what social workers should be able to do. In this section we shall look at the second question, by raising the following issues – do social workers aim to further the interests of their clients (long-term and short-term interests), to help their clients obtain what they want or help them to satisfy their needs? Briefly, we suggest that social work comprises each of these aims, but it is important for social workers to know which they are pursuing at any given time.

Wants

'Wanting' looks fairly simple, in terms both of what it is 'to want' and of how it can be established that what is wanted is actually required. Giving the client what he wants may not always be possible, but it looks a relatively straightforward aim to entertain. Yet are the objectives of wants so clear? 'I want three packets of brand X' conveys a clear instruction to the shopkeeper and selling the commodity satisfies the want, but situations of 'wanting' found in social work are more complex: 'I want people to be more spontaneous in this group.' In these and similar situations what is wanted seems to be altogether different from a commodity. Kenny (1963, p. 206) has suggested that wanting X is always wanting to get X and a description of getting X describes a state of affairs and not a thing. Whether or not this applies to all cases of wanting should not concern us now, but cases of wanting met by social workers seem to fall within this notion. Kenny goes on to give three conditions for saying '*A* wants something'. *A* must be able to say: what counts as getting what he wants; what he wants to do with it; and what is wanted must not already be in his power or at least must not be known by him to be in his power.

So, even in the apparently simple case of 'want' the social worker cannot avoid work with the client and work of a critical nature. People coming to social workers for help will often require help in describing the state of affairs that they want, in ensuring that they have some idea of what they wish to accomplish by means of that state of affairs, and in testing that the state of affairs cannot already be realised by means at their actual disposal. Even if social work is only to be described as 'giving to people what they want' at least two implications follow. As we have seen, 'wanting' is complex, wants cannot be simply slotted into a computer-like machine for an automatic response. Second, as we have seen in the consideration of other aspects of social work, the picture of the social worker as 'giver' cannot simply be accepted.

Needs

Considerations of 'needs' usually acknowledge the existence of complexity, even though, as far as social work is concerned, discussion is often launched in the absence of any deep sense of puzzlement about the concept. Towle's much-used text entitled *Common Human Needs* (1965) evinces no curiosity about the concept of need; its self-confident, indeed gnostic, treatise is unfolded with no hint of conceptual anxiety. Within the boundaries of other subjects, however, some attempt has been made to establish that need-statements may be of different kinds. So, within social administration, Forder (1974, 1976) adopts a general view of need and then distinguishes between the ways in which goals are set. According to Forder, 'To speak of a need is to imply a goal, a measurable deficiency from the goal and a means of achieving the goal' (1974, p. 39). He then differentiates between the ways in which the goals are set – by 'some sort of consensus either of the specific means of achieving particular aims or of a comparative approach.' Forder makes a crucial point when he attempts to link conceptually 'need' with an implicit assumption about what can and should be changed. 'Need' certainly has within it some, fairly forceful, suggestion that what is needed should be provided, but simply to state need is not to give at the same time either a description or a justification for change of a particular kind. As Taylor (1959) has argued, 'Whether human needs *ought* to be met must be established on grounds independent of the "need" claims themselves.' Social workers face a similar problem in relation to the concept of self-development: just because a course of action can be seen as a form of self-development or self-expression provides no justification for it.

Other classifications of 'need' have been used by other authors. Bradshaw (1972) distinguishes between normative need, established by experts, felt need (something nearer to 'want'), expressed need and comparative need. Slack (1966) emphasises the distinction between short-term and long-term needs, whilst Braybrooke (1968) sees 'two basic categories of needs; course-of-life needs, which people have all through their lives or at certain stages of life through which all must pass; and . . . "adventitious needs" which come and go with particular contingent projects'. These distinctions are important in any kind of social work since there is often some kind of conflict between the different kinds of need. More important, however, is the distinction that can be made within need, as it were, rather than between needs. Taylor (1959) speaks of four kinds of 'need' statement: the first refers to a situation in which something is required by a rule ('You'll need to give the receptionist certain details of your personal and family history'). Second, need statements refer to what is required as a necessary means to the attainment of a goal of the person who is said to have a need. Examples of this would be: 'You need a social worker (if you are ever to understand your social security rights)'; 'You need temporary shelter so that you can sort yourself out'; 'You need something to take your mind off your troubles – a job perhaps.' Third, need statements can refer to situations in which a person's behaviour is motivated by a strong drive or motive. It is this sense of need that Braybrooke uses when he talks of the dominion of need. Fourth, need statements may make some kind of recommendation: we need more generally trained social workers; we need more graduates in residential social work.

It is possible to give further examples of the ways in which 'needs' can be distinguished, but we have suggested sufficient distinctions at least to prompt the question, why should social workers concern themselves with these distinctions? Why, for example, is Taylor's fourfold distinction of significance? In our view social workers inveterately use 'need' statements and it is important to recognise that distinctions are to be found within this general category and that each kind of 'need' statement requires a different justification. Social workers frequently refer, for instance, to unconscious needs. Now in Taylor's classification statements about unconscious needs are a particular kind of statement and to say that a person has unconscious needs (e.g. to punish himself) is to say one of two things. He either does not know that his behaviour is so dominantly motivated or he does not know what the motivating factor is. So, in Taylor's view, we justify a statement about unconscious needs if the person concerned either is not aware of his seeking any goal which would provide a plausible reason for his action, or the reasons he gives for his behaviour do not furnish as plausible an explanation of his behaviour as other reasons which he does not acknowledge or of which he is unaware.

Distinguishing between need statements also helps social workers to see the different purposes statements about needs can serve and the place of values in judgments on needs of various kinds. As Campbell (1974) has said, 'A man may be in need of a spanner, a cigarette or a win in a lottery, as well as in need of food, shelter and clothing, and he may need any of these things for the pursuit of evil as well as of good.'

Interests

Acting in someone else's interests is an idea strongly associated with altruism; serving the interests of particularly vulnerable or inarticulate people (children for example) has for long been an objective in social work; more recently social workers have been encouraged to help oppressed groups in society to realise their own real interests through what is described as the raising of consciousness. On this threefold basis there seems to be a very good case for arguing that 'interest' is one of the concepts social workers should know how to use. From the point of view of social work a number of important themes should be extracted from recent discussions, predominantly in the field of political philosophy. These can be most usefully presented through raising the question, how can interests be discovered?

It is attractive to entertain the idea that social workers can avoid any interpretative work at all and simply go to their clients to ask what their policy preferences are. Interests are connected to policies rather than particular acts, but it seems a comparatively simple matter to ask people which policy (say in relation to the democratic organisation of their residential centre, or their neighbourhood group) they care most about, would put most effort into, would prefer. This is, as we have said, an attractive idea and its attraction is to be found in the hope that such a line of enquiry would rescue the social worker from appraisal and assessment, would render him or her purely instrumental. This hope can also be seen in discussions of 'want' and of 'need'. If we could discover by some relatively straightforward process of enquiry what people want or need or what is in their interest then we could avoid the tempting complexities of having to establish what people really want or really need or what is in their real interests.

However, as we have already seen in relation to wants and needs, such a simple splitting of description and appraisal is not possible. It seems that we could say that a person's interests *are* his policy preferences, but saying this presents two difficulties. If a man is asked which policy he *prefers*, he must be given the range within which the preferences are to be brought into play. As Connolly (1972) has stated, 'since one always *prefers* something to other specified alternatives, the range of alternatives taken into account is crucial to the preference adopted. I might prefer democracy to communism, communism to death, and death to prolonged torture by the agents of a democratic society.' In addition, people have grounds for their preferences and simply asking them which policies they prefer obscures the fact that policies can be preferred for moral or for self-regarding reasons. We may say we prefer policy X to policy Y (in relation, say, to the handling of children in a residential centre) because we are not attending to the moral appraisal of the situation.

If registering actual policy preferences is unlikely to lead to 'interests', can we reach that destination by following 'wants' more closely? Barry, for example (1964) believes that we can say a particular policy is in someone's interest if it increases his opportunity to get what he wants. This view has been amplified, successfully in our view, by Connolly on the grounds that we should emphasise more than the securing of objects and advantages for private enjoyment. In Connolly's view 'we can also speak sensibly about the interests a person has as a social being. . . . When my interests as a social being are at stake, more than private wants are involved. Certain kinds of relationship with others are fostered – relationships which involve trust, friendship, shared conventions. . . .' A man might decide to forgo certain material goods in the interests of maintaining a relationship of trust another. 'He is surely acting in his interest in this case.'

Connolly also considers interests in terms of needs, but concludes that

> Any view which anchors interest *exclusively* (italics added) in felt behaviour tendencies runs the risk of celebrating uncritically those inclinations cultivated by dominant socialization processes while deflecting conceptual attention from possible gratifying modes of existence by-passed by those same processes.

He concludes with his own view of interests by stating that 'Policy X is more in A's interest than policy Y if A, were he to experience the *results* of both X and Y, would choose X as the result he would rather have for himself'.

We have in this section considered very briefly a group of concepts (wants, needs and interests) which are, in our view, essential in social work. We have seen that they are related ideas, but also that 'wants', 'needs' and 'interests' are established through distinct criteria. It is important to note that people can be mistaken about their wants, their needs and their interests, but a man mistaken about what he really wants is not necessarily mistaken about the results of something, as is the man mistaken about his real interest. Working out what people want or need or what is in their interest can be complicated. There is no way in which we can enthrone 'wants' or 'needs' or 'interests' as separately sovereign for social workers. Social work is concerned with all three. Yet talk about 'wants', 'needs' and 'interests' can be pursued. A guiding rule can be found by contradicting Lear's admonition to Regan 'O, reason not the need' (or wish or interest).

Power

Power has been used as the title for this subsection but, as in the case of wishes, needs and interests, we are actually confronted by a small group or family of concepts. We should deal not only with 'power' but also with 'authority' and with 'influence'. These concepts are frequently used in social work and in writing about social work, but distinctions between the concepts are not always observed. An example of the failure to use such a distinction may help our case that the distinctions are important. It is sometimes suggested that social workers believe in something called the 'self-direction' of their clients, but that this belief is an illusion, since experimental work can demonstrate that clients respond faithfully to the suggestions of their therapists. If, for instance, a therapist 'rewards' certain responses, such as those containing positive judgments of the client's self, even though the reward takes the minimal form of the therapist's closer attention, then these responses increase in number. This kind of finding is used to demonstrate the mythical quality of the belief in self-direction. Self-direction is apparently defeated because a therapist (or social worker as therapist) achieves a result. This, however, is not what the concept of 'self-direction' rules out. 'Self-direction' is in no way contradicted by the presence of 'influence'. 'Self-direction' rules out forceful persuasion, coercion and so on, but influence is not a form of coercion. It may be at times a form of persuasion, but not a forceful kind.

So, in our opinion, distinctions are required between the terms we have now identified – authority, power and influence. Obviously these concepts have been considered at length and in depth in sociology, social psychology and social and political philosophy, but in our view, the most economical and clearly understood distinction has been made by Lucas (1966). He distinguishes between authority, power and influence as follows (p. 16):

> A man, or body of men, *has authority* if it follows from his saying, 'Let X happen', that X ought to happen. . . . A man, or body of men, *has power* if it results from his saying, 'Let X happen' that X does happen. . . . A man, or body of men, *has influence* if the result of his saying, 'Let X happen', is that other people will say (perhaps only to themselves), 'Let X happen'.

We can see from these simple distinctions some of the crucial elements in the concepts which we are discussing. It is clear that 'authority' can be seen as legitimate power and that different social consequences flow from each of the concepts. These are two important points, but we shall be dealing at more length with 'authority' when we consider the social worker's right to intervene in a later chapter. At this stage in the general argument we would only stress the different social contexts to which these and other related concepts refer. So coercion implies a conflict of some kind between two parties and the securing of compliance by the threat of deprivation. (With this rudimentary notion of coercion it is possible to see how good or bad a description of social work activity is Handler's (1973) concept of *The Coercive Social Worker*.) Similarly, force refers to success in achieving an objective despite the non-compliance of the other, but the success is achieved in a particular way. The other is simply deprived of any choice between complying and not complying (Bachrach and Baratz, summarised in Lukes, 1974).

We are not at this moment concerned with empirical questions about the sources of power or authority in our society. Nor do we wish to advance propositions concerning the extent to which social workers use authority, wield power, exert influence. We wish instead to say that these empirical questions cannot be satisfactorily answered if, as so often happens in social work discussion, conceptual slippage occurs between authority, power, force, coercion and so on. We wish also to say that social workers have to face those in authority, with power and so on, and that they themselves have to pick a careful way between the different relations implied in each concept. It seems to us, therefore, that knowing how to handle these different concepts is an essential part of being a social worker.

Equality

We have chosen to discuss equality, but there seems to be a cluster of political concepts that the social work student should be able to use: justice (particularly as it relates to and is contrasted with benevolence), liberty (in relation to self-determination), fraternity (as a basis for social work) as well as equality. In our view of social work there is little to be gained by the attempt to forge social work as a set of techniques of treatment that could be divorced from their social context and yet somehow remain the same. Our emphasis on 'social auspices' means that for us social and political concepts are at the heart of social work activity. We cannot in the space available discuss even one of the group of concepts chosen, but we hope that our treatment of equality will at least demonstrate the kind of issues raised by any attempt to grapple with the undoubted complexities. (As with other subjects we have suggested further reading so that students can take their exploration of the concepts further.)

The concept of 'equality' is one that students of social work often encounter in social work literature and practice, but discussion of its problematic nature and direct relevance for social work is mostly neglected. For some social workers the 'equality' they subscribe to is a remote and laudable ideal: it has very little human connection with how they undertake social work, for example, with a mentally subnormal prostitute; for such workers courses of training that concentrate on the analysis of concepts of 'equality' prepare students for social work practice in Utopia. For them 'equality' is a blessed concept as far as it goes but it does not go very far in solving the real problems of social workers. Other students feel fervent about 'equality' and see the tasks of the social worker as central to 'equality' but they are unsure about ways of achieving this. What often emerges is a muddled belief that students and practitioners can adhere to the idea of 'equality' without any obligation to explore and examine what is entailed in the concept. We believe that students must first try to distinguish between the different interpretations the concept has acquired in use. This is a considerable task and requires more extensive treatment than we can provide in this context.

What must be first recognised is that a belief in 'equality' has been espoused by a wide variety of thinkers, conservative, liberal and radical alike. The concept is problematic because we have a wide spectrum of 'understandings' ascribed to it. For our purposes we distinguish crudely between two modes of equality, partial and total. Few serious thinkers in either group would deny that men are equal in so far as they share the common characteristics of being men, i.e. they belong to the same species and share a common potential capacity to communicate through language. Divergence really occurs when theorists attempt to explain the source of inequalities evident in all historical societies (irrespective of whether such inequalities are extensive or limited). What is contested is both the origins of individual and social inequality and the means for, or the desirability of, trying to remedy this state of affairs. At one end of the spectrum we have the view that social inequalities are the inevitable consequence of the social structure of society, of the fact that all societies are moral communities that institutionalise norms of behaviour to which sanctions are attached. These sanctions in turn produce inequality of rank amongst men. This view argued by Dahrendorf (1962) maintains:

> Since human society without inequality is not realistically possible and the complete abolition of inequality is therefore excluded, the intrinsic explosiveness of every system of social stratification confirms the general view that there cannot be an ideal perfectly just and therefore non-historical human society.

At the other end of the spectrum Marxists argue that human and social inequalities are a product of the relations of production. Distinctions of capacity and rank are the product of evolving the capitalist system and with its inevitable demise will emerge a classless society of equals. Marx claimed that the mode of production in material life determines the general character of the social, political and spiritual processes of life. Whilst the proletariat are divorced from the means of production human capacity is stunted and exploitation and domination flourish. Total social equality will only emerge with the overthrow of the capitalist state.

Between these extremes of inherently limited 'equality' and future 'total' equality exist a variety of proponents who believe in the pursuit of 'equality' as a genuine political, religious or moral ideal. They tend to have expectations more extensive than Dahrendorf and more immediate than Marx. They attempt through the repair or reform of existing social structures to eradicate or control those processes they identify as inimical to the sustenance of an 'equal' society. The character of the policies they adopt reflects not only their views on 'equality' but implicitly or explicitly their view of human society. The range of possible positions is extensive and there is no way of summarising cogently the qualifications involved. (Indeed the brief summaries of views we have outlined are intended to be indicative rather than informative.)

It is important for social workers therefore to explore the range of meanings attached to notions of equality so that we can establish relevant criteria for judging what we are trying to achieve by the practice of social work. Obviously such criteria are not once and for all objectives of social work because they will always be open to new developments in understanding in psychology, sociology, philosophy, politics, but they will enable us to eschew what is patently contradictory or irrelevant or even absurd in relation to social work understanding.

If we believe that the notion of 'equality' is central to social work activity this will emerge in the kind of provisions we seek to establish and sustain. If we re-examine the case history at the beginning of this text we can see emerging a milieu that operates on a very weak notion of equality. The 'milieu' did not encourage the handicapped residents to formulate their own goals and purposes. When the 'community' attempted to establish a procedure for eliciting personal aspirations the process was 'judged' in terms of 'trouble-making'. The rules necessary in any community were imposed by people who felt they knew better the 'interests' of their clients than they did themselves. The handicapped residents were judged to be inferior at the task of working out realistic and humane arrangements for the organisation of their own communal life. Obviously many members of a community who have been institutionalised for a long period of time show little evident capacity for this task and are as susceptible to domination by their fellow members as by the staff. What seems to us to be necessary here is the grasp of what is entailed in the notion of equality cited by Williams (1962).

> For it is precisely a mark of extreme exploitation or degradation that those who suffer it do *not* see themselves differently from the way they are seen by the exploiters: either they do not see themselves as anything at all or they acquiesce passively in the role for which they have been cast. Here we evidently need something more than the precept that one should respect and try to understand another man's consciousness of his own activities; *it is also that one may not suppress or destroy that consciousness.*

What we are suggesting is that social workers often give notional assent to the idea of human equality without achieving its manifestation in practice. This enables them often to feel good without the spadework of doing good. We believe that training courses do not sufficiently help them to grasp that the theory and practice are not dual functions but a unit of understanding and behaviour. Bad social work practice is an ill-informed, improper statement – an abuse of proper communication between client and worker. Social work in any setting is a process of communication between equal persons engaged in attempting to resolve problems of loss and change.

Suggestions for further reading

We have already referred to Wilson's introductory work on concepts. We have also suggested that social workers would gain from knowledge of the controversies concerning historical explanation and understanding. On this see Dray (1964) and Gardiner (1971). A useful discussion of 'having the concept of emotion' can be found in Wilson's *Assessment of Morality* (1973). Kenny (1963) and Mischel (1969) should also be consulted on 'feelings' as well as 'wants'. There is no single source to be consulted on 'needs' and 'interests'. Forder (1974) has a chapter on the definition of need, but in addition readers should read Braybrooke (1968), whose title suggests another way of perceiving the objectives of social work as concerned with diminishing the dominion of needs so that actual preferences may be developed. Taylor's (1959) analysis of 'need' statements is brief and very informative. On 'interests' Connolly

(1972) and Barry (1964) and Rees (1964) are essential reading. These authors are concerned with public interest in the main. This is, of course, important for social workers in its own right. It can also easily be adapted to the consideration of an individual's interest. The best short introduction to 'power' is Lukes (1974), who identifies a one-dimensional, a two-dimensional and a three-dimensional view of power, stressing the ways in which non-decision-making and the suppression of latent conflicts in society should also be seen as the exercise of power. Bradshaw (1976) has written a short criticism of Lukes. See also Martin (1971) who reviews some of the criticism of the notion of power, arguing against the view adopted in the text that power is legitimated authority – 'definitions of legitimacy are themselves contingent upon power relations'. The related notion of social control has not been examined in the text of this chapter, but a relatively simple introduction can be found in Watkins (1975). For a brief but useful treatment of liberty, equality and fraternity see Donnison (in Timms and Watson, eds, 1976), also Wilson (1966) on equality, Rawls (1962) on justice as fairness and Williams (1962) and Dahrendorf (1962) on equality. Some of the implications for social work of fraternity can be seen in Reynolds' (1951) account of social work in what she terms 'a membership organisation'. The concept of emotion, with particular reference to social work, is examined at length in Ragg (1976).

Social work knowledge— findings and theories

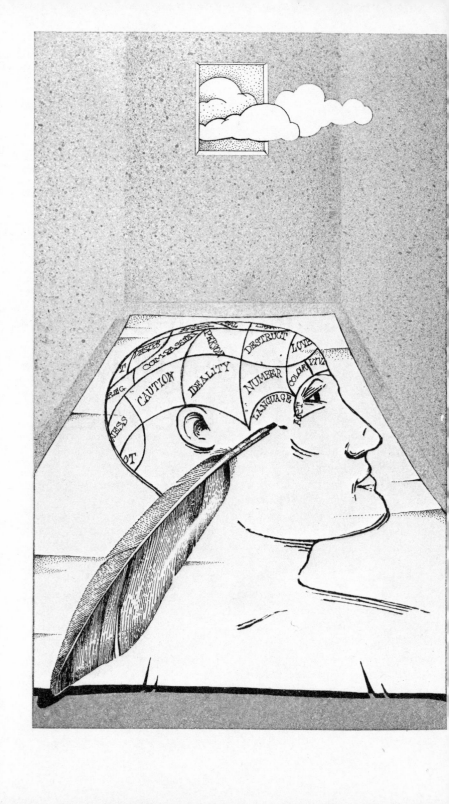

In this chapter we wish to consider what a social worker should know in the sense of 'knowing that'. It would be reassuring if we could produce a list of propositions or a list of facts that every social worker should know, but inevitably many propositions are held though few have been satisfactorily tested. Some social workers agree, for instance, that 'There is ample evidence that doing things for people does not help them' (Levitan, 1969, p. 115), but such a vague proposition does not really admit the possibility of evidence. Any occupation must at any time consist of a whole complex of ideas, half and fully formed, rather vague hunches, established propositions and so on, and such a complex cannot be articulated completely. What we aim to do in this chapter is to identify certain questions the practitioner must ask in relation to social work activity and to discuss some of the main theories that illuminate these questions. 'Theory' will be used very widely to encompass ideas and findings as well as propositions. There are, of course, some aspects of the knowledge a social worker should be able to use that are more or less factual. We have earlier referred to knowledge of legal provision and procedure. This will not be discussed, but we would make two points about this 'factual' knowledge. First, social workers often seem to have less than an expert's grip on this source of knowledge. This should not be taken as implying that social workers should have at their fingertips detailed knowledge, for instance, of the many kinds of benefit to which people might be entitled. On the contrary, scales of such benefit change from time to time and it is better to rely for accurate detailed and up-to-date information on literature or on a computerised system which would produce information in relation to the particular client concerned. Second, social workers should know the general principles that inform particular legal provision and should also be able to put this knowledge to use for the benefit of their client.

So we want in this chapter to outline some central questions and to suggest 'theories' which help to illuminate them. The questions we wish to examine are:

What am I doing when I do social work?
What problems can social work be directed towards?
What are clients doing at and with social agencies?
And, what are other people doing to clients and to agencies?

We believe that approaching knowledge through these simple questions concerning action is a more productive approach than approaching certain disciplines (usually sociology and, more particularly, psychology) and asking how social work can be helped. Certain areas of these disciplines may be identified as potentially helpful only as social workers become more clear about the questions that arise from their activity. The onus is on social workers to form and sharpen their own questions.

What am I doing when I do social work?

Historical study

We have seen that this is a central question, and one part of the answer comes from history. We suggested earlier in this book that social work should be seen in an historical perspective and also that such a perspective reveals significant and systematic criticisms of altruistic activity that have contemporary force and appeal. So social workers should be able to place themselves historically. This is not easy since history easily becomes tired and, as we have seen, crude interpretations become dominant. We need to attend to the development of historical enquiry and also to initiate new approaches. Two examples will show the kind of enquiry we have in mind. We think that in general C. S. Loch's injunction to social workers – Know your district – has been insufficiently heeded, even though contemporary social workers would perhaps wish to make clear that the district was not in any possessive sense theirs and that it could only be known satisfactorily if its articulation with other districts and with social institutions and groups were recognised. Knowing the district, however, is not just a matter of knowing it in the present. In this respect Margaret Simey's historical study (1951) of the social services of one particular district (Liverpool) can be taken as an example of the kind of historical work which, in our view, would provide helpful knowledge for the contemporary social worker. It remains, however, an 'experiment'; it has not become a precedent, and local welfare history has either been confined to social administration study or to providing the odd illustration whereby the superiority of the present can be instantly recognised.

The second example can be taken from a more recent volume, Walton's (1975) book on *Women in Social Work*. This book suggests the returns to be gained from taking a particular aspect of the occupation, i.e. the fact that for many decades it has been a woman's job. Thus, the beginnings of conceptualising modern social work were to be found in thinking about the models provided by certain female roles within the family.

> Nursing in sickness, tender love and comforting, education in its broadest sense and child care and nurture all demanded the ideal of service. It was, therefore, appropriate that women became involved in forms of social help which corresponded to these roles, as in almoning, psychiatric social work and child welfare (p. 257).

This presented the problem both within and outside social work of differentiating social work from what went on in ordinary, everyday situations. 'Even more than fieldwork, residential social work has suffered from the inability of outsiders to see anything other than domestic caring roles of the staff' (p. 293). Walton explores some of the implications of the predominance of women in social work but what remains curiously under-investigated is the effect of this predominance on clients. What do clients feel about receiving help from a woman? What does the sex of the social worker do to the process of help?

An historical approach, then, provides some answers to the question, What am I doing when I do social work? It is not, however, sufficient to develop historical curiosity. Some aspects of the problem are pressingly contemporary. The social worker is not an individual, somehow impossibly divorced from a social context, and with some historical curiosity. He or she needs to know the base from which they operate and to place this base from the point of view of social structure and of knowledge. These requirements call for knowledge and for decisions informed by knowledge.

Knowledge of the application of certain concepts to social services

It seems that more emphasis is given on training courses to theories that supply the social worker with an overall orientation to social work help. Such an orientation is inevitable and we shall return to this shortly, but we wish first to consider knowledge of the base from which the social worker operates. Some of this knowledge will come from studies of how consumers perceive and react to social agencies, and we have already discussed in some detail knowledge from this source. Social workers should also know the results of studies of interaction between agencies, of the adequacy of services, and of the application of certain concepts. Five examples will be given to illustrate the latter.

First, the notion of rationing has been applied by Parker (1967) and by Hall (1974) as a way of drawing attention to the problem of ever-increasing demand and static or slowly increasing or actually decreasing resources, and to ways in which the problem is met, often by social workers in face-to-face contact with clients. Parker suggests that among the various forms of rationing may be found the following: charging for service, creating physical barriers to access by encouraging the public to remain ignorant of the social services, the waiting list, dilution of service and so on. He recognises that rationing of some kind is inevitable, but argues that methods of rationing should be tested against three criteria: they should be rational and systematic, they should be explicit and they should be regularly reviewed. Clearly, rationing applies throughout social work and to all aspects of social work, whether this is material help or the social worker's time and attention.

The second example comes from the penal field. Davies's (1974a) study of prison after-care can be seen as an example both of a study of the adequacy of service and of the optimistic extension of the concept of after-care to increasing numbers and groups of people.

> The fact that the average after-care service cannot provide whisky, sex, or a dog to love, but is restricted not even to drama therapy and conceited compassion but often to a letter to the WRVS, a ticket to the Salvation Army Hostel and a few telephone calls to possible employers is something which ought to keep our view of the social services for ex-prisoners in clear perspective (p. 179).

Davies argues that difficulties of a similar kind are to be found in other areas of social work, where service is offered to those with the greatest need of help, for example to those with severe conditions of mental handicap, physical disability, addiction or terminal sickness. In his mind this raises a large and very important question concerning the provision of 'forms of social support and material aid irrespective of the probable response from the recipient'. This is in effect a good description of social work as caring work.

Our third example comes from the field of residential care, and involves the application of such concepts as boundary and primary task. Miller and Gwynne's study (1972) of some residential institutions for the physically handicapped and the young chronic sick identified two models of residential care, the warehousing and horticultural. These are not entirely happy expressions, but in the former (humanitarian) model the primary task is to prolong physical life through dependency, whilst in the latter (liberal) model it is to develop unfulfilled capacities through greater independence. The former gives staff control over the individual's boundary (and the boundary between the residential institution and the 'outside' world), whilst the latter asserts the right of the individual to control the boundary. They go on to argue that few inmates fit either model entirely, and that what is important is that 'the institution gives organizational (and also cultural) acknowledgement of the need for both' (p. 195). This study is important for several reasons. It pays attention to the boundary between the residential institution and 'society', arguing that the models are essentially 'social defence mechanisms set up to cope with the intolerable anxieties that are associated with the task that society implicitly defines for these institutions' (p. 88), that of coping with 'the socially dead'. It suggests that what is effectively in operation in social work is not so much a collection of theories consciously held, either in isolation or in some kind of interconnection, but a complex assumption, part of which may be a means of coping with the tasks of caring for disadvantaged and damaged people. We are reminded of the operation of ideologies in social service (which has already been discussed). Finally, whilst the study arose from particular institutions its main approach is at least suggestive for others.

The fourth example concerns the idea of the volunteer. Volunteers are an increasing feature of social work in many fields and their relationship to social workers raises a number of problems. Hadley, Webb and Farrell (1975) have recently studied the work of Task Force, which mobilises the work of young volunteers in the service of the old. What is important in our context is not so much the description of the old people and the volunteers, but the implications for voluntary work in general. So, for example, they suggest three models for organising a volunteer programme: an extensive model (through which service is provided widely but thinly); an intensive model (which concentrates upon the issue of quality); and a composite model which combines elements from both. It also is important for the general argument of this book to note that the authors do not believe that any one model can be canonised.

> Each has its merits and could be relevant in some situations. The choice of approach must largely depend upon the type and supply of volunteers, the clientele, the nature of the problem they present, as well as the careful costing of alternatives, and an assessment of the probability that appropriate staff could be recruited to run the organisation in the manner required (p. 182).

We believe that the imaginative and effective use of volunteers constitutes a special challenge to the contemporary social worker. This is primarily not because of economic forces (volunteers may in the long run be cheaper or dearer than professionals in full-time employment) but because the organising and facilitating of indirect help to clients (rather than a total preoccupation with direct treatment) is, as we noted earlier, an important aspect of social work activity.

The last example comes from a concept that 'belongs' to social work – foster care. Here we are concerned not so much with the extension of this idea, for instance to old people, or its variation (as in the case of special lodgings for people who have been in prison or residential care), but with its elaboration.

In 1963 Williston, writing on the foster parent role, identified the lay and the professional role. He suggested that the goals of the lay role were to ensure that the child dropped affectional ties and identification with the natural parents and conformed to the foster parents' standards. The professional role contrasted with this, so that, for example, discipline was to be carried out on the same basis as in the child's own home. Much more recently, Holman (1975) has developed the idea of exclusive and inclusive concepts of fostering. Exclusive fosterings are those that seek to exclude natural families. He cites as illustration the 56 per cent in Vic George's sample (1970) who did not think that real parents had even a conditional right to visit; 35 per cent of Holman's local authority foster mothers (1973) who thought that natural parents should not be encouraged to visit; 46 per cent of Adamson's sample (1973) who thought it best if foster children did not see their own families. Much of the orientation of the exclusive group echoes the 'fresh start' and 'rescue' notions of earlier child-care practice. A writer on boarding-out (Birchall 1904) commented that 'There can be no doubt that fresh country, fresh surroundings and a fresh home mean in most cases a fresh start, and *that* after all is what we want to give our children'. The inclusive foster parents are the 36 per cent in Holman's study (1973) who said 'I know he's not mine, but I treat him the same', or the 54 per cent in Adamson's group (1973) who thought that natural parents should see their children.

So here are two broadly similar ideas – lay and exclusive; professional and inclusive. But are these distinctions of any use? We think so, for two reasons. First, attitudes and behaviour towards social workers tend to follow the lines of these distinctions. Inclusive foster parents defined social workers as colleagues rather than friends and would immediately contact them if difficulty arose. Exclusive foster parents tended not to think contact necessary and regarded social workers as 'friends'.

Second, the characteristics of inclusive fostering seem to be associated with success, whether measured in terms of lack of breakdown or the condition of the child, his lack of problems, emotional adjustment, etc. Here the aspect most consistently measured has been contact. For example, Holman (1973) observed that in general the less contact the higher the incidence of certain emotional and physical symptoms such as soiling. Jenkins (1969) found that 57 per cent of foster children aged over $1\frac{1}{2}$ years at placement with no parental contact were 'disturbed' as against only 35 per cent in regular contact.

Activities placed in relation to society and to knowledge

So far we have indicated very briefly sources for knowledge about the agency base and the programmes which social workers carry out either directly or indirectly. But social workers operate within a wider framework: their agencies and their activities can be placed socially and in terms of a general orientation which has a considerable theoretical content. To some these two features are very closely connected, so that the social position of social workers dictates their general theoretical views. So Bitensky (1973) has indicated two approaches to understanding the development of social work: the first suggests that 'social work theory in a methodology such as casework advanced because theoreticians such as Mary Richmond, Gordon Hamilton and Jessie Taft used the newly created knowledge to think brilliant thoughts and conceptions'; the second maintains that 'while the role of the theoretician is important, the brilliant thoughts he produces are based on an agenda that is politically determined'. Bitensky believes that the second approach is the correct one. In our view it is essential, as we have indicated, to see social work in a perspective wider than the domestic. So a realistic view of the development of social work knowledge must include the kind of knowledge of political and social change that Bitensky suggests. It is, however, important to note that this concerns the source of ideas and beliefs, but, as we have already seen, these ideas and beliefs have to meet certain criteria before they can count as knowledge. Source has no necessary connection with validity. It is for this reason that we believe separate consideration should be given to the social position of social workers and to their theoretical orientation.

Part of the answer to questions concerning the social placing of social workers will come from empirical investigation. Social workers are often described as 'middle class' but we have no systematic information on the social origins of social workers. This information would produce, however, only part of the answer. It has also been argued that the way social workers understand society and the ease with which they adopt a social control function simply express middle-class values. We shall discuss the former shortly, but at this point the importance of concepts and theories of social class in the education of social workers should be stressed. In placing social work we have already implicitly made simple distinctions between ways in which class membership might be attained (by origin and by movement through education) and possibly between class membership and class consciousness. These are but two of the distinctions to be found in an extensive literature. A good grasp of social class is necessary to understand both social work and the problems of social work clients.

Such understanding, it has been suggested, is obscured by the social worker's insistence on treating situations in isolation and by what seems to be the model of society favoured by social workers. We refer here to the familiar distinction between a consensus and a conflict model. These can most usefully be described in the words of Dahrendorf. Dahrendorf (1959) contrasts an integration theory with a coercion theory of society in the following manner. According to integration theory

1) Every society is a relatively persistent, stable structure of elements.
2) Every society is a well-integrated structure of elements.

3) Every element in a society has a function, i.e. renders a contribution to its maintenance as a system.
4) Every functioning social structure is based on a consensus of values among its members (p. 161).

A coercion theory, on the other hand, makes very different assumptions:

1) Every society is at every point subject to processes of change; social change is ubiquitous.
2) Every society displays at every point dissensus and conflict; social conflict is ubiquitous.
3) Every element in a society renders a contribution to its disintegration and change.
4) Every society is based on the coercion of some of its members by others (p. 162).

Dahrendorf argues that both views are necessary if we are to understand society. It is certainly true that one view (the consensus) has predominated in social work, but in our opinion both views are required. This is sometimes denied. Mayo (Jones and Mayo 1974, p. 1), for example, refers briefly to a 'crude dichotomy between conflict and consensus as models of community work practice', adding that 'this is, of course, to assume that the worker or the group in question has a free choice between either as a tactic'. This question of 'a free choice' in knowledge is clearly crucial to the development of all kinds of social work. It is without doubt logically and psychologically very difficult to move from one model to the other and impossible to use both simultaneously, as it were. Yet social workers should already be practised in moving from one focus to another, as the client and his context are seen respectively now as foreground, now as background. Both models are required to understand society. Both are required if we are to develop a recent characterisation of social work that should attract considerable discussion. We refer to Olive Stevenson's comments (1974) following the Maria Colwell report: social workers must seek

> to mediate in the multiplicity of conflict in interpersonal relationships. They deal in shades of grey whereas the public looks for black and white. . . . They are 'brokers in lesser evils'. . . . In the precise sense of the word, society is deeply ambivalent about social work. . . .

We would suggest that such a description could be developed through applying to social work Rex and Moore's (1967) concept of 'institutions of the truce'. Rex and Moore argue generally against the assumption of limitless social conflict and refer to 'those organisational means through which conflicts and tensions are managed' (p. 617). In our view social work can usefully be seen as one of the 'institutions of the truce'.

Turning now to intellectual orientation we find that some social workers speak of themselves as influenced by or adopting some general approach which they have found helpful in understanding their work and also the problems of their clients. Some social workers would say they use an ego-psychology approach, others a learning theory or a systems theory. Some would say they were eclectic, others that they were using a predominantly sociological approach. So what workers are saying is that when they practise they are, in part, carrying out activities informed, at least to an extent, by certain theories or concepts of a particular kind. This book does not outline in detail any one theoretical orientation; partly because we argue that social workers can practise, and practise well, from a number of different theoretical orientations. We should note, however, one important aspect of a social worker's relationship to a body of ideas and theory (such as psychoanalysis): it is better described as a selective orientation; there will always be aspects of the theory or theories that will hardly be touched upon. In our view a great deal of ground can be covered through using some simple concepts and fairly rudimentary theory. This is why in an earlier chapter we drew attention to clients as often facing loss and change (Marris, 1974).

A number of factors will suggest which theory or group of theories is to be chosen. Some workers will be influenced by the group of concepts or theories that most advances the objective of making social work scientific, perhaps because this is for them the only way of being rational. Others will seek a theory or theories that seem to offer the best chance of liberalisation or that do justice to social work as clinical work. Everyone seeks a theory with which they feel personally 'at ease'. At least this is how one criterion is often described in ordinary social work language. In our view more work should be done on exploring the criteria that should govern the social worker's choice of general theoretical orientation. We can express the most important criteria in a simple phrase: the theoretical orientation must inform the practice. Each of the main terms in this statement will be examined so that the meaning is made more clear.

Emphasising the theoretical orientation implies that the social worker has a good grasp of the theory or theories and has a continuing interest in the way they develop: it should not be a once-for-all commitment to a theory or concept that happens to be at a particular state of development. It seems that sometimes social workers report their allegiance to a particular orientation but the orientation is only vaguely comprehended. Social workers might, for instance, say that they adopt the 'new deviancy' theory without appreciating the very different perspectives that can be encompassed under such a heading.

Two additional factors may hinder a social worker's grasp of a theory: uncritical acceptance, and the dominance of the psychological and the cultural.

By uncritical acceptance we refer to the fact that grasp cannot be established without considering some of the arguments or factors that might tell against the theory. It is rare for this to feature in social work texts. We give two examples of criticisms of theories which had attracted social workers: such criticisms should be taken seriously by those wishing to use the theories.

Bion's theory (1961), of the three basic assumptions that may, as it were, take hold of groups, therapeutic or not – fight/flight, pairing, and dependence – has been used frequently by social workers, but is not usually evaluated. Sherwood's (1964) criticism of the theory is directed not towards confirmation or refutation through the use of further clinical data, but towards logical issues. Some of these issues are not of immediate concern to the social worker: social workers do not have to settle for example, 'whether all group interactions are adaptations acquired in the face of social pressures or whether these are inherent drives to establish groups, and needs capable only of group satisfaction'. But it is of importance for someone trying to use Bion's theory whether it is the emotional states that accompany each assumption which are basic or whether it is the assumptions which are fundamental. It also matters whether or not conflict between individuals acting upon different basic assumptions is impossible. 'To lay down the dictum that such groups can only alternate is of course no answer at all, but science by fiat.' Sherwood calls his questions academic, but we believe it matters for practice that Sherwood can correctly describe the theory at certain points as 'clouds of confusion relieved only by clear patches of contradiction'.

The second example concerns Laing's theories concerning the family. These enjoy a considerable vogue in social work, but before social workers can be sure they have grasped them certain criticisms must be faced. One of the best statements of a critical position can be found in Morgan (1975). The relevance of his criticisms for social work understanding of and work with the family will be obvious. First, it is difficult to place, socially or temporally, the families about which Laing writes. Second, though Laing speaks of the totality of family relationships, he focuses mainly on the major roles involved in socialisation, parents and children. He takes, according to Morgan, a fairly orthodox model: failure to examine systematically the role of others and the tendency to see socialisation as flowing from parent to child. Third, it remains unclear whether Laing's pessimism about the family is a criticism of the institution or of the institution under certain cultural circumstances. We have drawn attention only to the negative criticism of Laing because absorption of this must be involved in claims to have grasped his theory. We believe that these (and other) criticisms are well grounded, not that they require of themselves any total dismissal of Laing. (See also Seigler *et al.* 1969.)

Part of Laing's fascination for the social worker may lie in those parts of his argument that detach the family from a social context and that resemble the 'culture-personality school'. According to Morgan (1975),

> At its simplest the culture-personality school (represented by Mead, Kardiner, Linton and others) assumed that personality was largely formed in early childhood; particularly important were the practices of weaning, bladder-control etc. Similar cultures have similar child-rearing patterns, therefore similar cultures have similar model personalities.

In other words, Laing's reception into social work may illustrate what we have described as the dominance of the psychological and the cultural. By this we mean that psychological understanding is preferred and that when sociological concepts are admitted they either slip back into the psychological or are seen in terms of culture or sub-culture. So, for example, conflict comes often to be viewed only as emotional conflict or as behaviour confined to the sub-culture of violence.

The dominance of the psychological stems from a basic conviction about the primacy of the individual and about the most satisfactory way of explaining social phenomena. It seems to be assumed by many social workers that explanations of social phenomena must refer exclusively to facts about individuals. Lukes (1970) has recently discussed this assumption in a way that sheds some light on the dominance of the psychological in social work. He describes a continuum of facts about individuals from the most non-social to the most social. We can talk about an ndividual's genetic make-up, his aggression or gratification, the esteem in which he is held, or various activities like cashing ۱ heques, voting and so on. These are descriptions at four different evels. Now explanation, the making intelligible of what was unintelligible, can take two forms. Sometimes explanation is given simply by identification, sometimes through deduction from generalisation. If we consider identification then, argues Lukes, to say that no explanation is possible unless it is framed in terms of brain-states, stimulus-response or exchange-reward arbitrarily rules out most acceptable explanations used in everyday life. If we consider explanation through deduction we are also in difficulty. Take the first level of individual description. To explain this we have either to develop a theory which will explain 'the sociological context' exclusively in terms of the central nervous system or which demonstrates that this context is simply a backdrop against which quasi-mechanical psychological foci are the only causal influences at work.

We have so far looked at some aspects of the first term in our phrase attempting to describe the criteria governing the social worker's choice of a theoretical orientation: the theoretical orientation must inform the practice. So far we have concentrated on ensuring that it is a theoretical orientation that is in question. We shall now consider, more briefly, 'inform' and 'practice'.

It does seem that theory is sometimes used as a kind of embroidery or that it is discarded in favour of an intensive reading of the individual situation. Certainly, individual situations have to be read, and this has been one of the main thrusts of social work since the middle of the nineteenth century. As the Annual Report of the COS for 1896-7 stated: 'Taking pains to go into each individual case shows us the great mistake is to give way to generalizing . . . it is worthwhile looking into each case, or we may lose a good opportunity.' Yet this concentration is only part of the process. We cannot in any event understand a particular situation without using generalisations; we cannot conceive of each situation simply in terms of its own individuality. We want to know in relation to the situation whether it is a case of X or of Y: Are we dealing with someone who is mentally ill or with an eccentric? Are we dealing with realistic complaints about the behaviour of officials or of group members? Thus, Skinner (1972) argues that if we wish to discover whether the 'autism' of an allegedly schizophrenic adolescent is a case of deliberate and meaningful behaviour, we do not begin by an intensive study of the particular case. We try instead to relate the particular case to other instances of adolescent withdrawal so that we may assess the extent to which the degree of 'autism' we see may not after all represent a form of adolescent protest. We should begin, according to Skinner, by trying to decode the agent's intentions by aligning his action with a more general awareness of the conventional standards which are generally found to apply to such types of social action. The reading of the particular situation, in other words, is important, but it is incomplete if it does not take a more general context into account.

Of course, a theory or idea may be related to practice in an indirect way. Some of its terms or part of its general message may indirectly lead to improvements in practice, even though the theory in its precise formulation has not survived empirical test. For example, one of the first studies of a mental hospital argued that there was a direct connection between disagreement amongst the staff and disturbance amongst the patients. Subsequent research which tried to test this hypothesis did not show this connection. However, this by no means rules out the possibility that thinking of a possible connection between the two groups has produced improvements in practice. Yet we would not wish to say that this would be a case of a theoretical proposition informing practice.

Our final criterion concerns practice, and practice provides a way of evaluating a theoretical orientation because 'practice' already has built into it some values. The orientation, we are saying, should not violate the values to be found in the practice we call social work. We shall consider these values in more detail later, but briefly we now need to show only the kind of value we have in mind. We think that some orientations could be ruled out if they led directly to or sanctioned behaviour that was exploitative of persons or that ignored them. In other words we would describe social work as a human practice, and we would argue that theories of non-intervention (even when described as healthy) are not compatible with that practice. Similarly, theories which exploit human unhappiness in some way would be incompatible, though it is important to note that it is exploitation that is ruled out, not, considered simply as such, the exercise of influence, authority or even power. 'Exploitation' picks out, as we have seen, some rather special behaviour.

What problems can social work be directed towards?

We want in this section to stress that one area of knowledge which receives less than its fair share of value in social work education is, to put it briefly and crudely, knowledge of social problems. Social workers should be experts, should have good information and imaginative ideas about the problematic conditions with which they have to deal. This requires up-to-date information on incidence and prevalence, on relevant legislation and appropriate sources of help. It also requires that attention is given to changes in the way social problems are conceptualised, and to the successful and unsuccessful claims that condition X be recognised as 'a new social problem', or that condition Y be no longer so recognised. This broad sweep of conditions and of the sometimes conflicting claims made on their behalf (e.g. that homosexuality is or is not an individual or a social problem) will help social workers to appreciate the limits of what they might expect their activities to achieve. One important aspect of a technology concerns the delineation of what cannot be accomplished. We must not, however, assume that unless social work can cure social problems it has nothing to say or do about those problems. In the past, perhaps, social workers have at least allowed rather extravagant claims to be made concerning the part they might play, if only numbers were increased, in reducing or removing social problems. It seems to us that social workers should play a role as informants. The knowledge they gain as a result of their work on social problems should inform their criticism of agency policy and of more general social policy.

The study of social problems has attracted increasing attention recently, particularly among sociologists. Sociologists (almost by definition) do not agree amongst themselves – and this must be remembered when social workers are told 'to use more sociology' (whose sociology? is the appropriate response). Yet, despite the basic disagreements, the sociologists have succeeded in bringing the study of social problems into the mainstream of sociology. This makes the appraisal of the different approaches easier. Psychological theory has not developed to the same extent, and much sociological theorising has been developed as a criticism of the predominantly psychological explanations usually accepted. Social workers should attend to the newly developed theories and to their criticism of explanations in terms of the 'kinds' of people who become deviant or 'the kinds' of emotional complexes that lead to deviancy. Of particular interest are those theories that raise one or more of three critical issues: To which group or groups is the particular social problem problematic? How do we obtain and respond to the accounts of experience that can be given by those who 'have' the problem? How do social work agencies explain, 'explain away', and cope with social problems?

A brief illustration of the last point will show the kind of question we have in mind and also the extent to which 'positive' conceptions of welfare may come to have a negative effect. At present we refer to some of our services as services for maladjusted children – residential and day schools, for example. The definition 'maladjusted' was probably considered an advance on 'criminal' or 'mentally defective', and in order to single out a group for special care and attention it is necessary to label them in some way, to describe their major significant characteristics. Yet the term carries with it some very undesirable implications. If we consider 'adjustment', we think of a process of alignment and agreement between two parties – 'they adjusted their differences' implies some kind of reciprocity – the change comes about as a result of action from both sides. To say, however, that someone *is* maladjusted is to imply that he becomes adjusted by action on his part; by some change as it were, on his side of the equation. It has been pointed out that this emphasis on the child's 'mal'-ness also goes with services that often take him out of the main stream of education and family life and thus emphasise his separateness (Higgins, 1963).

Yet social workers are faced with many social problems and even more theories to describe and explain them. They are faced with predominantly Marxian analysis in search of a social psychology (Walton and Taylor, 1973) and with more conservative analysts such as Lemert (1967). How can social workers begin to choose? We suggest two criteria: the extent to which the theory is internally coherent and to which it has been tested; the extent to which the theory produces results the social worker can use in ways that do not divert his attention exclusively either to private sorrows or to social problems. The formal criterion, at least in so far as it concerns testing, will be illustrated in the following section, but at this point we should try at least to illustrate what we mean by internal coherence. We refer to the simple question of whether the theory holds in terms of its own statements when these are critically examined. The romantic thrust of some of the theories is sometimes overwhelming and the reader is carried along (and away). Take, for example, one of the most frequently quoted of the new theorists and one of his most frequently quoted statements: 'Deviance is not a property *inherent* in certain forms of behaviour: it is a property *conferred* upon these forms by other audiences which directly or indirectly witness them' (Erikson, 1962). This way of talking appears to assume that behaviour occurs in a kind of neutral stream which at some point in the process has meaning stamped upon it. It also makes a romantic meal out of the truism that deviant behaviour is behaviour that is judged to be deviant.

We referred earlier to 'private sorrows', suggesting that these are a central interest for the social worker. We do not want to argue that these are the only interests of the social worker, but we wish to state that they are not synonymous with social problems and that both social problems and private sorrows should be of interest to the social worker. Theoretically this dual focus presents a considerable problem: this can be posed in the form, How can a social worker use more than one frame of reference when looking at 'the same' situation that requires some action? There are three possible responses and we shall refer briefly to these in terms of the use of a psychological and a sociological frame of reference.

The first response is to refuse the challenge and to adopt exclusively one of the two frames of reference. So social workers could decide to acknowledge only individual cases or series of cases understood in an individual, psychological fashion. Alternatively, they could deny the reality or the feasibility of working with the individual situation, relying on sociological generalisations for an understanding of general social problems which respond only to general social measures.

A second response is to work for some theoretical reconciliation of viewpoints derived from the different frameworks. This requires some hard work, and the chances of success are not high. Few sociologists recognise as valid one of the notions that has taken strong root in social work, that of common human needs. (There are some who have, notably Fletcher (1963) and Etzioni (1968).) On the other hand, the psychological theories most commonly used in social work (ego-psychology and, to a less extent, learning theory) are potentially capable of 'extension' so that they can incorporate social relationships and the social milieu. It is possible that at a very high level of abstraction certain general theories will be propounded which will use ideas from each of the two frameworks we are considering. Boulding's (1953) general theory of growth is a possible candidate, but our own view is that any reconciliation is more likely to come about through attention to more humble problems.

The third response is to eschew reconciliation (or integration) and to attend carefully to the differences between the frames of reference as they affect work in particular situations. In this way we shall gain in appreciation of what is involved from the point of view of action in the different frameworks and we shall begin to see the returns that can be gained from movement between the frameworks. Very little theoretical work has been done that would help us to do this, but a beginning has been made by Fraiberg (1963) who has attempted to show the difference 'role theory' and 'ego psychology' would make to an understanding of 'the same' case.

In this section we have concentrated on some of the difficulties that face the social work student as he considers the complex and growing theorising about social problems. We believe that the situation is far removed from that described by Moynihan (1969): 'A half century of international sociology had produced a set of propositions not far from Father Flanagan's assertion that, "There is no such thing as a bad boy".' Yet we should also note that the social worker's theoretical understanding is an event or series of events in a real world. This understanding is mediated through and constrained by social forms and institutions which have also to be understood. For example, it is sometimes asserted that social work activity and understanding is distorted or nullified because it is mediated through a bureaucracy. The concept of bureaucracy should be very critically examined by social workers so that they can assess the strength of these assertions. A very good analysis is fortunately available (Albrow, 1970).

What are clients doing at or with agencies and what are others doing to clients?

We have decided to discuss these two sections together since we are concerned with the interaction between them. It is worth noting that our concern is with the interaction, and we have emphasised action by referring in the heading to what clients are doing and what other people are doing to them. In one sense this is an over-emphasis, since it neglects the forceful constraints on people that arise from the material world. However, our description does serve to correct a view of man wholly determined by non-human forces, of an economic nature or arising from some impersonal id.

One answer to the questions raised in the heading of this section is that some people are subjecting clients or potential clients to stigma.

Stigma is a word of recent fashion in the social services, and in social work. It is a central concept in recent work (though social work students should note the differences between feelings of inferiority and inferior status) and it carries crucial significance for those theorists who claim that the one certain outcome of social service for its recipients is stigma. In some senses, this is not a new idea. Earlier thinkers on social service, particularly the rudimentary form we call the Poor Law, would have been somewhat surprised that help could be given without the imposition of a special moral identity on the one who was helped. How else to secure that only a minority were considered and considered themselves eligible for assistance?

But now our views are more heavily influenced by ideas of self-determination and by notions of the rights, the social rights, of the citizen. None the less, a number of writers are now drawing attention to the ways in which coming to the notice of, or being assisted by, our social services may confirm the recipient in a low, false, or unfavourable view of himself. Social work agencies, far from solving problems, add to and perpetuate them. They contribute to, or, in some cases, constitute the process by which a person is given and accepts a particular view of himself, a label.

Yet the question – Does this really happen? – is seldom raised, and, if it is raised, the questioner does not usually stay long for an answer. One interesting piece of empirical research published in America helps us to begin to see how difficult the labelling hypothesis is to test and reports the results of one attempt to discover the self-perceptions of presumably stigmatised people (Foster *et al.*, 1972).

First of all, it is important to appreciate that the labelling theory is not only popular but also complex. Police and court intervention must presumably vary in their impact according to previous experience with law enforcement agencies, the amount of public exposure of the intervention, the nature of the local community, the type of disposition (e.g. a fine or some kind of custodial disposal) and so on. In other words there are numerous important variables and most if not all of these are in themselves quite complex. Not all of these variables were covered in this study of 196 boys involved in activities definable as crimes under adult statistics, but there was a serious attempt to control the following: previous contact with a law enforcement agency, age, type of disposition and offence, and ethnicity. All subjects were interviewed fairly quickly after the disposition of their cases. In view of the fact that proponents of the labelling often refer to a cumulative and long-term process, it is encouraging to learn that the authors are planning a longitudinal follow-up specifically to investigate the effect time will have on the responses they discovered at one particular point in time.

In general the study was concerned to discover if the boys felt any sense of significant social liability as a result of their contact with 'the law'. Four areas of relationship were chosen – friends, parents, school, and future employers. As the boys perceived things – and we must recall that this was the focus of the research – there was little or no liability in terms of parents and of friends. They perceived no negative effect at all in the attitude of friends and only a slight negative effect in their parents. Indeed, parental attitudes had been settled some time before this brush with the law: parents who saw their children as troublesome were not surprised, parents who were surprised remained unconvinced that their children basically were troublesome.

Turning to perceived school reaction, the situation is more complex. Twenty-three of the boys had already been expelled or had quit, but we are given no information about them. The majority of the remainder felt that getting into trouble with the law would not create any special problems at school. Their belief in this view was based on a perception of 'the street' and the school as two distinct and unconnected 'societies': their 'crime' had nothing to do with the school and, in any case, the school would not know.

It is when they thought of future employers that the boys showed most apparent concern, and also when they considered future possible contact with the police. Just over half the boys expected an increase in police surveillance, and the more serious the disposition of the case, the more prevalent this was. The more serious the disposition, the more likely it was for the boy to consider that future employers would hold the incident against him. This type of disposition was closely associated with the existence of a previous record, but 40 per cent of the total groups believed they could have incurred a social liability through their offence in terms of a future employer. We have seen that in connection with school authorities the boys seemed to have confidence in secrecy – the school did not know and would not find out. However, in the case of future employers they seemed to have much less faith in secrecy. A great deal of concern was expressed that employers would 'check the record'. This is a small but interesting reminder to social workers that they have hardly made a start in examining the social significance of 'the record', whether it is compiled by them or by others.

The general finding that these delinquent boys perceived at the time of disposal little negative social liability as a consequence of their offence is of interest. It can, of course, be interpreted in a number of ways: from a social-work-action point of view this is, of course, always the trouble with 'findings'. It could begin, but only begin, to help us to question labelling theory more rigorously. Or, as the authors admit, the findings could be explained away. The perception of the boys is simply a function of their inability to project a stigmatised status into the future, as this group of predominantly lower-class boys had accepted and internalised a conception of very limited economic and social opportunities which social stigma would hardly decrease. They may already have neutralised the unfavourable consequences of stigma.

It is possible, of course, to review the range of available socio-logical and psychological knowledge and attempt to assess the utility of each item for social work. This has been attempted recently in relation to social science and with particular reference to community workers by Rothman (1974). The result is a very useful publication which would, in our view, have been consider-ably improved by greater attention to conceptual analysis and what we have described as theoretical coherence. Take for example the following:

'Generalisation 3.2: Whether in limited or extended role sets, many practitioners experience role conflict in the performance of their functions. . .' (p. 64). This generalisation leads to action guidelines (p. 67): 'The frequency with which role conflict situations are reported in the research literature suggests that agencies and practitioners should make it a point to   diagnose work assignments in terms of potential unproductive role disparities.'

Role conflict or role disparities are, in our view, not so much findings as notions that should be read 'off' the concept of role, at least as that concept is applied to modern industrialised societies.

In this section we are not attempting an inventory of theories, ideas or findings that social workers should use. We are trying to indicate the kinds of theory that social workers should examine in the attempt to answer the questions set at the beginning of this section.

So far we have considered stigma, but we should now widen our focus by appreciating what social workers have not always taken seriously, namely the fact that the contact of clients with agencies is often of rather brief duration. Even when clients sustain a long-term contact with an agency they are unlikely to be in the company of a social worker for less than an hour a week. So the attention of social workers should be less on the fine detail and nuance of 'the treatment session' and more on those social forms that do so much to shape the lives of clients – family, occupation, political institutions and so on.

Again, social workers are confronted with a multitude of theory to help them to understand family, work, leisure and so on. Is there any way in which they can begin to choose between them? A number of guidelines can be suggested. First, preference should be given to theories that link two or more of these areas of life. It is, for example, true that social workers remain relatively ignorant about work and that 'fathers' are always being rediscovered as an element in family life that social workers should do more to understand, but an approach that linked work and family is, in our view, preferable to the separate study of each. The task framework used by Robert and Rhona Rapoport (1965) is a good example of such an approach.

Second, social workers should also consider those theories that indicate a pervasive condition their clients may suffer, but they should give such theories critical examination. We shall give illustrations of what we mean from treatments of social class.

'Social class' should be used in a dynamic rather than a static way. Social workers should attend to those theorists of social class who stress change. Take, for example, Merrill's (1955) argument that 'Social problems are the products of a dynamic society, in which behaviour changes more rapidly than the values that define it.' He suggests that social problems have traditionally been defined in terms of the social character of the middle class. This character is changing, however, from one of inner-direction to one of other-direction, and this change may produce a changed reaction to social problems. Merrill suggests that this change will be away from the alleviation of distress and towards the manipulation of personality.

'Social class' should also be used critically when it is a question of appraising differences between classes. In particular, judgments concerning the culture of poverty or class sub-cultures should be carefully scrutinised. Social workers should be able to use the various concepts of poverty and of social and psychological deprivation; they should also know the extent to which such conditions exist and grow in our society. Yet poverty and deprivation are usually linked in terms of persuasive theories. It is these theories – for example, of deprivation transmitted through family membership and socialisation – that require critical scrutiny. Studies of child rearing, for example, have shown differences in practices between middle-class and working-class families, but, as Miller and Riessman (1961) argued, the meaning of the differences may have been mistaken. For instance, one study interpreted a long period of breast-feeding as part of a cluster of behaviour termed permissive child-care. This may have been accurate for middle-class families, but in the working class a long period of breast-feeding is not related to the permissive ideology of that class. In so far as reliable differences in class behaviour are found social workers are bound to consider the question, emphasised but not discovered by the recent American war on poverty. To what extent are the differences the result, over a period of time, of a massive denial of economic resources? If they are, will the life styles respond to an increase in financial resources or do we agree with Oscar Lewis that such measures including an annual minimum family income 'will in themselves not eliminate the pathology associated with the Culture of Poverty. They will not eliminate poor mothering, free unions, illegitimacy, alcoholism, gambling, wife beating, present-time orientation, impulse spending . . . to mention only a few traits.'

Suggestions for further reading

This chapter has covered a considerable amount of ground and many of the main ideas have been expressed in a very compressed manner. The suggestions for further reading are intended particularly to help students to extend their grasp of the most crucial areas covered.

Take first the problem of general orientation. Students will wish to cover a range of theoretical perspectives. If we consider psychology, there really is no substitute to reading Freud, but the best commentary, and the one most congruent with the approach of this book is Rieff (1965). Ruddock (1972) has edited a number of essays on theories of personality and the collection by Hepman and Heine (1964) contains a good range of approaches, including those based on phenomenology (Shlien) and personal constructs (Kelly). Of the various versions of psychoanalytic theory available the ill-named object-relations theory has most to contribute to a general interactionist approach. Guntrip (1961) covers this well, though part II of his earlier work (reissued in 1971) makes an easier beginning.

In relation to sociology students will have similar problems in finding their way through different schools. There are a number of ways of attempting to solve this problem. First, it is always possible to read the classics of sociology (Marx, Weber, Durkheim) – indeed some suggest that this is all sociologists do. Second, a number of books give material for a comparative approach. Rex (1974) introduces the major trends in sociology. An interesting variation on this approach is to read Colin Fletcher (1974), who describes his involvement in three different research projects using the quantitative method, the qualitative method and the method of social criticism. Third, the student may find it more rewarding to trace and study the application of one particular approach to a particular set of problems encountered in social work. Hence, Plummer (1975) discusses and applies a social interactionist approach to homosexuality and Taylor and Walton argue the application of Marx to radical deviancy theory (Taylor, Walton and Young, 1975). A collection of readings on ethnomethodology (ed. Turner, 1974) contains an essay by Garfinkel entitled ' "Good" Organizational Reasons for "Bad" Clinic Records'.

The chapter also raised questions concerning the reconciliation or integration of theories. Students can follow this theme in Maier (1965), who attempts an integration of Erikson, Piaget and Sears, but they should watch his way of coping with semantic differences between the theories. On an interesting attempt to reconcile conflict theory and social disorganisation theory as applied to social problems see Rose (1957).

We have stressed knowledge of social services and of social problems. Both should be seen as changing and not static. A good account of a number of comparatively small (but important) changes in social services can be found in Donnison et al. (1975). We have already referred to work which will be of use in the study of social problems. A collection of essays on social work and social problems (ed. Cohen) can still be read with profit, though students will have to read in the perspectives to be gained from later work, e.g. Rock and McIntosh (1974).

We have also stressed the importance of social workers having a firm critical grasp of the theories they espouse. It is only too easy in situations of application to be holding theories that have actually changed or been significantly challenged. See, for an example of the latter the assessment of the theory of need complementarity in marriage (Tharp, 1963) or of the effects of group size (Thomas and Fink, 1963).

Reference has been made to 'stigma', and this can be studied in Pinker's central treatment. It is, however, important to note how complex this treatment is. There are particular stigmas (e.g. of dependency and obligation); feelings of stigma contrasted with feelings of prestige or superordination; the equivalents of stigmas (e.g. lack oi money in market situations; degrees of stigma; and stigmative status). These are related in complex ways and also raise interesting questions. To take one only, to define stigma as a spoiled identity seems to rule out degrees of stigmatisation: identities are either spoilt or not; there cannot be degrees of spoiling where identities are concerned.

Social work beliefs
and attitudes

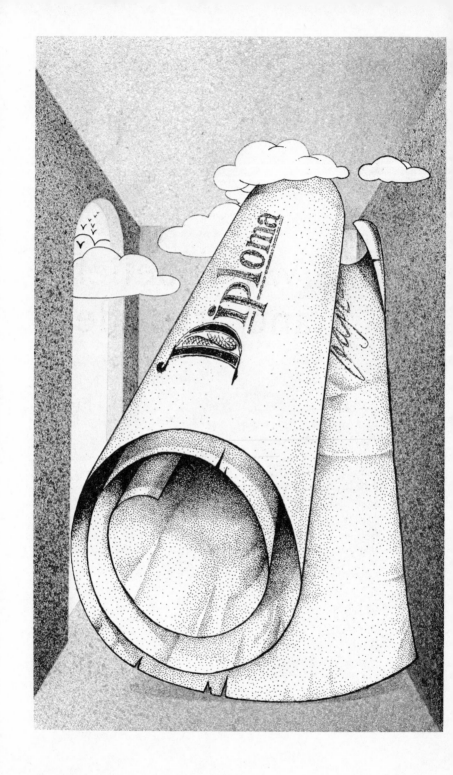

In this chapter we wish to discuss what are usually called 'the values' of social work. These are commonly presented as a list, including respect for persons, confidentiality, self-determination, acceptance and non-condemnation. The list is moreover often treated as an inventory of commodities – the values are as it were in the possession of the social worker. Treating what are in effect the beliefs and attitudes of social workers in this way suffers from a number of defects. The lists give a false impression of completeness, whereas some of the most important 'values' are hardly mentioned. The various 'commodities' are too blandly presented and their intrusive awkwardness is concealed. We shall illustrate briefly what we mean by these criticisms before turning to a more detailed exposition of an alternative approach. This would, in our opinion, take the form of a sustained critical treatment of the 'values' commonly given (we have chosen to discuss self-determination as an illustration) and discussions of some of the issues in the practice of social work which centrally involve belief and attitude. To illustrate the latter we have decided to examine 'the right to intervene' and 'the professional nature of social work and social work education'.

Introduction

We have just said that lists of 'values' strongly suggest an exhaustive quality, but some very important values seem always to avoid a mention. Flexibility seems to us to be a good example of a virtue much extolled but seldom critically noted. Pincus and Minahan (1973, p. 140) make a rather typical use of the notion when discussing one of the dilemmas facing a social worker who has to collect information. The worker 'must be selective in how he collects his data and approach the process with some orientation and assumptions to guide his effort. On the other hand, his orientation and assumptions can operate to bias and distort the data collection process to such an extent that all objectivity is lost.' The solution to this (not very sharply described) dilemma is 'flexibility': 'The worker must keep flexible enough to disregard his assumptions when they are not substantiated by the data, instead of building rigid frameworks which effectively filter out any data not supporting his original assumptions.' This gives considerable importance to 'flexibility' (and to its negative 'rigidity' which is so frequently a subject for avoidance in social work), but the result of the instruction is really no instruction at all. 'Flexibility' can be useful if we are given some idea of the extremes between which a flexible course has to be followed. It does not help social workers (or anyone else) to be told, taking another example from Pincus and Minahan, 'To cope with the ethical ambiguities of the change-agent role, the social worker must maintain a balance between flexibility and integrity' (p. 52). We are as much in favour of a flexible approach as anyone and have tried to avoid rigidity in our presentation of social work, but simply extolling 'flexibility' places a social worker precisely nowhere.

We have also suggested that the treatment of values in social work is often too bland (or too consensual). To illustrate this criticism we shall use the non-judgmental approach. Briefly, social work has avoided some of the most important issues in praise/blame. The kind of issues we have in mind can be seen in the following short passage from an author who could never be described as bland (Ivy Compton Burnett, *A Heritage and its History*, p. 31):

> 'We can find other people as little wrong as possible.'
> 'I find them as wrong as they are.'
> 'It may be difficult to judge that.'
> 'Can it be? Everyone finds it so easy.'
> 'There is no need to voice our judgments.'
> 'Silent ones are said to do more. And if we are never to blame anyone, what of the people who deserve praise?'

This passage can bear very careful scrutiny by those who accept 'praise' easily into their vocabulary but close the door on 'blame'. Is such a closure logically and psychologically effective? What is the effect of 'silent' judgment if judgment is unavoidable? Or is the social worker using the idea of blame, but always judging that, though a person has indeed done something and what has been done was undesirable, he was not to blame or is not blamed by the social worker (*I* don't blame you for that even though you may be blameworthy). One of the reasons why this subject is difficult for social workers to discuss is that it has been (incorrectly) assumed that blame has a necessary connection with condemnation.

We hope that by now we have sufficiently illustrated our general criticisms of the characteristic treatment of social work values: namely that omissions are often important, and that discussion of the values usually avoids the problem. We turn now to a more detailed discussion of one of the most frequently mentioned values, self-determination. We shall then discuss 'the right to intervene' and 'professionalism'.

Self-determination

Self-determination finds a place in any social work text and indeed in some writing about social administration. Perlman (1965) argues against an easy assumption that 'the concept is equally applicable across all the social work methods', wondering 'whether it is usable chiefly when the client can be designated as a "self" ', but since all clients must be so designated it does seem sensible to assume that in self-determination we have a central social work concept.

When we turn to consider the manner in which the concept is usually treated in the social work literature we are met with little short of confusion. Thus, one writer calls 'the right of self-determination . . . a most precious casework axiom' (Soyer, 1963), whereas another sees it as significant only because it is so misleading: '. . . much of the lip service paid to the notion amounts to little more than an argument about whether seduction is a more effective way of inducing behavioural change than direction' (Leighton, 1967). One writer at least believes that the principle of self-determination is incoherent: Keith-Lucas (1963) believes that the 'elusive principle of client self-determination' contains two distinct, and more or less relative, principles concerning a social worker's relationship with his clients. These are client participation in the solution of problems and the non-interference of the social worker except in essentials. Other writers see the problem not so much in the incoherence of the concept but rather in practical questions of application – the problem, for instance, as Whittington (1971) describes it, of 'reconciling client self-determination, the democratic ideal, with certain therapeutic methods'. In summary, for some, self-determination is essential for social work; for others, social work would be better off without it.

How can we find a way through this particular thicket of problems? It is basically a matter of trying to become clear about three questions. What do we mean by client self-determination? How much of social work should it describe? What is the relationship between self-determination and the vexed and complicated issues of determinism? We shall discuss each of these in turn.

When there is a wide conflict of opinion about a concept, it is at least possible that the people concerned have a different idea of its meaning. It is not easy to see immediately what 'self-determination' means but McDermott (1975) suggests how we can at least make a start by looking at the meaning the term has in a language other than the language of social work, namely that of politics. In his view the essence of the concept in social work can be found in a denial that the actions of a person described as self-determining are determined by anyone else. This view has to be very clearly distinguished from the opinion that self-determination is really what could be described as best-self-determination, i.e. the opinion that people are self-determining only when they are behaving maturely. This idea of self-determination stretches the core notion too far. Saying this does not rule out any concern that social workers may have with maturity. It is only to argue that defining self-determination with one or both eyes on maturity does not work.

Yet there is something built into the idea of self-determination over and above the notion that people should do what they wish, like, want or even fantasy. There is a discriminating element and this is to be found in what it is for an action to be determined. Not everything a man does could be described as determined, though we may wish to describe all human acts as determined. Clearly, we wish this if we have a special idea of what constitutes a human act. McDermott (1975) argues that for an act to be determined it 'must have direction and purpose, and this presupposes some degree of rationality – the rationality involved in choosing means towards ends, and being able to give reasons for one's actions in terms of one's beliefs and values'.

If we accept this kind of description of self-determination, then, it appears that self-determination could be used to describe a great deal of social work. Social work is well seen as a human activity concerned more with people's reasons for acting than causes which force them along predetermined lines. Yet it is sometimes the case that the necessary actions of a social worker clash with the principle, or that there are other principles in social work that may so clash. This is only a problem if self-determination is thought of as a means of describing social work exhaustively. We should take care, also, that what we think of as a clash actually is one. In another chapter we have already commented upon 'influence', and this concept appears again in discussions of self-determination. So Whittington (1971) argues that client self-determination 'must be interfered with by the other's *influence* on him' (italics added). Self-determination, however, is, as McDermott has stated, 'not the same as being insulated from all normal exchange of ideas and influence between adult human beings'. Self-determination is limited not by the beliefs of social workers about desirable solutions to problems, nor, as we have already suggested, by the client's propensity to immature behaviour, but by the law and by other principles of social work concerned with safeguarding the rights of those others in the situation who are especially vulnerable. If we wish to call self-determination a right (general questions concerning rights will be discussed in the following section), there is no reason to suppose it cannot clash with other rights or that the claim for it to be recognised cannot be supported or denied.

Finally, self-determination often becomes caught up with ideas of determinism. Whittington, for example, states that self-determination implies 'the converse of a purely deterministic position'. It is important to note that this is not necessarily the case. When we say that a man's action is free we are not saying at the same time that it was uncaused. A man's free action may be caused; it cannot have been subject to external constraint. 'Self-determination' requires social workers to treat their clients as free agents, i.e. social workers should not be coercive. In brief, self-determination can be discussed adequately without involving the complex question of whether or not the universe is determined. This is not, of course, to suggest that 'determinism' should not be discussed in any central consideration of social work.

The right to intervene

We have already drawn attention to the concept of intervention, suggesting that it has a strong and a weak sense. It can refer to particular actions (those of intervening between parties in some kind of conflict) or, apparently, any purposeful action at all. This is obviously a distinction of some importance, since the question before us could be concerned either with the social worker's right to a special and hence limited range of action or with the right simply to do social work. However, before we take this issue further we should consider the other term in the sub-heading, right. What kind of a right is involved?

Once again we have to note that such a question leads us towards a considerable mass of argument and material. Rights and duties have been the subject of a great deal of philosophical discussion, but two broad distinctions will help us to understand better the sorts of rights social workers may claim. First, we can distinguish legal from moral rights. In a brief but useful discussion Cranston (1967) sub-divides each of these in the following way. Legal rights are of five kinds: general positive rights (those rights 'that are enjoyed and fully assured to everyone living under a given jurisdiction'); traditional rights and liberties; nominal 'legal' rights; positive rights, liberties, privileges and immunities of a limited class of persons (such as doctors, freemen of the City of London); and such rights, liberties and so on of a single person (such as the Archbishop of Canterbury). Moral rights according to Cranston can be classified as follows: moral rights of one person only ('I, and I alone, have a network of rights which arise from the fact that I have done certain deeds, paid certain monies, been elected to certain places, and so forth'); the moral rights of anyone in a particular situation (e.g. a parent); and the moral rights of all people in all situations.

The second distinction which will be of some help concerns what is claimed when a right is asserted. Raphael (1967), for instance, makes a distinction between a right of action and a right of recipience. A right of action is a right to do something. 'Such a right is equivalent to an absence of obligation. If A has a right to sing in his bath, to cultivate his garden, or to give away his inheritance, this means that he has no obligation to refrain from these actions.' A right to recipience, on the other hand, is a right to receive something from someone else 'even if the something is simply the facility of being left alone'. 'If A has a right against B to have a contract fulfilled or a debt paid, this means that B has an obligation to A to fulfil the contract or pay the debt.'

Now the two distinctions we have made – between legal and moral rights, and the rights of action and of recipience – may appear plausible and sensible but, it may well be asked, what relevance have they for a discussion of the right of a social worker to intervene? The first distinction is quite crucial. If the right of a social worker to intervene is a legal right, then the existence of such a right is relatively easy to determine. As Cranston has argued, the most important question to ask in relation to supposed legal rights is 'Are they secured and enjoyed?' The existence of a moral right on the other hand depends on such questions as 'Is there a just title? Is there a sound moral claim?' Rights, it seems, must be either legal or moral, and the kind of right being claimed makes a difference to the areas one would explore to ascertain whether or not the right is recognised.

Similarly, the difference between rights of recipience and of action helps us to become clear about what the social worker's rights to intervention may claim of others. On the face of it, it does not appear that intervention by a social worker bears any relationship to singing in the bath or cultivating one's garden, though it is interesting to speculate on whether everyone can exercise a right of action in becoming a social worker. Rights to intervention appear to be rights of recipience and hence to be rights against other people. The interesting question in so far as social work is concerned is 'which other people'? Can it be argued, for example, that a client owes some duty or other corresponding to the social worker's right? If one accepted a general doctrine of the correlativity of rights and duties (i.e. for every duty there is a corresponding right) then some duty on the part of the client would be assumed for every right of a social worker. However, it now seems to be accepted that rights and duties go, as it were, so closely together only in relation to undertakings. As Mayo (1967) has argued, 'a person who is *concerned*, however, directly and specifically, in the duty-discharging act never has a right to that act unless there is an undertaking, express or implied, made *to* that person'. This question of the role of an undertaking in the generation of rights and duties is of considerable importance in social work, and it is interesting to note the recent emphasis given to the idea of the contract between social worker and client. Some rights to intervene in either the strong or the weak sense could be described as stemming from a previous agreement between the social worker and client, but not all interventive acts or all acts by a social worker are based on a previous agreement or contract with specific clients. In probation, for example, the client contracts with the court.

We have so far questioned whether the social worker's right to intervene is moral or legal. Some interventive acts may proceed from moral and some from legal rights. In so far as legal rights are concerned there is in principle no difficulty in discovering what the rights of a social worker are. We have also questioned the meaning of 'intervention'. Some actions of a social worker can be described as 'interventive' but only some. Acts that are strongly interventive require justification, but the justification they require and receive may not be extensive enough also to justify social work in its non-interventive aspects. (Action arising from undertakings cannot always be seen as intervention.) The legal rights of social workers, whether or not the actions to which they refer can be described as 'interventions', present no serious problems. They are or they are not discoverable in the law. Moral rights and duties that arise from undertakings between specific social workers and specific clients also present no serious problem, except in so far as the undertakings have not been freely entered into.

We can now see that the problem before us concerns the authority of social workers to offer help and to go beyond offering help to people in need.

The authority of the social worker

This is a complex subject for two main reasons: the term 'authority' carries a heavy burden of emotional and logical complication; second, there are tendencies for 'authority' in special situations (like child neglect) to spill over into general social work situations. Hence Keith-Lucas (1963) can draw attention to a social work vocabulary that 'increasingly includes such words as "intervention", "psychological authority", "responsibility" and "social control" '.

It is possible to discern in outline at least the development of the treatment of authority in social work. Social workers in the mid- and late nineteenth century were generally often authoritative in their behaviour towards clients and in their judgments of them. The source of this authority did not lie in some special expertise or legal power – social work agencies were characteristically voluntary, and social workers often volunteers – but directly in conviction about the moral and social order. It was probably the influence of psychoanalytic ideas that did most to undermine this basis for authority, but it also substituted one basis of authority for another. Psychoanalytic ideas helped the development of a claim that the authority of the social worker was based in his or her special knowledge and skill. Thus in 1949 Bibring stated:

> After listening to and observing the client, we may use our
> understanding of his personality structure, his patterns, his needs

> and conflicts and his defences, in order to 'manipulate' him in various ways. We may make suggestions as to what steps may or may not help this individual to cope with his problems . . . or we may purposely activate relevant emotional attitudes in the client for the sake of adjustive change.

Under the influence of psychoanalytic ideas social workers become hesitant concerning the exercise of legal authority, as in probation or in the compulsory admission of the mentally ill into hospital, and more secure in the use of psychological authority or the authority of professional knowledge. They could offer help and go beyond offering because they had become experts.

The next phase of development saw an enthusiasm for social work in settings of authority and in work with neglectful or problem families. 'We accept', said one writer, 'the parent's right to make his own decision but we question the wisdom of having him base it solely on his impulse to resist help and not include his wish to help his child' (Brunk, 1946). It was argued further that social workers needed to 'reach out' to neglectful families and that in offering what was sometimes called 'aggressive' casework the social worker should 'lead with strength and sustain that lead until the family can take on more responsibility' (Overton, 1953).

Consideration of this phase enables us to make two important points. First, certain interventive acts are defined as 'special' and hence are seen as requiring special justification in relation to assumptions about general or 'ordinary' social work. So, for example, some of the 'assertive' social work with problem families in the late 1940s and early 1950s is so defined (and has accordingly to be justified) because it is contrasted with the assumption that normally the social worker is more receptive and passive. At that time it would not have been considered appropriate to consider the extent to which 'intervention' in a strong sense was part and parcel of the daily life of the residential social worker. Second, social work writers often found it very difficult to find a path through the thicket of issues involved in authoritative intervention. So in the first major publication on *Problem Families* (Stephens, 1945), we can find the statements that 'the visitor cannot inflict his own remedies upon them (problem families) nor coerce them into social behaviour' and that 'the caseworker must make it his duty to see that the treatment he prescribes is carried out . . . whatever happens, the responsibility for the family's welfare is his'. It was even suggested that a basic division of view was at work – one writer suggested that assertive social work implies 'A casework philosophy that the worker must at times be his brother's keeper ... such a philosophy is not at the present time accepted in casework practice' (Wilsnak, 1946). Social workers may not be their brothers' keepers, but some room should surely be found for 'fraternity'.

The next stage in the development of ideas concerning authority marked a decisive move in the direction of a general assumption of authority. It was suggested that authority was not a feature only of certain fields in social work (such as probation), nor of work with certain client groups (the immature adolescent, for example), but of social work in general. This point of view was presented and argued by Foren and Bailey (1968), who stated that 'the caseworker's authority derives at least as much from knowledge and professional skill which he possesses or is believed to possess, as from the power conferred on him by society' (p. 19). They stressed the different sources of 'authorisation', legal and professional, but emphasised particularly the latter. Thus, they commended the statement of Hollis that 'All the negative connotations of the word "authority" can be removed simply by putting the word "professional" in front of it and thereby transforming "authoritativeness" into "strength" the clients can lean on.' This is, of course, to endorse not so much problem resolution as problem dissolution by magic.

This very brief review of some of the major developments in social work thinking on the subject of authority helps us to see some of the problems of meaning and of attitude. How can we make progress in disentangling the main issues? First, we have to be clear about attitudes to 'authority'. There seem to be, as Duncan Jones (1958) has suggested, two main approaches. 'One leads in the direction of annexing the word "authority" to what we approve or support. . . . The other leads us in the direction of withholding approval from anything to which the name "authority" is annexed until we have subjected it to some critical process.' Each of these attitudes has been, at different times, dominant, as we have seen, in social work. It is simply not the case that social workers have always unquestionably supported 'authority'. As Keith-Lucas (1963) has correctly observed, social workers in the 1930s in America

... considered the individual a better judge of his own interests than law, morality or ... culture. ... For that reason they quite shamelessly protected many of their clients from the social and legal consequences of their actions. . . . It is hard for us today to remember how much social workers in the 1930s felt themselves outside the culture and, indeed, opposed to it.

Second, we should clarify the meaning and the sources of authority. 'Authority' is sometimes used in company with 'authoritarian', but this refers to a manner of exercising power whether or not that power is legitimate. 'Authority' simply means 'legitimate power'. So we have to ask which powers of a social worker have been authorised, and by whom or by what process.

The authoritative offer of help by a social worker is secured from two possible sources, the agency and the profession. The force of claims based on the agency has possibly gained the greater public recognition, but it is not easy to see clearly the ways in which a wide social legitimisation, as it were, gets into the agency. The functionalist school of social work in America has perhaps given most thought to this. For the functionalists the social work agency is the place in which the interests of the individual and of society are joined and reconciled. The social work agency is seen as the direct expression of the will of society, and society is seen as charging the profession of social work with the development and administration of programmmes of social service. 'The way the social purpose of society, as manifest in a given agency, is interpreted and carried out becomes the responsibility of the agency' (Smalley, 1969). Briefly, society has directly authorised the social work agency and indirectly the professionals who work in it.

Similar theories have been pursued by Clare Winnicott (1964).

In functioning within an agency, a social caseworker, as well as being a trained professional person who uses his or her knowledge and skill to help people, also becomes something in relation to the clients on behalf of the whole community. The Probation Officer becomes an authority figure, the Child Care Officer becomes a parental figure, and the Medical Social Worker as part of the medical team becomes a healing person on whom the patient's health depends.

The fact that the child care officer and the medical social worker no longer exist in the sense they did when Winnicott wrote does not affect her arguments; social workers still carry out child care and medical social work functions. The core of the argument – that social workers become something on behalf of the whole community – is subject to criticism. Like the functionalists, Winnicott seems to be assuming a basic consensus, a will on behalf of the whole community, including clients, that certain institutions should be established to achieve particular ends, i.e. the establishment and maintenance of particular kinds of relationships. Unlike the functionalists, who shy away from parenting and healing, Winnicott particularises the sorts of relationship that are desired: the functionalists stress the facilitation of adult choice in the client.

Difficulties of the same kind face other attempts to describe the bond between social worker and society, the kind of bond that carries and conveys rights. So social workers have claimed rights to intervene, in the strong or the weak sense, on the grounds that they 'represent society'. However, 'representative' has to be disentangled before we can be sure whether or not it has the strength to convey rights. As we shall see, some senses of 'representative' seem too weak.

'Representative' is used in a number of different ways. A man may be a fairly typical 'representative' of a group or groups: he represents them. A man may symbolically stand for some belief or sentiment: we say that Florence Nightingale represents the tradition of middle-class service. One person may legally represent another or may represent another's interest. So a Member of Parliament may not be typical of his constituents and may stand for no particular tradition, but he may represent the interests of certain trade unions even though he has not been appointed by them as legal representative. Griffiths, who has made these distinctions, calls the four kinds of representation respectively descriptive, symbolic, ascriptive and the representation of interests. From the point of view of social work what matters is that the connection between the representative and those represented is in each case different, and this is of some importance if we are trying to ground some rights in the notion of 'being a representative' (Griffiths, 1960).

It seems to us that acting as 'the representative of society' is too wide a concept to be of much use. If, however, we try to specify a little more closely the kind of representation we may intend, then it would seem to be the case that a social worker acts as a representative. Sometimes, a client will entrust the social worker to speak on his behalf – perhaps in negotiation with a department of central or local government. Frequently, social workers will be representing the interests of their clients within the agency or to workers in other agencies. Characteristically, however, these actions as representative are sanctioned by the client.

Some writers stress the claims of social workers to act, if necessary without the express approval of the client, on the basis of the worker's professional competence and knowledge. The social worker's right to persist, insist, strongly advise (in the absence of a legal right) is, in this argument, based on the worker's status as a professional. Just as there are doctor's orders, so, it is suggested, are there social work orders which a social worker has a right to give. Thus if a social worker judges that a particular person or group requires the maintenance of strong boundaries the social worker will channel the topics of discussion or insist that certain behaviour is self-defeating. In this context it is important to note that authority – and this includes professional authority – conveys specific and not unlimited powers. To say that a social worker persists in 'presenting reality' to a very disturbed patient or that a residential social worker has authority to control the behaviour of a resident that threatens the well-being of others or their property, is not to claim a right to some kind of general control. It is not to say that the residential social worker, for example, should intervene to establish one particular pattern of eating habit or in what Keith-Lucas (1963) has called 'those small matters of taste, opinion, and day-to-day living that make one client different from another and give him a sense of being an individual'. It is also important to establish the role played by the beliefs and feelings of those over whom authority is exercised. The question here, quite simply, is how far acceptance by others is a part of the concept 'authority'. We would not perhaps say that Richard II had authority when he met Bolingbroke after his return from Ireland, though his legal rights to the crown were clear.

We have considered the authority of the social worker at some length, because it is a subject of historical and contemporary importance for social workers (and, of course, for clients and others). It is obviously also a difficult subject, but we would summarise our own views on it in the following way. The offer of social work help is authorised in a number of ways: by the agency, symbolically representing membership and the rights and duties of membership of a particular society; by the law; and by the social worker's reasoned conviction open to public debate and test that what he has to offer is of some value. Going beyond the offer of help is also authorised in these ways but in addition certain special circumstances must obtain – exploitation, serious danger to psychological or physical well-being, the social worker being placed in a position of parenting, and so on. We do not think that a convincing case has been made for assuming only one source of authority for social work or for social work intervention in the strong sense.

Social work as a profession and social workers as professional people

Study of the professions shows at least two major social processes at work: the ways in which certain occupations orient themselves to ideas of professionalism and the ways in which people who were previously lay people become fully fledged professionals. These two processes are referred to respectively as professionalisation (of occupations) and professional socialisation (of people). Both constitute important areas of study and of choice for those who are or those who would become social workers. Why is this so?

First, 'profession' and 'professional' are terms that have played a dominant part in the education of social workers and the ways in which they have described their practice. It was as early as 1915 that Flexner raised the question 'Is Social Work a Profession?' and his discussion of the subject, which is in our view still worth some attention, was clearly not the first occasion on which the subject had been raised. Since then treatment of the status and function of social work (e.g. Has the occupation the prestige of a profession?) and guidelines for social work practice (e.g. 'social workers should establish professional rather than personal relationship with their clients') has made essential use of the terms and ideas of professionalism. Take 'profession' and 'professional' out of the majority of social work articles and books and the texts would be peppered with holes.

Second, a study of professions bears centrally upon the concerns of social work because of the plausible and growing criticism of the ideas of professionalism applied to social work. This criticism refers to each of the processes already mentioned. Professional socialisation is scrutinised as a powerful form of conversion which moulds the lay entrant along predetermined lines. Professional education, in terms of this perspective, is not a liberalisation whereby a person chooses from a range of possibilities for himself, but an enforced repetition of the accepted models of behaviour and belief. The aims of the occupation are also criticised through the questioning of the desirability and the justification of professional status. So doubts are raised about the road social work is travelling. Should social work aim at becoming (or, for the more optimistic this would read 'remaining') a profession? If the answer to this is in the affirmative, should social work model itself on medicine and the law or is there an alternative model (social work could be seen as part of a new grouping of helping/human relations professions or as a radical semi-profession)? These questions, concerning the professionalisation of people and of occupations, will only be half-understood if they are studied exclusively as domestic matters. Their full appreciation requires a wider context.

Before considering them in the light of the systematic study of the professions, it is worth noting two important features of social work education illustrated by this topic. Social work education faces the very difficult task of teaching a basis for reasonably confident action and at the same time developing a systematically critical approach. In the case of 'professional' and 'professionalism' the teacher of social work must help the student to form an adequate idea of his or her work and of the boundaries around the relationships established in the course of that work, without denying the extent to which 'professionalism' and 'being professional' have rightly been criticised. The second feature of social work education that is graphically illustrated by the study of professionalism and professionalisation is the difficulty and also the importance of close and continuing contact with research and discussion in much wider fields of interest, in this case the general study not simply of professions but of occupations. Take the question of difficulty first. There are literally hundreds of articles on different aspects of professionalisation. Yet it is not, of course, merely a question of the extent of the ground to be covered, new perspectives often appear which seriously question earlier approaches. The study of the professions has fairly recently shifted significantly, moving from an almost exclusive preoccupation with the traits – and the 'good' traits at that – of professionalism towards an approach which both emphasises power and also questions the extent to which 'profession' is a meaningful category for sociological analysis. (So powerful is sociology that professionals may be forgiven for some unease if 'profession' is not a meaningful category for such analysis.) Students of the professions have also begun to question the assumption that a profession is actually a united group of peers rather than an association of often conflictual segments. Finally, the development of work in the area suggests that some false questions have been identified. Hughes (quoted in Vollmer and Mills, 1966, p. v), for example, has stated that in his own studies he 'passed from the false question, "Is this occupation a profession?" to the more fundamental one, "What are the circumstances in which people in an occupation attempt to turn it into a profession, and themselves into professional people?" ' And this in our view, represents an improvement on another formulation – not 'Is this occupation a profession?', but 'How professionalised has it become?' Each of these developments in the study of professions has implications for social workers. The cracks that have appeared in the concept perhaps enable social workers to explore the adequacy of 'professional' as the exclusive or main description of their activity. The term may describe some aspects of social work well, but other terms – social movement, for example – may highlight other features more successfully. The idea of a profession as a confederation, sometimes loose, between groups may help to lessen anxiety concerning 'splits' amongst social workers. Certainly, it is in line with the notion of catholicity that informs this book. This is not to say that if social work is a profession it is one in which anything goes. It is only to say that more things can go than we sometimes appear to imagine. Our own view, briefly stated, is that to describe the occupation of social work as a profession is not a very useful description. Applying 'professional' to the relations of social worker and clients succeeds in describing well some aspects, but not every one.

The process of professionalisation

The processes through and by which an occupation becomes accepted as a profession are complex and imperfectly understood. At least one writer has attempted to describe the natural history of occupations as they move towards full professional status, but his description does not apply universally. Such attempts should enliven curiosity about the history, particularly the recent history, of social work, which is not sufficiently studied, but we should be aware of two assumptions that could distort our understanding. First, it could be taken for granted that movement on the road to professionalisation is in one direction only: occupations cannot over the years lose some marks of professionalism. This is an important assumption to note in the light of the characteristic tendency to encapsulated optimism which we have already noted in many references to historical change in social work. It could also be assumed that any or certain kinds of occupation can become in the course of time fully professional: in other words, there is a single scale from 'totally without professional signs' or 'with the necessary starting minimum' to 'fully professional', with each occupation at a particular point. Such an assumption would rule out, for example, the concept of a semi-profession or an occupational group destined to be and to remain professional in only certain respects.

Suggesting that social work is and will remain a semi-profession provides in fact a useful starting-point for a discussion of professionalisation and has two additional advantages. First, it should mean that ideas of social work as a profession can be increasingly divorced from questions concerning the identity of social work. As we have seen earlier in this book, it is striking how closely these two have become intertwined. Second, taking seriously the idea of a semi-profession may help social workers to see that professionalisation is not a matter of meeting certain criteria established by some platonic process with quietly confident assertion, but a question of making public claims that require support and the ability to refute counter-arguments. The concept of semi-profession acknowledges the weakness of some social work claims to full professional status and the strength of the counter-arguments.

Definitions of a profession are numerous, but three elements appear in most – monopoly of knowledge, service orientation, autonomy of work. We may think of a semi-profession as an occupation whose claims in one or more of these areas do not receive sufficient support. In social work significant questions can be raised in connection with each area.

Knowledge and professionalism

A knowledge base is important for a profession because it helps to distinguish the layman from the expert and it gives the professional control over the application of certain skills that are informed by his knowledge. In recent years the knowledge base of social work has been considered an important concept, but for student and teacher many problems remain. First, as we have already noted, the differences between three types of knowledge – knowledge of facts (that something is the case; that a certain kind of marital role segregation tends to be associated with networks of a certain quality); knowledge by acquaintance (of particulars and universals); and what a person knows when he knows how to do something ('knowhow'). Some authorities would give this classification a particular rank order stressing the primacy of the second or third categories. Others would note that all occupations can be placed on a continuum between what Jamous and Peliolle (1970) have termed Indetermination and Technicality. Occupations have a high technicality ratio if members claim the knowledge base is technical (can be learned from textbooks, through apprenticeship), and a high indetermination ratio if their knowledge is private, tacit, the private property of the practitioner. This ratio could also be applied within professions or, if not in professions generally, then within social work. Similarly, we do not have to decide which form of knowledge is *the* form for social work: different practitioners may well decide to emphasise a different order of priority. It is important, however, that we are clear about the differences. Second, there are problems around the idea of monopoly. We will mention just two of these. All professions work on the basis of a range of knowledge, from the highly esoteric to the commonsensical. Occupations that are called professional tend to assume they operate only on the basis of one kind of knowledge (the highest or best) and this leads to a neglect of all the other kinds of information, common sense, etc., that are in fact used.

If this is so, then it presents a special problem for the social worker, who should be especially knowledgeable about ordinary social situations. The problem could be described briefly as that of the expert in common sense or that of the professional layman.

Monopoly is also in question if we consider the extent to which other groups have a stake in territory that social workers have begun to mark as their own. There is force in Flexner's (1915) early observation that social work

> appears not so much a definite field as an aspect of work in many fields. An aspect of medicine belongs to social work, as do certain aspects of law, education, architecture, etc. Social work is in touch with many professions rather than a profession itself.

Moreover, we should recall that social workers often undertake the responsibility (in casework as well as community work) of passing on both knowledge of facts and their own knowhow to others.

Third, we are unclear how knowledge connects with activity, and the connection between the two is of crucial importance in the context of establishing professional claims. Problems here are hidden rather than clarified under the time-honoured phrase, 'the integration of theory with practice'. We will mention just two of these problems:

(a) What counts as the application of a theory? Take, for example, Bott's (1957) theory already mentioned concerning the relationship between degree of role-segregation in a marital relationship and the quality of the couple's social network. Would such a theory be applied if a social worker found a loose-knit social network and deduced from this that the marital role relationship was of a certain kind? Or would the theory be applied if the social worker was able to think in terms of networks and roles, and of looseness and segregation?

(b) What empirical evidence there is suggests that social workers have *preferred ways of understanding* and intervening in social situations. Thus, studies by Reid (1967) and by Schmidt (1969) in America suggest that the idea of a worker's style is more important than the differential use of theory. Reid, for example, found that the caseworkers' treatment decisions were influenced in a predictable way by the severity of a client's disturbance, but that at least one kind of technique was characteristic of the worker's approach regardless of the severity of the client's disturbance – this was the probing response. Goldstein's study (1973) of the theoretical base that guided social work practice showed two patterns of practice representative of style which were used consistently, regardless of the nature of the problems or the objectives of the service given.

Service orientation and autonomy

It is here that the claims of social work as a profession receive perhaps their most severe contemporary test. Social workers in Britain are increasingly employed by the state: they have for long worked in courts and prisons, but now in comparatively large local authority bureaucracies which, it is argued, so constrain 'the professional' that they force him to abandon his service orientation. In any case, social critics, such as Raymond Williams (1961), have taught us to suspect the idea of service, at least in so far as it reflects the emphasis of the mid- and late nineteenth century. Pearson (1975) has argued forcibly that the governmental service aspects of social work have produced a set of values which are the direct contradiction of the commonly listed values of social work. For example, 'Clients as the objects of a large-scale organization with many bureaucratic features, will be treated within an administration machinery as cyphers' (p. 53). Or, 'The client's communications to officials of a public service, involving as they do matters of public money, and in the last analysis public order, have the character of public knowledge' (p. 53).

The dangers (and also the advantages) of placing social work predominantly in the governmental sector have to be acknowledged. Yet facing and overcoming these dangers (and exploiting the advantages) are among the special tasks of social work. If social work counts as a profession – and, as we have already indicated, we see it as a profession only in certain limited respects – then it is rather a special kind of profession. Earlier in this book we supported the idea of the functionalist school that social work should be seen as an institutionalised profession, i.e. one which worked exclusively in and by means of social work agencies. Yet such an occupation can, we believe, still maintain a service orientation. Raymond Williams (1961, p. 317) may say that 'The idea of service, ultimately, is no substitute for the idea of active mutual responsibility', but service is not incompatible with active mutual responsibility and, in any case, 'ultimately' is a long way off.

Other writers have urged that the special nature of the social work 'profession' should be recognised: a profession of reformers, a radical profession, a human relations profession. Yet it is not always clear how far, if at all, these descriptions qualify or contradict the term 'profession'. Bennett and Hokenstad (1973) however, believe that the special kind of profession social work is makes a considerable difference to the claim to autonomy.

> Very few aspects of the jobs of teachers and social workers, especially, do not come under political scrutiny. In even fewer cases do the actions of these workers fail to possess some political meaning of their own. . . . In fact, the bureaucratic and political involvement of the personal service professions must be seen as a normal condition of their work.

In this situation the authors suggest that the criterion of autonomy be replaced by that of political accountability, but it is difficult to see to whom, other than the elected representative, the social worker would be responsible. In our view of social work autonomy is hardly possible or desirable, but the social worker is accountable both to his or her clients and to the agency for ensuring that as far as possible practical reason holds sway. We shall return to this notion of practical reason in the concluding chapter.

Professional socialisation

This process whereby a layman becomes a professional has recently received attention in the study of the professions. It used hardly to be considered in social work, partly because becoming a member of a profession was taken to be an unquestionable good. It was not so long ago that Clare Winnicott observed in a much-quoted remark that the professional contains the best elements in our personality, and clearly the pioneers of psychiatric social work were convinced that they were solving and not creating problems when they extolled and advocated a professional approach. Today, of course, the valuation of 'professional' as a preferred manner of behaviour and conviction about the problems the term solves are much less firmly rooted.

Two aspects of the moulding influence of professional socialis-ation have been emphasised in recent discussions. That relatively intensive courses of training tend to produce people with par-ticular views on the world is not perhaps surprising, though knowledge of many social workers suggests that they are much less made in one mould than is commonly asserted. What have been discussed are the methods and the results of the socialisation of training. So, Deacon and Bartley (ed. Jones, 1975) argue that the supervisor in the group they studied was not teaching, but making out. 'The language-style . . . is used to socialise, to instil ways of behaving, of making out, rather than to convey ideas and information. In this very much of the latent political and con-troversial content of the work is filtered out.' Similarly, Pearson (ed. Jones, 1975), states that 'this professional representation of the work scene provides a powerful guiding imagery for both students and teachers of social work; but it is a *routine* solution to the task at hand, and it glides through the thorny moral and pol-itical dilemmas of organisational policy'.

There seems to be some rough justice in these criticisms of professional socialisation, but to take the question further requires consideration of three questions – the extent to which professional training actually achieves its supposed effects; the adequacy of the diagnosis of the problems to which 'becoming a professional person' is a solution and the extent to which the solution is ade-quate.

The first question is comparatively simple and can be dealt with briefly. Descriptions of the process of social work training, in so far as they existed, used to be bland reports from the per-spective of the educator. They tend now to be rhetorical and from the point of view of the student. What is required is research which attempts to measure the effects (not the same things as the effectiveness) of training. When these have been carried out the results have sometimes been surprising. Cypher (ed. Jones, p. 835) after noting some of the empirical work, concluded:

> There is nothing to suggest that a uniform and conservatizing professional ideology is transmitted – the very diversity amongst schools of social work staff members concerning practice and models of change must operate against the transmission of a uniform ideology – to say nothing about variation in student receptivity in the teaching situation.

'Becoming a professional' may result in an emphasis on expertise and social distance, in overrating complexity and the esoteric, but it can also refer to a process of critical scrutiny which holds the student to answer a number of questions and confirms, contrary to Pearson, that there are no routine answers. These are questions concerning the nature of a universalised friendship, the boundaries and the texture of a helping relationship, the place of a sense of obligation, the whole ambiguity and ambivalence of help, all the questions of altruism practised under social auspices. These are the questions we referred to earlier when we suggested that 'becoming a professional person' constituted an attempt to solve certain problems. We shall now consider some of the more important problems from the point of view of the client and the social worker.

From the point of view of the client

Notice first that 'client' goes with 'professional': if a worker is 'professional' then those to whom he attends become 'clients'. Frequent references are made to the unsatisfactory nature of the term. For some it is somewhat fanciful, especially when applied to consumers of the probation officer's services. Others see something more sinister in the term. Tropp (1974), who begins to raise some useful questions concerning what he sees as the problematic concepts of client, help and worker, states that, '. . . by implication in our society today, *client* means a person not worthy of much respect'. It is not easy to be sure, but this seems to be the sort of conclusion that would be derived 'by implication'. It seems to us that if we consider the use of the term client, it is not used to mean a person not worthy of much respect. The question to be asked rather is to what extent the term represents an improvement on earlier descriptions, such as applicant, or conveys a more realistic and helpful description than two new descriptions that are currently canvassed, user or customer.

How can we begin to assess the adequacy of these, and other terms? What work do we want them to do? We want a term which does not offend against human dignity – 'supplicant' will not do. We require a term which carries some claims that can be rightly made, which gives some protection to those who need or want help at times of crisis. Those who seek help or who are offered help are asked to entrust personal information to social workers, and the relationship of trust requires some delineation. Many of those who have supported professionalisation and the increasing effectiveness of professional socialisation have done so on the ground that 'professionals' have 'clients', and 'clients' have rights and are the willing recipients of individualised services.

The term 'client' does meet some of the criteria reasonably well. It does not offend against human dignity: no one could reasonably object to the status of client; and it carries some claims on the social worker and the agency. Sometimes these claims have to be forcibly pressed by social workers. Pearson has contrasted the value system explicitly espoused by professional social workers with the systematic isolation of that code occasioned by the fact that social work activity is undertaken largely under government auspices. In accordance with this anti-professional code the clients' communications to officials of a public service have the character of public knowledge; his actions are judged; the client's rights as citizen do not entitle him to anticipate that he will be 'accepted'; clients will be treated within an administrative machinery as cyphers. This list does undoubtedly describe dangers, perhaps systematic dangers, to the client, but these dangers do not derive from the concept professional–client.

This is not to say that the term 'client' cannot be criticised. Its use may give a misleadingly firm impression of those directly served by social workers. Is 'the client' of a social worker holding a group each individual member of the group? Is the beneficiary of social work with a delinquent gang, the members of the group or residents in the locality? Is the 'client' of a community worker a community? Who are the clients of a residential social worker? The term client may also convey a misleading impression of the amount of control possessed by the user of social service. Clients of lawyers can terminate the relationship with their professionals, can freely criticise its process and outcome, and judge its results. It is also important to note that 'clients', when their opinions are sought, do not seem to be preoccupied with the need for 'protection' from the personal intrusions of social workers. It is the friendliness of social workers that seems to impress, and the absence of friendliness that is criticised. One client of a Family Service Unit said of one worker they found unsatisfactory, 'He didn't seem so warm. He gave you the impression it was just his job . . .' (Sainsbury, 1975).

So it is possible to assess how far 'client' is a satisfactory term. Our own conclusion is that no one term is satisfactory for all situations, but that a combination of 'client' (characteristically where people are recipients of a counselling service) and 'user' will probably serve most purposes.

From the social worker's viewpoint

'Becoming a professional person' solves or attempts to solve a range of problems for the social worker. A professional offers service to those in need, not on the basis of colour or creed: his service has a universalised basis. Now in saying this it may seem that we are simply treating 'profession' as synonymous with virtue, but this is not so. To aim at being professional solves some of the problems arising from the need to disentangle some elements in friendship which do not offer a helpful model. The effort to be and remain 'professional' renders down some of the protruding problems in friendship. A character in *The Black Prince* by Iris Murdoch describes one such problem. 'We naturally take in the catastrophe of our friends a pleasure which genuinely does not preclude friendship. This is partly but not entirely because we enjoy being empowered as helpers.' This analysis of friendship seems more subtle and hence more rewarding for our purposes of contrast than those usually assumed in social work writing.

So 'professional' helps a social worker to pick his or her way through the attractions and disorientations of the different models available for his activity. It also helps to place some boundaries around interactions, often of a deep, intensive nature, between himself and his 'clients'. Perhaps most importantly of all, it establishes a basis for responsibility. A professional offers a service of expertise: briefly he knows his job and can be relied upon to take responsibility for his part in the transaction. He has traversed the country before and knows what he is about.

So far 'being a professional person' seems to be entirely advantageous for the social worker. It has, however, some negative connotations. It is easy, for example, to mistake 'being professional' for emphasising formality in behaviour, dress and attitude. Training courses used to devote considerable time to the mode in which clients should be addressed, by Christian name, or such title as Mr, Mrs, etc. Such discussion is not without importance, but the mistake often made was in the judgments that 'being professional' ruled out one or more forms of address completely. In our view, 'being professional' in this situation leads a social worker to consider the matter in a wider context than that provided by the endless discussion of minutiae; not to slide into easy assumptions about 'what people like to be called'; and to make a decision on the form of address most likely to advance the work in hand.

Suggestions for further reading

General statements concerning the values of social work can be found in Pumphrey (1959) and Younghusband (1967). Empirical work attempting to describe the values social workers actually hold has not developed very far, but McLeod and Meyer (1967) should be consulted. Readers who like a concrete approach may like to do some analysis of their own on a working document which attempts a formulation of some social work values for practical use (BASW *Discussion Paper* No. 2, 'A Code of Ethics for Social Work').

We have suggested that in social work ideas of praise/blame and the place of criticism have been neglected. Those who wish to follow up this line of enquiry should read Feinberg (1970), Downie (1969) and Holborow (1972). For those who take the view that any important differences in belief and attitude stem from fundamental differences in ideas of human nature, Stevenson (1974) offers a good summary of seven such ideas, those of Plato, Christianity, Marx, Freud, Sartre, Skinner and Lorenz. This is a particularly useful selection for social workers since many of these theorists also had specific ideas about methods of changing the world. Most of the theories have been adopted by social workers at one time or another.

Self-determination, as we indicated in the text, has been widely discussed. Fortunately, the main social work articles have recently been collected by McDermott (1975) who has also chosen some philosophical texts that should be read in conjunction with the social work contributions. Questions of determinism, we have suggested, can be avoided in a discussion of self-determination, but they cannot be avoided in other contexts. For a brief critical treatment of a recent social work essay which discussed some aspects of determinism see Watson (1975). On the more general problem see D'Angelo (1968).

The best introduction to rights is Raphael (1967), particularly since the essays are concerned with those rights in which social workers can be said to have a special interest – human rights. A good survey of writing on social work authority can be found in Foren and Bailey (1968).

Writing on 'the professions' is extensive, but some of the most important issues can be grasped through Toren (1972), Halmos (ed.) (1973) and Johnson (1972). See also Hamilton (1974).

A social worker
takes bearings

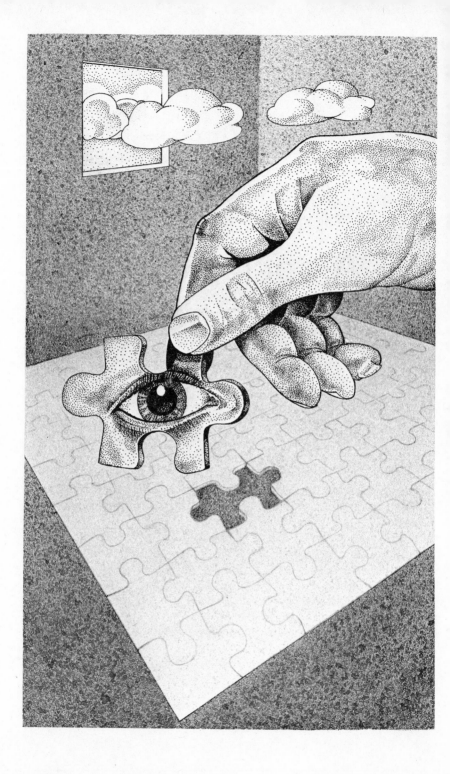

As we said at the beginning of this book, this is not an easy time in which to write on social work. So much seems to have become or to have been made unstable. In addition it has seemed important to write critically so that the current literature of social work is examined and alternatives explored. We have sought to discover and analyse key concepts and to advocate a reasonable approach, which recognises but finds some way through the real problems. We do not underestimate the problems our approach may pose to those reared on a diet of Biestek (1957) marinated in diluted Freud.

We believe that a great deal of social work writing has been along the wrong lines. Direct treatment (in a strong sense) has been exclusively emphasised rather than dialogue and the direct and indirect provision of milieux: when 'environmental manipulation' has been given more than a residual role it has been seen as a method of treatment. Social work has been seen as a passive reflection of the client's talk rather than as planned action. The conflicts in 'professional friendship' or expertise in common sense have not been recognised. The social worker has been seen – often by social workers – essentially as a private practitioner and not as an agency worker. Professional petticoats have been drawn aside to avoid contact with those aspects of ordinary life that are most crucial to a person's milieu, chores in family and residential life, politicking in advocacy, the physical and socio-psychological care of bodies.

We have pursued this critical approach throughout the book, but we have also been conscious that the student of social work needs more than a series of discrete analyses. Before turning to this question of how a social worker may take bearings on social work, it will be helpful if we review the argument advanced in this book.

This will serve as a pointed summary which will show the way towards the answer to the question on bearings.

Chapter 2

We argued that definitions and short descriptions did not work very well in illuminating social work. They raised some interesting questions, but their authors have, on the whole, not seen the problematic nature of the questions. In this situation it is hardly surprising that they offered no guidance on how the questions might be answered. This guidance is similarly lacking if we try to take a practical approach – well, social work is just helping people. Obviously, different people are helped in all kinds of ways by different others. Consequently, the concept of social work and of right and wrong ways of practising it are essential in the task of clarifying what social work is.

Historical studies show a long-established tradition of altruism and of the criticism of policies of altruism. We suggest that this provides a perspective for exploring the identity and problems of social work, provided we see social work as a special case of altruistic activity, namely altruism under social auspices. Such a perspective constitutes a fresh approach and illumination to the problems of social work. Bishop Butler may seem as remote in time as in subject matter from modern social work, but his description of the altruist's reaction to those in distress still poses problems to the social worker that are glossed over in contemporary treatments:

> There are often three distinct perceptions or inward feelings upon sight of persons in distress: real sorrow and concern for the misery of our fellow-creatures; some degree of satisfaction from a consciousness of our freedom from that misery; and as the mind passes on from one thing to another, it is not unnatural from such an occasion to reflect upon our own liableness to the same or other collaboration. (Sermon Five)

'Social auspice' may seem vague, but we intend it to be forceful enough to rule out private practice, on the one hand, and direct revolutionary action, on the other. It does not rule out criticism of the agency, its procedures or its policies, nor confrontations of different kinds. It does not assume one way of being a member of society, but it accepts that there must be some on-going social arrangements. Social workers can be radical or conservative, irrespective of the 'method' of social work they use: there can be radical caseworkers and conservative community workers. Yet this qualifies and does not constitute their social work. They are social workers who are radical, reformists, etc. They are social workers because they stand in particular relationship to society, which they do not totally reject. We see one of their main tasks as that of criticism and this can only be pursued within an accepted context.

Chapter 3

In this chapter we presented the results of evaluative research into social work. Such an early consideration of evaluation was not perverse, since the main result of evaluative studies so far undertaken is to tell us more about the kinds of questions we should be asking about social work. The way in which the results of the studies have often been received by social workers is also instructive – a rather wholesale gloom has set in. This illustrates the importance of what should be one of the golden rules in social work – try to specify. To ensure that the maximum possible specification has been attempted and secured does not rob a subject of its humanity or subtlety.

Our consideration of evaluation research led us to discuss the meaning social work had for clients and for social workers. We can distinguish in many activities between what something is and what it means to particular groups of people, but in social work, especially if it is viewed as a kind of altruism, this distinction is much less easily upheld: social work is an activity which essentially should have personal significance for social workers and their clients, however fleeting the contact.

Chapter 4

Here we attempted to describe in simple terms the kind of things social workers should be able to do. Some items in our list may appear formal (calling encounters 'interviews', for example) or biased in the direction of casework or forgetful of 'the relationship'. Obviously, we would not agree. 'Interviews', formal or informal, can cover most of the encounters in social work, whether this is casework or community work. The relationships formed in social work arise out of and are based upon the work in hand. Sometimes the work requires simple human courtesy, but on many other occasions much more is required. In residential social work more is always required, but this does not make residential social work itself a kind of counselling.

We believe that the activities we have described – planning, delivering services and so on – are of considerable importance in social work, and we have tried to specify them closely. We believe that a concentration on these elements will lead to a situation rather different from that described by a father in George and Wilding's study (1972, p. 155):

> All they did was listen. They couldn't actually do anything. It was useless in the end. The situation was the same, the facts were not altered. The only good thing was that you had a sense of being able to tell someone your troubles. I would recommend it to others whose problems are not so serious.

It is possible that in this, as in other parts of the book, readers may find an approach that is 'too rational', but in our view social work is a reasonable activity (often a reasoning activity). We should not, as social workers, begin by assuming pathology and irrational behaviour, so that clients are seen as incapable of planning or choosing from and deriving benefit from a range of services. One of the rules in social work should be that social workers should begin with the client's purpose, plan or project and only when this fails to make any sense at all should the social worker fall back on the consideration of causes, and 'pushes and pulls', whether 'internal' or 'external'.

Chapter 5

This chapter raised some very basic questions concerning knowledge in social work. We saw, on the one hand, the considerable emphasis given quite recently to the importance of knowledge in social work. Knowledge, after all, helps considerably to make professionals. On the other hand, there is also a strain of scepticism about the value or even the possibility of the kind of knowledge claimed as the actual possession or the intended objective of the social worker. This apparent contradiction exposes a number of problems, including the role of 'intellectualisation' in social work. We believe that the crude distinctions used in the chapter between kinds of knowledge – knowing that, knowing a person or thing (or class of person or thing), and knowing how – will help to clarify and re-focus problems in a crucial area.

We believe that a fundamentally sceptical position is untenable.

We think that social workers do know certain things and can recognise patterns of behaviour that are connected to the provision of service. It would be baffling if this was not the case.

> Strange to know nothing, never to be sure
> Of what is true or right or real,
> But forced to qualify or so I feel,
> Or Well, it does seem so:
> Someone must know.

(Philip Larkin, 'Ignorance')

Chapter 6

In one sense it was difficult to know whether it was appropriate to consider the content of this chapter under the general heading of what a social worker should be able to do. The concepts discussed in this chapter are concepts that a social worker should be able to handle with some ease. If he cannot handle them, then, in our view, he simply has not got them. We would like to have given more space to each of the concepts considered – understanding, emotion, power, needs, etc. – and we are aware of compressing a great deal of material and argument. The arguments spread, of course, to areas adjacent to social work which sometimes exercise a strong influence on developments in social work. Take, for example, the concept of emotion and a historical study in theories of deviancy which has attracted attention in social work, Erikson (1965). In this study Erikson is concerned with the creation of deviancy. At one point he suggests that a particular process is at work: 'Men who fear witches soon find themselves surrounded by them.' This process in time seems to explain particular witch-hunts, but a firmer grasp of the emotion of fear would have shown that this explanation is illusory. People who fear witches are surrounded by them.

We could not hope to follow all the implications even of the particular concepts we have chosen, but this chapter will have succeeded if readers have been convinced that social workers should be able to use certain key concepts and if they recognise that such concepts have work to do. Otherwise we shall not have moved from the present unsatisfactory situation in social work, where concepts abound but their life is either very short or entirely decorative.

Chapter 7

Here we considered what is usually discussed when reference is made to social work knowledge: the kind of theoretical information a social worker should have. Social work knowledge can refer to a general orientation based on a school of psychology or sociology, or to findings or theory 'borrowed' from psychology or sociology, or to findings or theory developed within the perspective of social work itself. We have stressed the latter, namely theory and findings about the social services, their rationale and use. We also believe that social workers will seek a general basis for action. Such a basis can take one of a number of forms, but it must be founded on a firm, critical grasp of the theory and the theory must actually inform the practice. In choosing a general orientation social work students will encounter theories that cannot easily be reconciled (e.g. a conflict and a disorganisation theory of social problems). It is tempting to assume that each of these differences can be reconciled, even 'integrated'. We believe that the attempt to achieve reconciliation is worthwhile, but difficult, and that integration is largely illusory. We think that social workers can move between frames of reference, even though more than one frame cannot be used at any one time. We believe that no one frame of reference should be used exclusively and that always the social worker should attend to the individual embedded in his social context. It is, we believe, mistaken to argue that the social worker 'must be sure she is listening to an individual in trouble, not to a member of a group' (Raynor, 1970, p. 55).

Chapter 8

This chapter referred to what are usually called the values of social work. We discussed in some detail one of the values usually listed, namely that of self-determination. This discussion illustrated the value of appreciating the wider context for the exploration of social work problems – in this case, we forget easily the political context in which self-determination has some immediate meaning. It was also part of our argument that the most important values upheld in social work often systematically elude analysis. We believe that greater returns can be expected from analysing the beliefs that social workers hold. We examined two of these beliefs in detail; the belief that social work is a profession and the belief in a right to intervene. We believe that too much time has been given to the simple assertion or assumption that social work is a profession, and insufficient attention paid to the fact that these assertions are claims made by one particular occupational group. It would have been preferable, in our view, to press on with particular tasks and with discrete claims, rather than with the attempt, often subject to easy ridicule, to dress social work in the borrowed, ill-fitting clothes of professionalism. The right to intervene raises again the crucial question, touched on at the beginning of this book, concerning the relationship between the social worker and 'society'. Just as the individual should not be abstracted from society, so, we believe, the social worker should not be abstracted from his agency and its legal and social basis. It is the agency that connects the social worker to the client and to society.

We have now summarised the main arguments of our book. We have tried to present them clearly and in a way that recognises and attempts to meet possible objections. Perhaps the most central objection can be stated in the following response: the book amounts to a series of thoughts (possibly interesting, possibly not), but not to any basis for action; the book diagnoses liberally the problems of social work, it constitutes no programme. In our view such a response has more to do with the unfamiliarity of our approach than with any basic fault. We have stressed throughout the values of clarity and of specificity, and we have argued that the problems of social work should be acknowledged and not left hidden in the confident phrase and the implicit contradiction. We also believe that social work is a very worthwhile enterprise which can be seen and experienced as reasonably coherent.

Students should begin by appreciating that their orientation should be to social work rather than to what have so far been identified as the methods of social work. In this book we have often referred to casework, groupwork, residential and so on, since these terms are in very common use, but a widespread and consistent attention to social work as the main organising concept will have beneficial results. It will avoid the ontological anxiety implicit in the question 'What am I doing as a social worker when what I am doing cannot with any ease be called casework, community work and so on?' It also safeguards us from what we can call creeping methodology. By this we mean the tendency to assume that everything a social worker does must be forced into one of the methodologies; everything in work with a family, for instance, has to be interpreted as a form of treatment, in a strong sense. It is because of creeping methodology that social workers have come to think of financial aid, for example, as a tool in casework treatment.

'Social worker' does not, of course, describe very well, but it does encompass a number of features. It is not easy to grasp these, and previous attempts have not sufficiently acknowledged the problems. Some writers, for example, refer to social work as a unique constellation of knowledge, values and so on, but their treatment of the connections between these elements suggests that they might as well have spoken of a simple conjunction. What can be said about the main features of social work that will help the student to take his or her bearings?

Social workers work in and through social work agencies. Within agencies social workers will adopt different orientations and different ideologies, but private practice is a contradiction in terms when applied to social work. It is because of the central role of the agency that we have emphasised that social workers should be knowledgeable about the operation of the social services. This orientation does not turn the social worker exclusively into a bureaucrat; as we have seen, some aspects of social work admit of a description as professional activity, some of a description as a social movement. We would now add that some can be described by using the concept of bureaucracy.

But what are social workers doing in social work agencies? In our view they are acting on behalf of others (acting altruistically). This means they seek to establish non-exploitative relationships. They are also acting critically, by which we mean that they offer a critical attention to people as they choose between services and use services, and that they become critically informed of the operation of their own and other services. Social workers will vary in the emphasis they give to particular services. Some, for example, will emphasise counselling, and within that service they will again vary in terms of theoretical and practical orientation. Some will adopt a radically critical perspective and see counselling as directed towards raising people's consciousness of their historical and social position. Others will adopt a client-centred approach of a Rogerian kind. Much will depend on the worker's own decision and the form of work sanctioned by the agency and by the law. In reaching a decision the social worker must consider the general criteria governing the choice of theoretical position. It is not just a case of the worker finding a theoretical position with which he is comfortable. His comfort must depend, at least in part, on the degree to which a theory or theories can make an impact on his activity, can contribute to the service of *persons*, and can stand up to critical scrutiny and test.

We believe that in the past social work has emphasised too insistently the pathological and the causative force of the irrational. We think that the time has come to emphasise a reasoning and reasonable approach (rather than treatment in any strong sense) to what should increasingly be seen as situations of practical reason. Peters (1973) has suggested that we make five assumptions in relation to people in such situations: that there is more than one type of end which can function for them as a goal; that they are capable of weighing the pros and cons of alternatives without being paralysed by indecision; that the weight which people attach to different beliefs can be influenced by relevant information; that changes in people's beliefs can modify their decisions; that people's decisions can be translated into appropriate action. Of course, these criteria rule out, for one reason or another, people like psychopaths, drug addicts and some kinds of hysteric. These constitute a certain proportion of social workers' caseload, but even in these cases it is the social work task to help to make such situations as like situations of practical reason as possible.

We have throughout emphasised a catholic approach to social work: there is not just one way to do social work, and the differences between professional social work and 'lay' social work cannot always be sharply drawn. Protagonists of a highly professionalised social work and their critics sometimes assume that social work can only be practised in one way. This situation is similar to that pertaining to studies in residential provision. As Tizard *et al.* (1975) have pointed out, criticism of what can be called the 'steampress' model of institutions shares with that model the assumption that variations in staff, organisation and so on make little difference to the quality of life in residential centres. Tizard *et al.* question this and suggest that there are four factors crucial for the pattern and quality of life in residential centres: ideological variation (the centre is seen as school, hospital, house, etc.); organisational variation; staffing; and variation in the response of residents. These factors are also of significance for the quality of general social work that is actually offered and delivered.

As we said in the introductory chapter, we have not attempted to present a complete inventory of what every social worker should know, believe, be able to do. We have tried to raise questions and also to indicate plausible answers. We hope we have unsettled ill-founded certainty and also encouraged social workers towards a more fine appreciation of the things they do when they practise social work. We shall have achieved a great deal if it can be said of this book in relation to social work, as was said of the work of Henry James, that it has 'added the sharp taste of uncertainty to a quickened sense of life' (Bayley, 1966, p. 246).

BIBLIOGRAPHY

ADAMSON, G. (1973), *The Care-Takers*, Bookstall Publications.
ADDAMS, J. et al. (1893), *Philanthropy and Social Progress*, New York.
ALBROW, M. (1970), *Bureaucracy*, Macmillan.
ALEXANDER, L. B. (1972), 'Social Work's Freudian Deluge: Myth or Reality?', *Social Service Review*, 46, 517–38.
ANONYMOUS (1919), *Charity Organisation Review*, June.
ASHCROFT, B. and JACKSON, K. (1974), 'Adult Education and Social Action' in *Community Work: One*, ed. D. Jones and M. Mayo, Routledge & Kegan Paul.
ATTLEE, C. R. (1920), *The Social Worker*, Bell.
BAILEY, R. and BRAKE, M. (eds) (1975), *Radical Social Work*, Edward Arnold.
BAKER, R. (1975), 'Toward Generic Social Work Practice – A Review and Some Innovations', *British Journal of Social Work*, 5, 193–216.
BALDOCK, P. (1974), *Community Work and Social Work*, Routledge & Kegan Paul.
BARNETT, H. (1918), *Canon Barnett, his Life, Work and Friends*, John Murray.
BARRY, B. M. (1964), 'Public Interest', *Proceedings of the Aristotelian Society*, Supplementary Volume XXXVIII, 1–18.
BARTLETT, H. (1958), 'Towards Clarification and Improvement of Social Work Practice', *Social Work* (USA), 3, 3–9.
BASW (BRITISH ASSOCIATION OF SOCIAL WORKERS) (1973), 'The Inalienable Element in Social Work', *Discussion Paper* No. 3, *Social Work Today*, 4.
BASW (undated), 'A Code of Ethics for Social Work', *Discussion Paper* No. 2.
BAYLEY, J. (1966), *The Characters of Love*, Constable.
BAYLEY, M. (1973), *Mental Handicap and Community Care*, Routledge & Kegan Paul.
BECK, D. F. (1973), 'Research Findings on the Outcome of Marital Counselling', *Social Casework*, 56, 153–81.
BECK, H. and JONES, M. (1974), 'A New Look at the Clientele and Services of Family Agencies', *Social Casework*, 53, 589–99.
BECKER, H. (1968), *Institutions and the Person*, Aldine.
BECKER, H. (1974), 'Labelling Theory Reconsidered' in *Deviance and Social Control*, ed. P. Rock and M. McIntosh, Tavistock Publications.

BEEDELL, C. (1970), *Residential Life with Children*, Routledge & Kegan Paul.

BENINGTON, J. (1974), 'Strategies for Change at the Local Level: Some Reflections' in *Community Work: One*, ed. D. Jones and M. Mayo, Routledge & Kegan Paul.

BENNETT, W. S. JR. and HOKENSTAD, M. JR. (1973), 'Full-time People Workers and Conceptions of the "Professional" ' in *Professionalisation and Social Change*, ed. P. Halmos, Sociological Review Monograph no. 20, University of Keele.

BENNIS, W. G. (1971), 'Changing Organisations' in *Social Intervention*, ed. H. A. Hornstein *et al.*, Free Press.

BERRY, J. (1975), *Daily Experience in Residential Life*, Routledge & Kegan Paul.

BESSELL, R. (1971), *Interviewing and Counselling*, Batsford.

BIBRING, J. (1949), 'Psychiatric Principles in Casework, *Journal of Social Casework*, 30.

BIDDLE, B. and THOMAS, E. J. (eds) (1966), *Role Theory: Concepts and Research*, John Wiley.

BIESTEK, F. (1957), *The Casework Relationship*, Allen & Unwin.

BION, W. R. (1961), *Experiences in Groups*, Tavistock Publications.

BIRCHALL, J. (1904), 'Boarded-out'. Paper read to the 25th Annual Poor Law Conference for the West Midland District.

BITENSKY, R. (1973), 'The Influence of Political Power in Determining the Theoretical Development of Social Work', *Journal of Social Policy*, 2, 119–30.

BLUMER, H. (1955), 'Attitudes and the Social Act', *Social Problems*, 3, 59–65.

BOTT, E. (1957), *Family and Social Networks*, Tavistock Publications.

BOULDING, K. (1953), 'Towards a General Theory of Growth', *Canadian Journal of Economics and Political Science*, 19, 326–40.

BOWERS, S. (1949), 'The Nature and Definition of Social Casework', *Social Casework*.

BRADSHAW, A. (1976), 'A Critique of Steven Lukes' *Power: A Radical View*', *Sociology*, 10, 121–7.

BRADSHAW, J. (1972), 'Taxonomy of Social Need' in *Problems and Progress in Medical Care*, ed. G. McLachlan, Oxford University Press.

BRAGER, G. (1968), 'Advocacy and Political Behaviour', *Social Work*, 13, 5–15.

BRAGER, G. and SPECHT, H. (1973), *Community Organising*, Columbia University Press.

BRAYBROOKE, D. (1968), 'Let Needs Diminish that Preferences may Prosper' in *Studies in Moral Philosophy*, ed. N. Rescher, Blackwell.

BROWN, G. E. (ed.) (1968), *The Multi-Problem Dilemma*, Scarecrow Press.

BROWN, G. W. and RUTTER, M. (1966), 'The Measurement of Family Activities and Relationships', *Human Relations*, 19, 241–63.

BRUNK, C. (1946), 'Protective Casework in a Family Agency', *American Journal of Orthopsychiatry*, 16, 312–28.

BUCHLER, J. (1961), *The Concept of Method*, Columbia University Press.

BUTRYM, Z. (1968), *Medical Social Work in Action* (Occasional Papers in Social Administration), Bell.

BYWATERS, P. (1975), 'Ending Casework Relationships (1)', *Social Work Today*, 6, 301–4; 'Ending Casework Relationships (2)', *Social Work Today*, 6, 336–8.

CAMPBELL, T. D. (1974), 'Humanity before Justice', *British Journal of Political Science*, 4, 1–16.

CARKHUFF, R. R. (1969), *Helping and Human Relations* (2 vols.), Holt, Rinehart & Winston.

CARKHUFF, R. R. and TRUAX, C. B. (1967), *Toward Effective Counselling and Psychotherapy*, Aldine.

CASE, L. and LINGERFELT, N. (1974), 'The Labelling Process in the Social Work Interview', *Social Service Review*, 48, 75–86.

CCETSW (1975), *Day Services: An Action Plan for Training*, CCETSW Paper 12.

COCKERILL, E. *et al.* (1952), *A Conceptual Framework for Social Casework*, University of Pittsburgh Press.

COHEN, A. (1971), 'The Consumer's View: Retarded Mothers and the Social Services', *Social Work Today*, 1, 12, 39–43.

COHEN, N. E. (ed.) (1964), *Social Work and Social Problems*, National Association of Social Workers, New York.

COHEN, S. (1975), 'It's All Right for You to Talk: Political and Sociological Manifestos for Social Action' in *Radical Social Work*, ed. R. Bailey and M. Brake, Edward Arnold.

CONNOLLY, W. E. (1972), 'On "Interests" in Politics', *Politics and Society*, 2, 459–77.

COX, MURRAY (1973), 'The Group Therapy Interaction Chronogram', *British Journal of Social Work*, 3, 243–56.

CRANSTON, M. (1967), 'Human Rights, Real and Supposed' in *Political Theory and the Rights of Man*, ed. D. D. Raphael, Macmillan.

CYPHER, J. (1973), 'Sections and Strife', *Social Work Today*, 4, 104–8.

DAHRENDORF, R. (1959), *Class and Class Conflict*, Routledge & Kegan Paul.

DAHRENDORF, R. (1962), 'On the Origin of Social Inequality' in *Philosophy, Politics and Society*, 2nd series, ed. P. Laslett and W. G. Runciman, Blackwell.

D'ANGELO, E. (1968), *The Problem of Freedom and Determinism* (University of Missouri Studies, Vol. XLVIII), University of Missouri Press.

DAVIES, B. (1975), *The Use of Groups in Social Work Practice*, Routledge & Kegan Paul.

DAVIES, M. (1969), *Probationers in their Social Environment*, HMSO.

DAVIES, M. (1974a), *Prisoners of Society*, Routledge & Kegan Paul.

DAVIES, M. (1974b), 'The Current Status of Social Work Research', *British Journal of Social Work*, 4, 281–303.

DENNIS, N. (1970), *People and Planning*, Faber & Faber.

DE SCHWEINITZ, E. and DE SCHWEINITZ, K. (1962), *Interviewing in the Social Services*, National Council of Social Service.

DILMAN, G. (1959), 'The Unconscious', *Mind*, LXVIII, 446–73.

DONNISON, D. *et al.* (1975), *Social Policy and Administration Revisited*, Allen & Unwin.

DOWNIE, R. (1969), 'The Right to Criticise', *Philosophy*, XLIV, 116–26.

DOWNIE, R. and TELFER, E. (1969), *Respect for Persons*, Allen & Unwin.

DRAY, W. (1964), *Philosophy of History*, Prentice-Hall.

EMMET, D. and MCINTYRE, A. (eds.) (1970), *Sociological Theory and Philosophical Analysis*, Macmillan.

ERIKSON, K. T. (1962), 'Notes on the Sociology of Deviance', *Social Problems*, 9, 307–13.

ERIKSON, K. T. (1965), *Wayward Puritans*, John Wiley.

ETZIONI, A. (1968), 'Basic Human Needs, Alienation and Inauthenticity', *American Sociological Review*, 33, 870–85.

ETZIONI, A. (ed.) (1969), *The Semi-Professions and their Organisation*, Free Press.

FEINBERG, J. (1970), *Doing and Deserving*, Princeton University Press.

FISCHER, J. (1973), 'Is Casework Effective?', *Social Work* (USA), 18, 5–20.

FITZJOHN, J. (1974), 'An Interactionist View of the Social Work Interview', *British Journal of Social Work*, 4, 425–34.

FLETCHER, C. (1974), *Beneath the Surface: An Account of Three Styles of Sociological Research*, Routledge & Kegan Paul.

FLETCHER, R. (1963), *Human Needs and the Social Order*, Michael Joseph.

FLEXNER, A. (1915), 'Is Social Work a Profession?', *Proceedings of the 42nd National Conference of Charities*.

FORDER, A. (1974), *Concepts in Social Administration*, Routledge & Kegan Paul.

FORDER, A. (1976), 'Social Work and System Theory', *British Journal of Social Work*, 6, 23–42.

FOREN, R. and BAILEY, R. (1968), *Authority in Social Casework*, Pergamon.

FOSTER, J. D. *et al.* (1972), 'Perceptions of Stigma Following Public Intervention for Delinquent Behaviour', *Social Problems*, 20, 202–9.

FOWLER, D. (1975), 'Ends and Means' in *Towards a New Social Work*, ed. H. Jones, Routledge & Kegan Paul.

FRAIBERG, S. (1963), 'Psychoanalysis and the Education of Caseworkers', in *Ego-oriented Casework: Problems and Perspectives*, Family Service Association of America.

GALLIE, W. (1964), *Philosophy and the Historical Understanding*, Chatto & Windus.

GARDINER, P. L. (1971), 'The Concept of Man Presupposed by the Historical Studies' in *The Proper Study*, ed. G. N. A. Vesey, Macmillan.

GARLAND, J. A. *et al.* (1972), 'A Model for Stages of Development in Social Work Groups' in *Explorations in Group Work*, ed. S. Bernstein, Bookstall Publications.

GARRETT, A. (1942), *Interviewing: Principles and Methods*, Family Service Association of America.

GELLNER, E. (1970), 'Concepts and Society' in *Sociological Theory and Philosophical Analysis*, ed. D. Emmet and A. McIntyre, Macmillan.

GELLNER, E. (1974), *The Devil in Modern Philosophy*, Routledge & Kegan Paul.

GEORGE, V. (1970), *Foster Care: Theory and Practice*, Routledge & Kegan Paul.

GEORGE, V. and WILDING, P. (1972), *Motherless Families*, Routledge & Kegan Paul.

GILBERT, N. and SPECHT, H. (1974), *Dimensions of Social Welfare Policy*, Prentice-Hall.

GILPIN, R. (1963), *Theory and Practice as a Single Reality*, University of North Carolina Press.

GOLDBERG, E. M. *et al.* (1970), *Helping the Aged*, Allen & Unwin.

GOLDSTEIN, H. (1973), *Social Work Practice: a Unitary Approach*, University of South Carolina Press.

GONOPKA, G. (1970), *Group-Work in the Institution*, Association Press.

GREVE, S. (1969), 'Financial Help as Part of Social Work', *Social Work* (UK), 26, 13–23.

GRIFFITHS, A. P. (1960), 'How Can One Person Represent Another?', *Proceedings of the Aristotelian Society*, Supplementary Volume XXXIV, 187–208.

GUNTRIP H. (1961), *Personality Structure and Human Interaction*, Hogarth Press.

GUNTRIP, H. (1971), *Psychology for Ministers and Social Workers*, Allen & Unwin.

GYARFAS, G. (1969), 'Social Science, Technology and Social Work: A Caseworker's View', *Social Service Review* 43, 259–73.

HADLEY, R., WEBB, A. and FARRELL, C. (1975), *Across the Generations*, Allen & Unwin.

HAINES, J. (1975), *Skills and Methods in Social Work*, Constable.

HALL, A. (1974), *The Point of Entry*, Allen & Unwin.

HALL, A. R. (1974), 'Science and the Industrial Revolution', in *Studies in English Thought and Society in Honour of J. H. Plumb*, ed. N. McKendrick, Europa Publications.

HALMOS, P. (ed.) (1973), *Professionalization and Social Change*, Sociological Review Monograph 20, University of Keele.

HAMILTON, G. (1940), *Theory and Practice of Social Casework*, Columbia University Press.

HAMILTON, R. (1974), 'Social Work: an Aspiring Profession and its Difficulties', *British Journal of Social Work*, 4, 333–42.

HAMLYN, D. W. (1970), *The Theory of Knowledge*, Macmillan.

HANDLER, J. F. (1973), *The Coercive Social Worker* (Institute for Research on Poverty Monograph Series), Rand McNally.

HARTFORD, M. (1972), *Groups in Social Work*, Columbia University Press.

HARTMAN, A. (1969), 'Anomie and Social Casework', *Social Casework*, 50, 131–7.

HARTMAN, A. (1971), 'But What is Social Casework', *Social Casework*, 52, 411–15.

HEPMAN, J. and HEINE, R. (1964), *Concepts of Personality*, Methuen.

HEYWOOD, J. and ALLEN, B. (1971), *Financial Help in Social Work*, Manchester University Press.

HIGGINS, R. (1963), 'The Concept of Maladjustment: its Social Consequences', *Human Relations*, 16, 60–74.

HIRSCHMAN, A. and LINDBLOM, C. (1969), 'Economic Development, Research and Policy Making: Some Converging Views' in *Systems Thinking*, ed. F. E. Emery, Penguin.

HOLBOROW, L. C. (1972), 'Blame, Praise and Credit', *Proceedings of the Aristotelian Society*, LXXII, 85–100.

HOLLIS, F. (1958), 'Personality Diagnosis in Casework' in *Ego Psychology and Dynamic Casework*, ed. H. J. Parad, Family Service Association of America.

HOLLIS, F. (1964), *Social Casework: A Psycho-social Therapy*, Random House.

HOLMAN, R. (1973), *Trading in Children*, Routledge & Kegan Paul.

HOLMAN, R. (1975), 'The Place of Fostering in Social Work', *British Journal of Social Work*, 5, 3–30.

HOWE, M. W. (1974), 'Casework Self-Education: A Single-Subject Approach', *Social Service Review*, 48, 1–23.

HUDSON, W. (1974), 'Casework as a Causative Agent in Client Deterioration: A Research Note on the Fischer Assessment', *Social Service Review*, 48, 442–9.

HUGHES, M. W. (1973), 'Our Concern with Others' in *Philosophy and Personal Relations*, ed. A. Montefiore, Routledge & Kegan Paul.

IRVINE, E. E. (1964), 'The Right to Intervene', *Social Work* (UK), 21, 2, 13–18.

JAMOUS, H. and PELIOLLE, B. (1970), 'Professions or Self-perpetuating Systems' in *Professions and Professionalization*, ed. J. A. Jackson, Columbia University Press.

JANCHILL, M. P. (1969), 'Systems Concepts in Casework Theory and Practice', *Social Casework*, 50, 74–82.

JEHU, D. (1967), *Learning Theory and Social Work*, Routledge & Kegan Paul.

JEHU, D. (1972), *Behaviour Modification in Social Work*, Wiley Interscience.

JENKINS, D. E. (1971), 'The Concept of the Human' in *Technology and Social Justice*, ed. R. H. Preston, SCM Press.

JENKINS, R. (1969), 'Long Term Fostering', *Case Conference*, 15, 349–53.

JOHNSON, T. (1972), *Professions and Power*, Macmillan.

JONES, DUNCAN (1958), 'Authority', *Proceedings Aristotelian Society*, Supplementary Volume XXXII, 241–60.

JONES, D. and MAYO, M. (1974), *Community Work: One*, Routledge & Kegan Paul.

JONES, D. and MAYO, M. (1975), *Community Work: Two*, Routledge & Kegan Paul.

JONES, E. O. (1975), 'A Study of Those who Cease to Foster', *British Journal of Social Work*, 5, 31–42.

JONES, H. (ed.) (1975), *Towards a New Social Work*, Routledge & Kegan Paul.

KADUSHIN, A. (1972), *The Social Work Interview*, Columbia University Press.

KAHN, A. J. (ed.) (1973), 'A Policy Base for Social Work Practice' in *Shaping the New in Social Work*, ed. A. J. Kahn, Columbia University Press.

KARP, M. (1931), *The Scientific Basis of Social Work*, Columbia University Press.

KASSMAN, A. (1973), *Knowledge and Belief*, Open University.

KATZ, D. and KAHN, R. (1969), 'Common Characteristics of Open Systems' in *Systems Thinking*, ed. F. E. Emery, Penguin.

KEITH-LUCAS, A. (1963), 'A Critique of the Principle of Client Self-Determination', *Social Work* (USA), 8, 66–71.

KENNY, A. (1963), *Action, Emotion and Will*, Routledge & Kegan Paul.

KING, J. (1969), *The Probation and After-Care Service*, Butterworth.

KING, R., RAYNES, N. and TIZARD, J. (1971), *Patterns of Residential Care*, Routledge & Kegan Paul.

KUHN, M. (1962), 'The Interview and the Professional Relationship' in *Human Behaviour and Social Processes*, ed. A. M. Rose, Routledge & Kegan Paul.

LAKATOS, G. and MUSGRAVE, A. (eds) (1965), *Criticism and the Growth of Knowledge*, Cambridge University Press.

LEICHTER, H. and MITCHELL, W. (1967), *Kinship and Casework*, Russell Sage Foundation, 1967.

LEIGHTON, N. (1967), 'The Myth of Self-determination', *New Society*, no. 230.

LEMERT, E. (1967), *Human Deviance, Social Problems and Social Control*, Prentice-Hall.

LEONARD, P. (1975), 'Explanation and Education in Social Work', *British Journal of Social Work*, 5, 325–33.

LEVITAN, S. (1969), *The Great Society's Poor Law: A New Approach to Poverty*, Johns Hopkins University Press.

LEWIS, O. (1969), quoted in Sundquist J. (ed.), *Perspectives on Poverty*, Vol. II, *On Fighting Poverty*, Basic Books, p. 246.

LOCH, C. S. (1910), *Charity and Social Life*, Macmillan.

LONERGAN, B. (1972), *Method in Theology*, Darton, Longman & Todd.

LUBOVE, R. (1965), *The Professional Altruist*, Harvard University Press.

LUCAS, J. R. (1966), *The Principles of Politics*, Clarendon Press.

LUKES, S. (1967), 'Alienation and Anomie' in *Philosophy, Politics and Society* 3rd series, ed. P. Laslett and W. G. Runciman, Blackwell.

LUKES, S. (1970), 'Methodological Individualism' in *Sociological Theory and Philosophical Analysis*, ed. D. Emmet and A. MacIntyre, Macmillan.

LUKES, S. (1973), *Individualism*, Blackwell.

LUKES, S. (1974), *Power: A Radical View*, Macmillan.

MACAULAY, J. and BERKOWITZ, L. (1970), *Altruism and Helping Behaviour*, Academic Press.

MCCLEAN, J. (1975), *The Legal Context of Social Work*, Butterworth.

MCDERMOTT, F. (1975), *Self-determination in Social Work*, Routledge & Kegan Paul.

MACDONALD, M. (1966), 'Reunion at Vocational High: An Analysis of Girls at Vocational High', *Social Service Review*, XL, 175–89.

MCGOWAN, J. and SCHMIDT, L. (1962), *Counseling: Readings in Theory and Practice*, Holt, Rinehart & Winston.

MCKAY, A. *et al.* (1973), 'Consumers and a Social Service Department', *Social Work Today*, 4, 486–91.

MCLEOD, D. and MEYER, H. (1967), 'A Study of the Values of Social Workers' in *Behavioural Science for Social Workers*, ed. E. J. Thomas, Collier-Macmillan.

MAIER, H. W. (1965), *Three Theories of Child Development*, Harper.

MARRIS, P. (1974), *Loss and Change*, Routledge & Kegan Paul.

MARTENS, W. and HOLMSTRUP, E. (1974), 'Problem-oriented Recording', *Social Casework*, 55, 554–61.

MARTIN, R. (1971), 'The Concept of Power: a Critical Defence', *British Journal of Sociology*, XXII, 240–56.

MAYER, J. and ROSENBLATT, A. (1974), 'Sources of Stress among Student Practitioners in Social Work: A Sociological View', *Journal of Education for Social Work*, 10, 56–66.

MAYER, J. and TIMMS, N. (1970), *The Client Speaks*, Routledge & Kegan Paul.

MAYO, B. (1967), 'What are Human Rights?' in *Political Theory and the Rights of Man*, ed. D. D. Raphael, Macmillan.

MELDEN, A. I. (1969), 'The Conceptual Dimension of Emotions' in *Human Action*, ed. T. Mischel, Academic Press.

MENCHER, S. (1964), 'The Influence of Romanticism on Nineteenth Century British Social Work', *Social Service Review*, 38, 174–90.

MERRILL, F. E. (1955), 'Social Character and Social Problems', *Social Problems*, 3, 7–12.

MEYER, H. *et al.* (1964), 'A Study of the Interview Process: the Case-worker–Client Relationship', *Genetic Psychology Monographs*, 69, 247–295.

MEYER, H. *et al.* (1965), *Girls at Vocational High*, Russell Sage Foundation.

MEYER, H. *et al.* (1968), 'Social Work and Social Welfare' in *The Uses of Sociology*, ed. P. Lazarsfeld *et al.*, Weidenfeld & Nicolson.

MILLER, E. and GWYNNE, G. (1972), *A Life Apart*, Tavistock Publications.

MILLER, S. and RIESSMAN, F. (1961), 'The Working Class Subculture: A New View', *Social Problems*, 9, 86–97.

MISCHEL, T. (ed.) (1969), *Human Action*, Academic Press.

MITCHELL, J. CLYDE (1969), *Social Networks in Urban Situations: Analyses of Personal Relations in Central African Towns*, Manchester University Press.

MONTEFIORE, A. (ed.) (1973), *Philosophy and Personal Relations*, Routledge & Kegan Paul.

MORGAN, D. H. (1975), *Social Theory and the Family*, Routledge & Kegan Paul.

MORRIS, C. (1972), *The Discovery of the Individual, 1050–1200*, SPCK.

MORRIS, P. *et al.* (1973), 'Public Attitudes to Problem Definition and Problem Solving', *British Journal of Social Work*, 3, 301–20.

MOYNIHAN, D. (1969), *Maximum Feasible Misunderstanding*, Free Press.

MULLEN, E. J. and DUMPSON, J. R. *et al.* (1972), *Evaluation of Social Intervention*, Jossey-Bass.

MURDOCH, IRIS (1969), 'On "God" and "Good" ' in *The Anatomy of Knowledge*, ed. M. Grene, Routledge & Kegan Paul.

MURO, J. and FREEMAN, S. (1968), *Readings in Group Counseling*, International Textbook Company.

NEILSEN, K. (1976), 'Alienation and Self-Realisation' in *Talking About Welfare*, ed. Noel Timms and David Watson, Routledge & Kegan Paul.

NOTT, K. (1970), *Philosophy and Human Nature*, Hodder & Stoughton.

NURSE, J. (1973), 'The Client, the Caseworker and the Absent Third Person', *British Journal of Social Work*, 3, 39–53.

OAKESHOTT, M. (1975), *On Human Conduct*, Oxford University Press.

OLDS, V. (1962), 'Role Theory and Casework: A Review of the Literature', *Social Casework*, XLIII, 3–7.

OVERTON, A. (1953), 'Serving Families who "Don't Want Help" ', *Social Casework*, XXXIV, 304–9.

PALMER, T. (1973), 'Matching Worker and Client in Connections', *Social Work*, 18, 95–103.

PARKER, R. A. (1966), *Decision in Child Care*, Allen & Unwin.

PARKER, R. A. (1967), 'Social Administration and Scarcity: the Problem of Rationing', *Social Work* (UK), 24, 9–14.

PARKER, R. A. (1971), *Planning for Deprived Children*, National Children's Homes.

PARSLOE, P. (1971), 'What Social Workers Say in Groups of Clients', *British Journal of Social Work*, 1, 39–62.

PEARS, D. (1972), *What is Knowledge?*, Allen & Unwin.

PEARSON, G. (1975), 'Making Social Workers: Bad Promises and Good Omens' in *Radical Social Work*, ed. R. Bailey and M. Brake, Edward Arnold.

PERLMAN, H. H. (1957), *Social Casework – A Problem Solving Process*, University of Chicago Press.

PERLMAN, H. H. (1965), 'Self-determination: Reality or Illusion?', *Social Service Review*, 39, 410–21.

PERLMAN, H. H. (1972), 'Once more with Feeling' in *Evaluation of Social Intervention*, ed. E. J. Mullen *et al.*, Jossey-Bass.

PETERS, R. S. (1973), 'Freedom and the Development of the Free Man' in *Educational Judgements*, ed. J. F. Doyle, Routledge & Kegan Paul.

PHILIP, A. E., MCCULLOCH, W. and SMITH, N. (1975), *Social Work Research and the Analysis of Social Data*, Pergamon.

PHILLIPS, H. (1972), *The Essentials of Social Group Work Skill*, University of Pennsylvania and Folcroft Press.

PINCUS, A. and MINAHAN, A. (1973), *Social Work Practice: Model and Method*, Ithaca, Illinois: Peacock.

PINKER, R. (1971), *Social Theory and Social Policy*, Heinemann.

PINS, A. M. (1963), *Who Chooses Social Work, When and Why?*, Council of Social Work Education, USA.

PLANT, R. (1973), *Hegel*, Allen & Unwin.

PLATT, A. M. (1969), *The Child Savers*, University of Chicago Press.

PLOWMAN, D. E. G. (1969), 'What are the Outcomes of Casework?', *Social Work* (UK), 26, 10–19.

PLUMMER, K. (1975), *Sexual Stigma: An Interactionist Account*, Routledge & Kegan Paul.

POPPER, K. (1952), *The Open Society and its Enemies*, Routledge & Kegan Paul.

POYNTER, J. R. (1969), *Society and Pauperism: English Ideas on Poor Relief, 1795–1834*, Routledge & Kegan Paul.

PRINS, H. (1974), 'Motivation in Social Work', *Social Work Today*, 5, 40–3.

PULLAN, B. (1971), *Rich and Poor in Renaissance Venice*, Blackwell.

PUMPHREY, M. (1959), *The Teaching of Values and Ethics in Social Work Education*, Project Report of the Curriculum Study, Vol. XIII, Council on Social Work Education, USA.

RAGG, N. (1976), *People not Cases*, Routledge & Kegan Paul.

RAPHAEL, D. D. (ed.) (1967), *Political Theory and the Rights of Man*, Macmillan.

RAPOPORT, R. and RAPOPORT, R. (1965), 'Work and Family in Contemporary Society', *American Sociological Review*, 30, 381–94.

RAWLS, J. (1962), 'Justice as Fairness' in *Philosophy, Politics and Society*, 2nd series, ed. P. Laslett and W. G. Runciman, Blackwell.

RAYNOR, L. (1970), *Adoption of Non-white Children*, Allen & Unwin.

REES, R. (1964), 'Symposium on the Public Interest', *Proceedings of the Aristotelian Society*, Supplementary Volume XXXVIII, 3–18.

REES, S. (1973), 'Patronage and Participation, Problem and Paradox: A Case Study in Community Work', *British Journal of Social Work*, 3, 3–18.

REES, S. (1974), 'No more than Contact: an Outcome of Social Work', *British Journal of Social Work*, 4, 255–80.

REID, W. (1967), 'A Study of Caseworkers' Use of Insight-Oriented Techniques', *Social Casework* 1, 3–9.

REID, W. and SHAPIRO, B. (1969), 'Client Reactions to Advice', *Social Service Review*, 43, 165–73.

REID, W. and SHYNE, A. (1969), *Brief and Extended Casework*, Columbia University Press.

REID, W. and SHYNE, A. (1972), *Task-centred Casework*, Columbia University Press.

REIN, M. (1970), 'Social Work in Search of a Radical Profession' in M. Rein (ed.), *Social Policy*, Random House.

REITH, D. (1975), 'I wonder if you can help me?', *Social Work Today*, 6, 66–9.

REYNOLDS, B. (1951), *Social Work and Social Living*, Citadel Press.

REX, J. (1974), *Approaches to Sociology*, Routledge & Kegan Paul.

REX, J. and MOORE, R. (1967), *Race, Community and Conflict*, Oxford University Press.

RICHMOND, M. (1917), *Social Diagnosis*, Russell Sage Foundation.

RIEFF, P. (1965), *Freud: the Mind of the Moralist*, Methuen.

RILEY, P. V. (1974), 'Family Advocacy: Case to Cause and Back to Case' in *The Practice of Social Work*, ed. R. W. Klenk and R. M. Ryan, Wadsworth Publishing Company.

ROBERTS, R. W. and NEE, R. H. (eds) (1970), *Theories of Social Casework*, University of Chicago Press.

ROBINSON, J. (1971), 'Experimental Research in Social Casework', *British Journal of Social Work*, 1, 463–79.

ROBINSON, R. (1968), *Definition*, Clarendon Press.

ROCK, P. and MCINTOSH, M. (1974), *Deviance and Social Control*, Tavistock Publications.

RODGERS, B. and DIXON, J. (1960), *Portrait of Social Work*, Oxford University Press.

ROGERS, C. R. (1942), *Counseling and Psychotherapy*, Houghton Mifflin.

ROSE, A. (1957), 'Theory for the Study of Social Problems', *Social Problems*, 4, 189–99.

ROSE, A. M. (ed.) (1962), *Human Behaviour and Social Processes*, Routledge & Kegan Paul.

ROSENBLATT, A. (1962), 'The Application of Role Concepts to the Intake Process', *Social Casework*, XLIII, 8–14.

ROSENHAM, D. (1970), 'A Natural Socialization of Altruistic Autonomy' in *Altruism and Helping Behaviour*, ed. J. Macaulay and L. Berkowitz, Academic Press.

ROTHMAN, J. (1974), *Planning and Organising for Social Change: Action Principles from Social Science Research*, Columbia University Press.

ROWE, J. and LAMBERT, L. (1973), *Children Who Wait*, Association of British Adoption Agencies.

RUDDOCK, R. (1970), *Roles and Relationships*, Routledge & Kegan Paul.

RUDDOCK, R. (1972), *Theories of Personality*, Routledge & Kegan Paul.

RYLE, G. (1968), 'Jane Austen and the Moralists' in *Critical Essays on Jane Austen*, ed. B. C. Southam, Routledge & Kegan Paul.

SACHS, J., *et al.* (1970), *Clients' Progress within Five Interviews: an Exploratory Study Comparing Workers' and Clients' Views*, FSAA.

SAINSBURY, E. (1975), *Social Work with Families*, Routledge & Kegan Paul.

SCHELER, M. (1954), *The Nature of Sympathy*, Routledge & Kegan Paul.

SCHMIDT, J. T. (1969), 'The Use of Purpose in Casework Practice', *Social Work* (USA), 14, 77–84.

SEED, P. (1973), *The Expansion of Social Work in Britain*, Routledge & Kegan Paul.

SEIGLER, M. *et al.* (1969), 'Laing's Models of Madness', *British Journal of Psychiatry*, 115, 947–58.

SHAW, I. (1974), 'Justifying Social Concern', *Christian Graduate*, 27, 65–70.

SHAW, I. (1975), 'Consumer Opinion and Social Policy: A Research Review', *Journal of Social Policy*, 5, 19–32.

SHAW, J. (1974), *The Self in Social Work*, Routledge & Kegan Paul.

SHAW, M. (1974), *Social Work in Prison*, Research Studies 22, Home Office (HMSO).

SHERWOOD, M. (1964), 'Bion's Experiences in Groups: a Critical Evaluation', *Human Relations*, 17, 113–30.

SIMEY, M. (1951), *Charitable Effort in Liverpool in the Nineteenth Century*, National Children's Home.

SIMEY, T. S. (1960), *The Concept of Love in Child Care*, National Children's Home Convocation Lecture.

SINCLAIR, I. (1971), *Hostels for Probationers*, Home Office Research Unit Report (HMSO).

SKINNER, Q. (1972), ' "Social Meaning" and the Explanation of Social Action' in *Philosophy, Politics and Society*, 4th series, ed. P. Laslett *et al.*, Blackwell.

SLACK, K. (1966), *Social Administration and the Citizen*, Michael Joseph.

SMALE, G. (1976), *Prophecy, Behaviour and Change*, Routledge & Kegan Paul.

SMALLEY, R. (1967), *Theory for Social Work Practice*, Columbia University Press.

SMITH, G. and HARRIS, R. (1972), 'Ideologies of Need and the Organisation of Social Work', *British Journal of Social Work*, 2, 27–46.

SOYER, D. (1963), 'The Right to Fail', *Social Work* (USA), 8, 72–8.

SPECHT, H. (1968), 'Casework Practice and Social Policy Formulation', *Social Work* (USA), 13, 42–51.

STEPHENS, T. (ed.) (1945), *Problem Families*, Pacifist Service Units (out of print).

STEVENSON, L. (1974), *Seven Theories of Human Nature*, Clarendon Press.

STEVENSON, O. (1973), *Claimant or Client*, Allen & Unwin.

STEVENSON, O. (1974), Editorial, *British Journal of Social Work*, 4, 1–13.

STREAN, H. (ed.) (1971), *Social Casework: Theories in Action*, Scarecrow Press.

TAYLOR, I., WALTON, P. and YOUNG, J. (1973), *The New Criminology*, Routledge & Kegan Paul.

TAYLOR, I., WALTON, P. and YOUNG, J. (1975), *Critical Criminology*, Routledge & Kegan Paul.

TAYLOR, P. (1959), ' "Need" Statements', *Analysis*, XIX, 106–11.

TELFER, E. (1970), 'Friendship', *Proceedings of the Aristotelian Society*, V, 223–42.

THARP, R. G. (1963), 'Psychological Patterning in Marriage', *Psychological Bulletin*, 60, 97–117.

THOMAS, E. J. (1970), 'Behavioural Modification and Casework' in *Theories of Social Casework*, ed. R. W. Roberts and R. H. Nee, University of Chicago Press.

THOMAS, E. J. and FINK, C. F. (1963), 'Effects of Group Size', *Psychological Bulletin*, 60, 371–84.

TIERNEY, B. (1959), *Medieval Poor Law*, University of California Press.

TIMMS, N. (1962), *Casework in the Child Care Service*, Butterworth.

TIMMS, N. (1970), *Social Work: An Outline for the Intending Student*, Routledge & Kegan Paul.

TIMMS, N. (1971), 'And Renoir, and Matisse, and . . .', An inaugural Lecture, Bradford University.

TIMMS, N. (1972), *Recording in Social Work*, Routledge & Kegan Paul.

TIMMS, N. (1976), with D. WATSON (ed.), *Talking about Welfare*, Routledge & Kegan Paul.

TITMUSS, R. M. (1970), Foreword to *Helping the Aged*, by E. M. Goldbert *et al.*, Allen & Unwin.

TIZARD, J. *et al.* (eds) (1975), *Varieties of Residential Experience*, Routledge & Kegan Paul.

TOD, R. (ed.) (1968), *Children in Care*, Longmans.

TOD, R. (ed.) (1971), *Social Work in Foster Care: Collected Papers*, Longmans.

TOREN, N. (1972), *Social Work: the Case of a Semi-Profession*, Sage Publications.

TOWLE, C. (1965), *Common Human Needs*, National Association of Social Workers (USA).

TRIGG, R. (1973), *Reason and Commitment*, Columbia University Press.

TROPP, E. (1974), 'Three Problematic Concepts: Client, Help, Worker', *Social Casework*, 55, 19–29.

TURNER, R. (1974), *Ethnomethodology*, Penguin.

URBANSOURSKI, M. (1974), 'Recording to Measure Effectiveness', *Social Casework*, 55, 546–53.

VICKERY, A. (1974), 'A Systems Approach to Social Work Intervention its Uses for Work with Individuals and Families', *British Journal of Social Work*, 4, 389–404.

VOLLMER, H. and MILLS, D. (1966), *Professionalization*, Prentice Hall.

WALTON, R. G. (1975), *Women in Social Work*, Routledge & Kegan Paul.

WASSERMAN, H. (1970), 'Early Careers of Professional Social Workers in a Public Child Welfare Agency', *Social Work* (USA), 15, 93–101.

WATKINS, G. (1975), *Social Control*, Longman.

WATSON, D. (1975), 'Ethical Implications of a Behavioural Approach in Social Work – A Response', *International Social Work*, XVII, 32–5.

WHITTINGTON, C. (1971), 'Self-determination Re-examined', *British Journal of Social Work*, 1, 293–303.

WILDING, P. and GEORGE, V. (1975), 'Social Values and Social Policy', *Journal of Social Policy*, 4, 373–90.

WILLIAMS, B. (1962), 'The Idea of Equality' in *Philosophy, Politics and Society*, 2nd series, ed. P. Laslett and W. G. Runciman, Blackwell.

WILLIAMS, R. (1961), *Culture and Society*, Penguin.

WILLISTON, G. (1963), 'The Foster Parent Role', *Journal of Social Psychology*, 60, 263–72.

WILSNAK, W. (1946), 'Handling Resistance in Social Casework', *American Journal of Orthopsychiatry*, 16, 297–311.

WILSON, J. (1963), *Thinking with Concepts*, Cambridge University Press.

WILSON, J. (1966), *Equality*, Hutchinson.

WILSON, J. (1973), *The Assessment of Morality*, NFER Publishing Company.

WINNICOTT, C. (1964), *Childcare and Social Work*, Codicote Press.

WITMER, H. and POWERS, L. (1951), *An Experiment in the Prevention of Delinquency*, Columbia University Press.

WOOD, K. (1971), 'The Contribution of Psychoanalysis and Ego Psychology to Social Casework' in *Social Casework: Theories in Action*, ed. H. Strean, Scarecrow Press.

WOODROOFE, E. (1963), *From Charity to Social Work*, Routledge & Kegan Paul.

WOOTTON, B. (1959), *Social Science and Social Pathology*, Allen & Unwin.

YOUNGHUSBAND, E. (1962), *Community Work and Social Change*, Report of a Study Group, Longmans.

YOUNGHUSBAND, E. (1967), *Social Work and Social Values*, Allen & Unwin.

ZANDER, M. (1974), *Social Workers, their Clients and the Law*, Sweet & Maxwell.